The Art of Managing Human Resources

The
Executive
Bookshelf

Sloan
Management
Review

Arnoldo C. Hax (Editor), *Planning Strategies That Work*

Stuart E. Madnick (Editor), *The Strategic Use of Information Technology* (in press)

Edward B. Roberts (Editor), *Generating Technological Innovation*

Edgar H. Schein (Editor), *The Art of Managing Human Resources*

The Art of Managing Human Resources

Edited by

Edgar H. Schein

New York   Oxford

OXFORD UNIVERSITY PRESS

1987

Oxford University Press

Oxford   New York   Toronto
Delhi   Bombay   Calcutta   Madras   Karachi
Petaling Jaya   Singapore   Hong Kong   Tokyo
Nairobi   Dar es Salaam   Cape Town
Melbourne   Auckland

and associated companies in
Beirut   Berlin   Ibadan   Nicosia

Copyright © 1987 by Sloan Management Review

Published by Oxford University Press, Inc.,
200 Madison Avenue, New York, New York 10016

Oxford is a registered trademark of Oxford University Press

Library of Congress Cataloging-in-Publication Data
The Art of managing human resources.
Bibliography: p.
Includes index.
1. Manpower planning. 2. Organizational effectiveness.
I. Schein, Edgar H.
HF5549.5.M3A78   1987   658.3'01   86-31107
ISBN 0-19-504882-2

9 8 7 6 5 4 3 2 1

Printed in the United States of America
on acid-free paper

Foreword

The Executive Bookshelf reflects the mission of the *Sloan Management Review,* which is to bridge the gap between the practicing manager and the management scholar. Based on real-world business concerns, *SMR* articles provide the practicing manager with state-of-the-art information on management theory and practice. These articles are of particular benefit to the executive who wants to stay abreast of some of the best research and analysis coming from top business schools.

This series draws together *SMR* articles that make significant contributions to the management fields they cover. Each book is edited by one of the Sloan School of Management's most respected professors in the field, and begins with the editor's introduction, which guides and broadens the reader's understanding of the subject at hand.

The great value of these collections lies in how the articles complement one another. The authors do not always agree, but each has something important to say. Consequently, when read in its entirety, each book will challenge the reader to think more carefully about specific management issues. The editors' selection of, and introduction to, the articles will help readers interpret the various perspectives that are presented.

The usefulness of this series is enhanced by the *Sloan Management Review*'s rigorous editorial standards. Articles must not only have a practical focus, but they must also be accessible to the reader. Before an article is accepted for publication, it must be reviewed and accepted by an independent referee. The combination of applicability, academic seriousness, and solid writing assures that the series is readable and authoritative. The language is nontechnical, with minimum discussion of research and methodology, and the authors are influential leaders in the field of management.

The qualities that make these books useful to managers also make them invaluable as assigned readings in academic executive development programs and in private sector management training. In addition, they are helpful to students needing practical information to complement the theoretical materials in standard textbooks.

On a broader scale, this series is an extension of the Alfred P. Sloan School of Management. As one of the leading business schools in the country, the Sloan School complements its educational programs with research intended to produce new and better solutions to management problems. The *Sloan Management Review* in general, and this series in particular, reflects this combined research and training orientation.

The *Review* has a tradition of facilitating communication between executives and academics, and this series is an exciting addition to that tradition. We hope that you share our enthusiasm and that these books help you to become increasingly challenged, informed, and successful.

Cambridge, Mass.   Abraham J. Siegel
March 1987   Dean, Alfred P. Sloan School
                           of Management
                           Massachusetts Institute of Technology

Preface

The Art of Managing Human Resources brings together for the first time some of the best and most influential articles that have appeared in the *Sloan Management Review*. The book is intended to provide practicing managers with a systematic range of ideas and applications in the ever-important area of the management of people in organizations. Designed for easy reading and reference, the book should be equally valuable to line managers and human resource specialists alike.

The strength of these articles is that they are conceptual. They present ideas and perspectives—ways of looking at and solving the very complex problems that managers have to think about. The willingness of the *Sloan Management Review* to publish such articles in an age obsessed by quantification and hypothesis testing is testimony to its editorial wisdom. I believe that good ideas and concepts always have been and continue to be more valuable than rigorous analysis of invalid, unreliable, or unimportant data.

This is not to say that empirical data gathering is unimportant. A number of the articles reprinted in this volume are based on empirical studies, but the primary emphasis in my selection has been to find those articles that identify and elucidate important ideas and concepts. There has been much knowledge accumulated in the field of the management of human relations, and it is time to put that knowledge to practical use in the hands of managers.

Cambridge, Mass.   E.H.S.
October 1986

Contents

Part III. Organizational Change

Part IV. Organizational Culture

Contributors

Yvan Allaire is Professor of Strategy, Marketing, and Research Methodology in the Department of Administrative Sciences at the University of Quebec, Montreal. He is also a consultant to many large Canadian firms.

Richard Beckhard, who is retired, was the Adjunct Professor of Management at the Sloan School of Management, MIT, and Director of Richard Beckhard Associates. Mr. Beckhard's most recent book is *Organizational Transitions: Managing Complex Change,* coauthored with Reuben Harris.

Warren G. Bennis is Distinguished Professor of Business Administration at the School of Business Administration, the University of Southern California, Los Angeles. His latest book is entitled *Leaders,* coauthored with Burt Nanus.

Mihaela Firsirotu is Professor of Strategy in the Department of Administrative Sciences at the University of Quebec, Montreal.

Marc Gerstein is President of Marc Gerstein Associates, Ltd., Managing Director of the Delta Consulting Group Inc., and Adjunct Professor at Columbia Business School. As a consultant, he specializes in areas of strategic management, organization development and senior management recruitment, and assessment and development.

Mason Haire, who is deceased, was a Visiting Professor of Organizational Psychology and Management at MIT and Professor of Psychology at the University of California, Berkeley.

James N. Kelly is cofounder and Senior Vice President of Management Analysis Center, Inc., London. His consulting activities have included strategic planning and the design of management systems.

Leo B. Moore is retired. He was Professor of Management at the Sloan School of Management, MIT. He has written extensively on the subjects of standards and management problems.

Edwin C. Nevis is Senior Lecturer, Organization Studies Group at the Sloan School of Management, MIT. He is also Coordinator of the Executive Education Program Development at MIT.

Heather Reisman is the Managing Director of Paradigm Consulting, Inc., a firm specializing in competitive strategy and organization change. As a consultant, she specializes in the areas of strategy formulation, organization structure, and equal employment opportunity.

Edgar H. Schein is the Sloan Fellows Professor of Management at the Sloan School of Management, MIT. Dr. Schein has published a number of books and articles ranging from organitional psychology and process consultation to professional education and occupational socialization. His most recent book is *Organizational Culture and Leadership*.

W. Brooke Tunstall was Assistant Vice President and Director of Corporate Planning of AT&T. As Chairman of AT&T's Restructure Implementation Board, he was responsible for corporate-level coordination and planning of the divestiture of the twenty-two operating companies from AT&T. He was active in the redesign of AT&T's new System of Management in preparation for the post-divestiture business environment.

The Art of Managing Human Resources

Introduction

Edgar H. Schein

The study of organizational effectiveness, leadership, and management has a long and venerable history. Social scientists and practitioners of every persuasion have had a crack at telling managers how to do it better. But the complexity of organizational and managerial phenomena is still keeping us from those clear insights that we hope for.

Why then another volume dealing with partial insights? There are several persuasive reasons. First, this volume, by drawing only on material published in the *Sloan Management Review,* presents a number of highly insightful but not very widely circulated articles that span the various social-science disciplines. Eclecticism has always been a hallmark of the Sloan School's Organization Studies Group, founded originally by Douglas McGregor in 1952. Many of the articles reprinted here broke new ground and became classics, because they did not fit into traditional categories. In fact, it is to the credit of the *Sloan Management Review* that some of them were published at all, given their nontraditional essaylike approaches.

Second, the problems addressed in this volume continue to be central in our field, and many of the insights provided in the individual articles are as fresh and relevant today as they were at the time of their original publication. It is especially important to bring together into one volume material that covers more than two decades of research.

Third, the Organization Studies Group of the Sloan School has been influential in shaping contemporary points of view toward management and organizational change. Critical pioneering efforts in organization development were made by Doug McGregor, Mason Haire, Warren Bennis, Richard Beckhard, and Leo Moore, all of whose work, except McGregor's, has appeared in the *Sloan Management Review*. Three of the articles were original talks given in honor of Doug McGregor afer his untimely death. The articles of my own that I have included reflect my early thinking on topics that only later became the focus of popular research. In a very real sense, then, this volume is also a kind of history of the work of those members of the Organization Studies Group who focused particularly on problems of organizational change.

The articles are grouped around four major themes. The themes are, of course, interconnected, but at the same time they reflect different focuses of attention. In Part I, I have grouped three articles dealing with the problem of what makes an organization effective, one by Mason Haire, one by Warren Bennis, and one of my own. The difficulty of determining what *causes* effectiveness is, in the first instance, due to the difficulty of defining what we mean by "effectiveness" when we deal with a multipurpose complex system. The article by Warren Bennis is a brilliant review of this topic and leads to some sound conclusions on how to be scientific about effectiveness and what it means to be scientific when we deal with dynamic open systems.

It is clear that all effectiveness criteria involve the management and development of human resources. The dilemmas of how to integrate education with indoctrination, of how to meet both the needs of the organization and the individual, of how to ensure that employee behavior, whether at the shop floor or managerial level, meets ethical standards without sacrificing effectiveness, continue to perplex us. All five articles in Part II, including those by Richard Beckhard, Marc Gerstein and Heather Reisman, and myself, attempt to shed light on various aspects of these dilemmas. Finally, I have included here also one of the few published papers of our longtime colleague, Leo B. Moore. His analysis of how managers can improve their own management of time is must reading for any manager interested in improving his or her own overall effectiveness.

Part III deals with the crucial problem of organizational change. It is a clear conclusion from Parts I and II that the ability to learn and to adapt is a central criterion of organizational effectiveness. But organizations are homeostatic systems—i.e., they are made up of interdependent elements tending toward a state of equilibrium. They resist change, in other words, which is why the development of concepts and technologies of how to initiate and manage change has been a central concern of our field. Richard Beckhard's classic article on managing large system change leads off this section. James N. Kelly's article on how new CEOs conceptualize their own role in managing change reveals a fascinating variety of views, many of which destroy some of our stereotypes of how new executives operate. And the final article, by Yvan Allaire and Mihaela Firsirotu, confronts the ultimate issue of how to think about *radical* strategies for change, if and when that becomes necessary.

Part IV focuses on culture, both national and organizational. Culture has become an important concern lately, because of claims that the right kind of culture or a strong culture leads to greater organizational effectiveness. I examine this argument vis-à-vis claims made for Japanese management styles, and Edwin C. Nevis, who visited the People's Republic of China as a teacher of management, analyzes his experiences in a comparative perspective. The final two articles in the volume, by W. Brooke Tunstall and myself, focus specifically on *organizational* culture and show that culture change is at best a difficult and complex phenomenon. In fact, it is the discovery of how strong cultures can be a real constraint on desired change that illuminates in a special way the problem of resistance to change, which all change managers and consultants have noted over and over again.

Culture has become a popular concept, and managers who want to get real attention often label what they are trying to do as "culture change" to give it a special importance. But the danger in this casual labeling is that the real significance and importance of organizational culture as a force toward and constraint on change will be lost. I have, therefore, ended the book with my own effort to describe in a serious way what culture is all about.

PART I

What Is Organizational Effectiveness?

1

Coming of Age in the Social Sciences

Mason Haire

This article was prepared to read as one of the annual Douglas McGregor Memorial Lectures in honor of the late Douglas McGregor, Alfred P. Sloan Professor of Management at MIT. It assesses the contributions of the behavioral sciences to the practice of management and discusses the barriers to free interchange between the two groups. It presents a systematic theoretical approach to the management of human resources and to manpower planning, and it deals with the kind of industry-university research organization that seems best adapted to advanced work on this problem. *SMR*.

It is with a bewildering variety of feelings that I approach the Douglas McGregor Memorial Lecture. My feelings are compounded of a number of elements. There is a strong sense of personal indebtedness to Doug for my own life in the field he did so much to create and shape. There is a deep humility in approaching the task of commenting on the field in his name. Finally, there is a profound realization of the degree to which he gave character to the field and made possible the work of many individuals and developments within the area. A great many of the people whose work was made possible by Doug never came into contact with him; those who did were doubly benefited. Still, the burgeoning field of the relevance of the behavioral sciences to industry is what it is to a large extent because of the existence of Doug McGregor, and his hand reaches out to support us today in the many corners into which the field has gone.

One can point to a variety of specific senses in which this is true: the widespread and highly leveraged activities of the National Training Laboratories—T-groups, Bethel, and the like—had their origin in the idea and the atmosphere he created. The productive and prestigious Institute for

From *Sloan Management Review,* Spring 1967, Vol. 8, No. 2. Reprinted with permission.

Social Research at Ann Arbor—contributing more empirical research to the field than any other one center—is largely staffed by people who first saw their problems in a situation he created. MIT's own active and productive group in the behavioral sciences is deeply indebted to him. Whenever companies realize that management development is not simply a mechanical addition of more information, or that performance appraisal is not best managed like a classroom grading system, his spirit is present. Theory X and Theory Y have become part of the international vocabulary of management. Still, it is not in these specifics that his influence is best understood, but rather in his broad view of the field. He was one of the first who dared to believe that the problem of human nature was central to the problem of industry. He saw psychology not as a discipline for tinkering on the edge of the issues—a little selection here, a little training research there, a little human engineering here—but as the heart of the matter. He saw the relevance of perception, development, motivation, and personality. He saw the transactional adaptive character of the firm. He saw that theory was the only practical tool, and that the criterion must be extended well beyond traditional productivity measures to include initiative, innovation, and growth as dependent variables. For him "human relations" was not something loosely added on to the firm as if with a band-aid. *The Human Side of Enterprise* emphasizes the conviction that human relations is one of the integral facets of the social institution.

So much of the field is his product that it is particularly important to look at its historical development—what it is and what it has been and what it may be—and remember, as part of the McGregor Memorial Lectures, that Doug is a large part of the answer to each of those questions.

The Bits-and-Pieces Approach

In this context, let me raise some issues and point to some things that seem to me to be happening, some things that ought to happen, and what may come of them. Let me say at the outset that I find the contribution of the social sciences to the present practice of management disappointingly small. We should look at why this may be so and what, if anything, may be done to remedy it.

When I say the contribution of the behavioral sciences to management has been disappointingly small, I mean this: In the past 15 years there have been perhaps 150 books and 1500 articles written on the subject. And yet the practice of management remains almost the same. To be sure, managerial vocabulary has changed. The well-rounded manager now speaks of T-groups, cognitive dissonance, and role conflicts, but he does just about the same things he's always done. The social scientist, on the other hand, has made his field tremendously larger and more complex, but in general he has considered very few of the manager's pressing problems. We are in danger of realizing a situation in which the two groups talk to themselves but not to one another—a complicated gavotte whose partners endlessly circle but never make contact. Why is this so?

One of the reasons is the tendency of the behavioral sciences to approach the management problem with a bit of this and a piece of that. Instead of facing the whole of the organizational problem, we have been seduced by the apparent relevance of psychological concepts to particular problems. We have felt that there should be more participation in the system; the effect of participation on various kinds of behavior is clear. There should be a dash of achievement motivation thrown in. "Achievement motivation" is obviously related to the problems of the business organization. We should have some sensitivity training. Why? Surely the name itself makes it clear. More sensitivity is, on the face of it, better than less. We should study satisfactions at work. Why? Well, again, satisfactions, like sensitivity, are a good thing, and surely more of them must be better than less.

This is what I mean by the "bits and pieces" approach to the problem. Instead of directing themselves to the broad organizational issues, it seems to me that the social sciences raised the issues that seemed relevant to social science. The things that were done were those that were cute, superficially relevant, and had a short-term payoff. In the face of this, the manager was often intrigued, or even convinced, but it was hard for him to know how to use the contributions, because it was hard for him to see just how they applied and toward what end their main thrust was directed.

A faddish interest in organization theory helped somewhat to overcome the bits-and-pieces approach. It properly raised the question of the dynamic interrelation of the parts within the system and asked how the parts relate optimally to one another. However, behavioral scientific research and theory has in only a few instances responded to this system view.

A Little History

Let's turn to history to see what happened. The question "What is the point of all this social science business?" came up in the course of the field's development, but it was soon clouded in the details of everyday work. Let me reconstruct the issue and oversimplify a little to bring it out. The human-relations movement at one point seemed to say to managers, "You ought to run your companies so that people at work get more satisfaction from work-ing." Managers, in brief, replied (though more elegantly), "Yeah, why?" The human-relations answer tended to be that it was socially desirable, that it gave reality and importance to human dignity. Faced with this argument from moral principles, the manager fell back on moral principles of his own. He retreated into his fiduciary responsibility and said "But how much of the stockholder's money am I justified in spending to produce satisfactions?" (It was at this point that the managerial school of "Let them be happy on their own time" was born.) The calculus involved in the apparently conflicting responsibilities to shareowners and to human dignity was a poser to the social scientists, and it split the human-relations field into two camps in reply. One group—which persists today—stuck to the simple social point: "You ought to provide more human values at work, and the stockholders' returns are secondary." The second group resolved the dilemma by a device with a long tradition in the social sciences: They said it was no dilemma at all. The position became that the more satisfaction one has at work, the better he works; human dignity and return on investment are simultaneously satisfied in one fell swoop.

The argument was an interesting inversion of John Stuart Mill's more traditional one. Mill said that if you manage your business to maximize its success, social good will automatically flow from it. The human-relations argument seems to be an even more convenient example of preordained harmony. It says: "If you manage your business in the interest of social good, business effectiveness will flow from it." In spite of the ingenious dialectics, however, the argument that more satisfied employees would be-come more effective employees led to a morass: It led to the investigation of the relation between morale and productivity—a miasmic welter of confused data whose upshot seemed to be that there was no consistent association between the two.

In the face of the discouraging empirical datum that the correlation be-tween morale and short-term productivity seems to average out at zero, the field again shattered into pieces. One segment pursued the study of satisfac-tions, arguing that more of them are still a better thing than less. Another fraction sidestepped the empirical datum and withdrew into the construction of theoretical models showing that at least people ought to make more contribution if they have a positive feeling about their work. Only a very small portion took the position that seems to me to be the moral of this story: The correlation between morale and short-term productivity used the wrong criterion. Short-term productivity is the result of long-term causal factors. The proper object of variables introduced by the social sciences is a longer-term and more complex criterion. Such a criterion must include commitment, integration, initiative, and the development over time of the kinds of skills, motives, and attitudes relevant to performance on a specific job at a specific time. Short-term productivity will flow from these and will be included in them, but only indirectly, and the simple use of it as a criterion will only cloud the issue.

Short-Term Productivity as a Criterion

We have been bemused by short-term productivity. As we look at the success stories of social science research in industry, the argument is typically from short-term success, although the main thrust is elsewhere.

The Hawthorne studies showed that taking girls off a line and treating them specially created a group where none had existed before. Surely this is the real effect, and its potential leverage for a variety of managerial tasks is considerable. But when we want to give a real clincher, we say that with the change their productivity went up.

The Coch and French studies showed that participation in change radically altered the response to that change. Surely here, too, there is an effect that goes well beyond the argument that is finally produced to show the force of the exercise: Their productivity went up.

A variety of experiments—by Bavelas and others—have shown that designing a job one's self, self-pacing, or independent action makes a major difference in one's approach to the job. Once more we have a powerful lever that goes well beyond the anticlimactic demonstration that in the short run they produce more.

If one goes on endlessly listing classic experiments, the same thing seems to stand out; we have fallen into the trap of trying to win friends by demonstrating short-term productivity, and, in the process, have missed the larger essential organizational problems to which the social sciences are relevant. Let me be clear about this: I am not opposed to short-term productivity. It is an essential criterion. It is, however, only one of several criteria essential to the firm. The exclusive concentration on this single criterion may mislead and confuse social scientists about the relevance and leverage of phenomena in their investigations.

So far I have argued that the social sciences have contributed relatively little to management practice because a bits-and-pieces approach has dominated research. There is an undue fascination with short-term productivity as a criterion. We must come to two questions: What kind of integrated approach will supplant the bits and pieces, and what general objectives will override short-term productivity? Before we do, however, let us look at managerial practices. I have castigated the social sciences for failing to contribute maximally to the management of human resources. What have the companies done?

Management's Version of the Bits-and-Pieces Approach

I would argue that an exactly parallel course has occurred here: Management has largely ignored the clearly present, but very complex, long-term criterion on the one hand, and, on the other, has operated in the most disparate bits-and-pieces manner possible with respect to the management of human resources. Consider the situation. In any organization there are at least two tasks with respect to the people. We must deploy them and support them technologically, so as to optimize present productivity. At the same time we must operate in such a way as to guarantee future manpower needs. Future needs can be budgeted at least as well as capital needs. We'll need, say, one new president every ten years. We'll need five new vice-presidents every ten years. They must be such that they can do the present vice-presidenting well and also provide the pool from which the president will be drawn. We'll need twenty new general managers every ten years, and they have the same demands as the vice-presidents. Whatever the correct numbers are, they can be filled in, with a margin of error, for any organization, and the two criteria—present productivity and future promotability—can be specified for each need at each time. The problem of planning over time is not, however, simply a problem of providing warm bodies in the right numbers at certain places at specified times. It includes a projection of requirements in terms of skills and experience and the explicit management of the process of producing them.

It seems to me that very few organizations face the problems of managing their human resources as squarely as this. We have a tradition of planning expansion in terms of market growth, product diversification, and capital availability, and trusting that the flexibility of people and a loose labor market will protect us from the results of not planning in the human area. When the crisis comes, we can hire or fire or pirate from our competition to take care of the needs we did not foresee. We have not, in general, taken responsibility for what is, from the side of the organization, manpower planning, or what is, from the side of the individual, career development. At the same time, any company controls a portfolio of the most powerful tools for changing behavior. Pay, promotion, training, job rotation or cross-functional assignment, performance evaluation, supervision—all of these are immensely strong levers to modify behavior. They can be considered usefully in organizational terms, as variable inputs that can be applied at the discretion of management to shape the manpower pool for present productivity and future promotability. Or, on the other hand, they can be viewed as optional interventions in the career-development process. In either case, they are the company's repertoire of things it can do or not do in treating the problem of human resources.

In utilizing these weapons, I would argue that the company has been guilty of exactly the same two errors as the social scientist: first, of committing its resources piecemeal, and second, of focusing too narrowly on a short-term criterion. Most companies do a little training, a little worrying about the effect of the compensation plan, and a lot of supervisory exhortation. I don't know of any that treats the optional interventions as an integrated whole. I have never seen a case where one said, "If we change our compensation plan in this manner, we will have to change our supervisory practices in that way, to modify our techniques for controlling turnover, and to reshape our training to meet the changed conditions." Instead, each of these is treated on a one-shot basis. We don't treat them as an integrated whole.

One of the reasons why we don't treat them as an integrated whole is that we don't know how. One of the reasons we don't know how is that we've never faced squarely what we're trying to do with our variable treatments of the human side and have never asked what any of the treatments do or how they affect one another. We have not generally dealt with the discretionary possibilities as an integrated system of parts interacting with one another and differentially related to the various goals of the organization.

For example, cross-functional assignments are presumably designed to improve future promotability, even though they are probably at the expense of present productivity. I have never seen an attempt to assess the cost in productivity or to demonstrate the hypothetically attendant benefit to promotability. These commitments of resources tend to be made in the quite untested hope that the benefit is great and the cost is not too bad. Similarly, if a man is assigned to a new function to improve his promotability, do we adjust our other mechanisms to this? Does he get an incentive bonus for doing less well than other people at the same job because we know he's doing well, considering the fact that he was deliberately stretched beyond his specialty? Does his performance evaluation give him a pat on the back and say "Congratulations. You're doing poorly. It's a wonder you're not doing worse"? These things don't happen. We do a shot of one and a shot of the other, with little planning for the way the whole system works.

It is time we stated the system explicitly, time we treated explicitly the multiple objectives with respect to human resources and the degree to which each of the treatments affects the outcomes, as well as the way in which they interact with one another. It is technologically possible to do this now. We have the concepts, instruments, and hardware to do it. We need the will to treat the whole system in an integrated way. We need to do for the management of human resources what the general adoption of budget procedures did for manufacturing processes some years ago.

There is a manpower squeeze at the moment. Companies are going to face a much worse squeeze on management in the future. We know, for example, that in the 1970s there will be a million fewer men aged thirty-five to forty-five than there are today—a reduction of about 8 percent. This development is inexorably approaching on the basis of births already laid down. Any expansion or diversification will have to be done in the face of a reduced pool of management manpower. We can't solve the problem as we have in the past by pirating from our neighbors. There will be fewer for all. Even to stand still, much less to grow, we must find ways to make more use of the human resources—particularly managerial—we have. The management manpower squeeze promises, in the future, to make the credit squeeze seem, in retrospect, like a pleasant time. We must begin to face this problem. Let us look at it in detail.

An Integrated Model

What are the things that can happen to change the effectiveness of people in organizations? There are, fortunately, a small number of them:

1. New people move into the organization.
2. Some people move out of it.
3. Some people move up in the organization.
4. Some people move sideways, i.e., don't change their job or level from t_1 to t_2.
5. Some people change their behavior from t_1 to t_2.

I would like to argue that these are all the things that can happen to people in an organization. Out of these five variables, management has to do today's job and provide for the future. What tools does the company have with which to try to do the job?

I would argue that management's tools to change the effectiveness of people, though immensely powerful and diverse in their specifics, are relatively few:

1. Recruitment.
2. Selection and classification.

3. Training.
4. Supervision.
5. Job assignment.
6. Performance evaluation.
7. Pay.
8. Promotion.

It will be useful, I think, to put these two sets of variables together in a matrix to see how they relate to one another. (See Table 1.1.) When we put the two lists together it helps us to see to what purpose each of the optional interventions may be used. We can already begin a resource allocation as we see what we are trying to do.

I have also put some numbers in the boxes to indicate the effect of the variable treatments in the column on each outcome in the rows. You may not agree with the numbers. No matter. These will do for illustration. What they mean is that, for instance, recruitment has a primary effect on who moves in, and is given a value of 1. On the other hand, it has only an indirect effect on the character of those moving up, or on their change, and is given a lower weight of 3. Training, on the other hand, has little to do with who comes in, and gets a 5, but a lot to do with who changes, and gets a 1 there. Never mind whether these are the correct numbers. They serve to focus, so far, on several things:

1. They emphasize what a particular variable will do for a particular outcome.
2. The row totals give some idea of the overall effectiveness of various optional inputs. Here, supervision, assignment, and promotion are the most powerful factors. Pay is, surprisingly, the least.

Table 1.1

	Moving In	Moving Out	Moving Up	Moving Over	Changing	
Recruitment	1	3	3	3	3	13
Selection and classification	1	3	3	3	3	13
Training	5	2	2	2	1	12
Supervision	4	1	1	1	1	8
Assignment	3	1	1	1	2	8
Performance evaluation	5	2	2	2	2	13
Pay	2	2	3	4	4	15
Promotion	2	1	1	1	3	8
	23	15	16	17	19	

3. The column totals give some idea of the responsiveness of various out-comes to treatment. Recruitment is least amenable to change; turnover is most. Costs being equal, unit investment in one is much more productive than in the other.
4. The matrix could be used diagnostically, to assess what a company is doing as opposed to what it might be doing, and to make guesses about what it would cost to do better. (And what it would cost not to.)
5. Finally, one begins to see the interaction of outcomes and inputs. If recruitment works splendidly, some of the pressure is taken off training and vice versa. Recruitment makes more difference than anything as to who comes in; supervision, assignment, and promotion make more dif-ference as to who goes out. It is foolish to invest in recruitment without stopping the leaks in turnover. Lateral movement in the organization may call for a variety of special responses in the categories of pay, training, assignments, and the like.
6. A matrix like this forces us to see some of the hard empirical facts we don't know. We generally don't know the transitional probabilities from time to time in an organizational matrix—what the probability is of someone moving in, up, out, over, or changing from t_1 to t_2. We don't know how much turnover costs, how much change takes place, or what the effect of moving sideways is. To manage the matrix, we need to know a great many things we don't know now. A responsible approach to the utilization of human resources requires the generation of empirical data in many of the boxes shown here.

Let us take the matrix one step further. We have spoken of the things management can do and the effects they can have, but we haven't dealt with the reasons for doing them. What are the organizational goals in the man-agement of human resources? Once more, by using broad categories, we can list a small number of them.

1. Productivity.
2. Promotability.
3. Innovation and flexibility.
4. Special skills.

Now we can put the three lists together and make a new matrix, Figure 1.1.

In this three-dimensional matrix we see even more the interactive effects of variables on one another. Pay may well increase change in productivity, but perhaps not in innovation or flexibility. Cross-functional job assignments may lead to change, facilitating promotability, special skills, and flexibility,

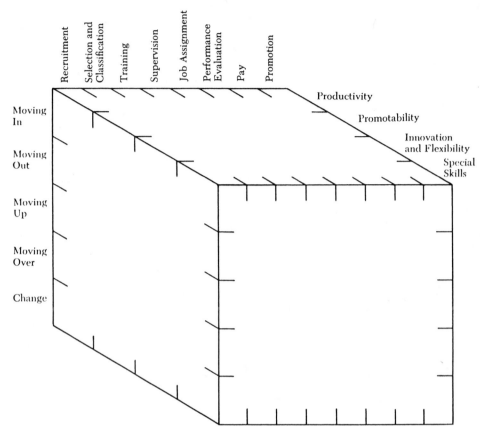

Figure 1.1

but they may inhibit productivity and cause some difficulties in pay and performance evaluation, and they may lead to turnover. Recruitment may raise the level of productivity and promotability, but it places special demands on pay, promotion, and training. The dynamic character of the variables is clear. We no longer treat them in bits and pieces, but as integrated parts of a whole system.

Incidentally, it is possible to isolate one variable, collapse the matrix across each of the other dimensions, and ask what is important to the goals of productivity, promotability, flexibility, and special skills. I put numbers in each of the boxes and tried it. With my numbers I found that pay and training stood out as the most important variable inputs, and that turnover and change were the most important intermediate variables. I hold no special brief for the numbers I put in, but they yielded some surprising results—

results that don't accord well with the attention given to them in common practice. It is also possible, by collapsing the matrix, to ask which of the four goals—productivity, promotability, flexibility, and special skills—yield best to optional interventions or intermediate variables. I find that productivity is easily the simplest one to influence, promotability next, skills next, and flexibility least. This order may not surprise anyone, but at least it sets part of our problem, and we are now further armed with the ways to attack whichever one we need to get at.

Now we have got away from both the bits-and-pieces approach and the overdependence on a short-term criterion. Management's job is clearer. I think the social scientist's job is also clearer. It becomes easier to identify where things like group processes, individual differences, or participation fit. It also becomes easier to identify where we need more work and, to some extent, what kind of work. That is, where we need simple nose-counting empirical facts, where new concepts and techniques, and where developmental research that will make available to practice basic research notions already well-established.

I might point out in passing that there is a research project in process at MIT in which Dr. James Miller and I are working at formalizing and computerizing a model of variable inputs and organizational outcomes along this line. No insuperable problems seem to be appearing. In its barest outline, the model includes the following characteristics:

1. A technique for formalizing management's evaluation of the worth of various behaviors in various jobs at different levels of the organization.
2. An allocation by members of the organization of their time (effort) among various behaviors in an attempt to maximize reward.
3. Organizational rewards on the basis of the (previously evaluated) worth of the members' behaviors. Future behaviors (i.e., allocations among alternative behaviors) are modified somewhat in the manner of formal learning models.
4. The system can be made to operate in this fashion over time periods. Error can be introduced at will—for instance, in the member's perception of reward and its relation to past performance. Alternative decision rules regarding promotion, the function connecting behavior and reward, and the like can be manipulated.

The model and its programming would let us simulate interventions and determine their effect over any period of time, would gauge the sensitivity of the system to various treatments, and could, in this way, generate normative implications, given management's values for outcomes. Such a model may have analytical value, too, in unearthing interactive effects among parameters and in highlighting what may be hidden aspects of customary treatments on the total process. As it stands, it is an abstract model, a kind of logical chess game. In order for it to make contact with reality, it is necessary for management to say exactly what is wanted and to provide the mechanisms for measuring it. For example, one must say what measurable behaviors one wants in specific slots in the company in order to accomplish any one of the outcomes. If these can be defined and measured, the model can go beyond an abstract set of relationships and become a tool for monitoring the effectiveness of the management of human resources.

It may seem like a lot to ask management to define what behaviors it wants in order to accomplish certain goals. On the other hand, if we are to progress beyond a seat-of-the-pants navigation, we will have to have such specification. It became possible to use budgeting as a monitoring device when we specified exactly what things were needed, in what amounts, with what priority, and at what times. Exactly the same requirement arises here.

I emphasize the problem of the kind of attention and specificity that management will have to give the problem not to frighten people off, but because it is an integral part of the matter. Similarly, social scientists will have to turn, on the one hand, to fact-grubbing in some places where we don't have data, and on the other, away from the seductive ease of applying a bit of psychological lore that seems superficially relevant to the industrial scene. Both sides must accept the discipline of the problem. In general, neither one has done so.

Organizational Problems

Now we are back very near to the beginning. The social sciences have contributed very little to the practice of business in the management of human resources. Neither companies nor scholars have made an attempt to see the repertoire of influence mechanisms as a single, integrated system of possibilities. Neither of them has stated the short- and long-run objectives explicitly and weighed the variety of treatments in terms of their effectiveness in moving toward each of the criterion variables. Why haven't they done so, and what can be done differently?

I mentioned before that there have been published a tremendous number of books and articles on human problems. There is no dearth of talented people. Why haven't they done more? For one thing, we have concentrated on short-term variables. Partly this is to prove to management quickly that the work is worthwhile. Partly it is because the university reward system is geared to short-term payoffs. Two papers a year are a kind of minimum for promotion. There is a negative incentive attached to a broader, longer-term study of the impact of influence treatments on the firm. The much better strategy is to do a series of cute insightful studies and sit back and bask. That they don't add up to much is the field's problem, not the individual's.

At the same time, the university's reward system is not well geared to recognize applied or developmental research. Basic research, a theoretical model, and the grand concept are what pay off. Consequently, when the manager finds something that looks interesting and wonders how to apply it, he is apt to find very little support in this step. For this reason the problem is not to fill the pipeline of basic research. The pipeline is full, because virtually nothing has been drawn from it. The problem is how to get more out of it, rather than to put more into it.

Faced with this problem, several companies have begun in-house programs in the behavioral sciences, hoping thus to harness this potential to their problems. Here, too, my assessment is that the result is discouraging, and for a variety of reasons. For one thing, the company has seldom stated clearly to itself what its objectives for the program are. It is enough that the organization has decided that it should have a little of this behavioral business. To ask, in addition, "What for?" is too much.

Since behavioral research is vaguely connected with people, the operation is usually attached somehow to the personnel department. The personnel department hasn't very much influence in the company councils anyway, and what little it has isn't enough to go around among the other things that it is already doing. Consequently, a broader look at social science issues never gets much attention at best. If it begins to raise matters that need some steam to carry them through, they're apt to be shunted aside in competition with other themes of longer standing—the IR problem, retailoring compensation in an inflating market, and the like. The organization structure is against it.

The problem is made doubly difficult by the fact that behavioral research tends to suggest basic changes in the way management itself does things and in the very philosophy of management. Other forms of research—hardware research, for example—typically lead to taking something new on and leaving the basic process unchanged but improved. It is small wonder, then, that behavioral research meets a large share of resistance. After all, every man is necessarily his own psychologist. He has acquired his present eminence, he feels, by practicing this trade. To suggest that he change his approach is to challenge the very basis of his success. Once more, the closer it approaches relevance, the more pressure there is to sweep behavioral research under the rug.

Finally, the point I have labored before—the bits-and-pieces approach and the short-term criterion—works against behavioral research in the organization. Small contributions and picayune evidence of effectiveness do not lead to change. The very short-term criterion is often used against it. It is commonplace, for instance, for an accounting type who is opposed to an executive-development program to suggest that an evaluation study be done of it. "Let us see," he says with all apparent good faith, "what the costs and benefits are." There are many people who have not avoided this cul-de-sac and have gone on to try to measure changes in productivity with simple pre- and post-training measures. The result is much the same as the studies that show that a college graduate earns $2000 more per year for a lifetime than a noncollege graduate. The fact is true, but the simple criterion does not evaluate the process. If this is truly the result of the community's investment in higher education, it isn't worth it. Similarly, if short-term productivity is truly the company's goal, it isn't worth it. A much longer and more comprehensive study would be needed to begin to evaluate.

All of these organizational factors—the failure of the social sciences to be integrated into top management's philosophy, the lack of power of personnel, the tendency to sweep the project under the rug as its findings and implications pinch—act to keep behavioral research from being effective. At the same time, universities have special liabilities that seem to make it difficult to supply the needed work. Despite the fact that graduate programs are running full steam, both universities and companies face a severe shortage in competent personnel largely due to problems of mobility. What can be done to resolve the situation?

A Proposal

We need a large, broad-scale, integrated attack on the problem of utilizing human resources. It must be set up for longer studies than have been the practice so far, and it must be protected from intervention at the point at which studies begin to bear critically on company practice. To do this, I think we must set up one or more centers for social science research in the utilization of human resources. I think they should be located physically at major universities, to draw on the small pool of specialized talent. Each of the centers should have a consortium of two or more companies as integral parts of it. The plurality of companies seems to me an essential. In a single company it is too easy to turn aside the research if it begins to threaten or pinch. With two or more of them it is my hope that they would shame one another into continuing in cases where any one alone would have stopped. In addition to the universities and companies, I suggest that the federal government be involved formally and actually in such centers. The problem of utilization of resources and the kind of concepts dealt with—participation, the distribution of influence within a social system—are an important part of our national goals. The government should be a part in order to represent the community and to be influenced by the major attack on our most pressing problems. Such centers could take responsibility for the broad integrated attack on human problems and could afford the longer-term studies that offer some hope for research. All the partners—management, scientists, and the government—could now be part of the shaping of the problem and part of the task of carrying the results back to practice.

It is not easy to say what the output of such centers would amount to. It is by no means certain, on the evidence at hand, that the results will come surely enough or soon enough to weigh conclusively in the issue of what system is most productive of human values and of material goods. However, the fragmentary evidence certainly suggests that it is a businessman's risk. Furthermore, the other side of the picture is quite clear. If we don't mount a concerted attack on the broad problem of human resources at work, we are condemned to the continuation of the ineptitude of the past. With these alternatives, there is little choice.

2

Increasing Organizational Effectiveness Through Better Human Resource Planning and Development

Edgar H. Schein

Planning for and managing human resources is emerging as an increasingly important determinant of organizational effectiveness. It is an area all too often ignored by line managers. As organizations evolve, the complexity of the environments within which they operate will cause increased dependence upon the very people making up the organization. This article focuses upon two key issues: the increasing importance of human resource planning and development in organizational effectiveness, and how the major components of a human resource planning and development system should be coordinated for maximum effectiveness. The author concludes that these multiple components must be managed by both line managers and staff specialists as part of a total system to be effective. *SMR.*

In this article I would like to address two basic questions. First, why is human resource planning and development becoming increasingly important as a determinant of organizational effectiveness? Second, what are the major components of a human resource planning and career development system, and how should these components be linked for maximum organizational effectiveness?

The field of personnel management has for some time addressed issues such as these, and much of the technology of planning for and managing human resources has been worked out to a considerable degree.[1] Nevertheless there continues to be in organizations a failure, particularly on the part of line managers and functional managers in areas other than personnel, to recognize the true importance of planning for and managing human re-

From *Sloan Management Review*, Fall 1977, Vol. 19, No. 1. Reprinted with permission.

sources. This article is not intended to be a review of what is known, but rather a kind of position paper for line managers to bring to their attention some important and all too often neglected issues. These issues are important for organizational effectiveness, quite apart from their relevance to the issue of humanizing work or improving the quality of working life.[2]

The observations and analyses made below are based on several kinds of information:

- Formal research on management development, career development, and human development through the adult life cycle conducted in the Sloan School and at other places for the past several decades;[3]
- Analysis of consulting relationships, field observations, and other involvements over the past several decades with all kinds of organizations dealing with the planning for and implementation of human resource development programs and organization development projects.[4]

Why is Human Resource Planning and Development Increasingly Important?

The Changing Managerial Job

The first answer to the question is simple, though paradoxical. Organizations are becoming more dependent upon people, because they are increasingly involved in more complex technologies and are attempting to function in more complex economic, political, and sociocultural environments. The more different technical skills there are involved in the design, manufacture, marketing, and sales of a product, the more vulnerable the organization will be to critical shortages of the right kinds of human resources. The more complex the process, the higher the interdependence among the various specialists. The higher the interdependence, the greater the need for effective integration of all the specialities, because the entire process is only as strong as its weakest link.

In simpler technologies, managers could often compensate for the technical or communication failures of their subordinates. General managers today are much more dependent upon their technically trained subordinates, because they usually do not understand the details of the engineering, marketing, financial, and other decisions that their subordinates are making. Even the general manager who grew up in finance may find that, since his day, the field of finance has outrun him, and his subordinates are using models and methods that he cannot entirely understand.

What all this means for the general manager is that he cannot any longer safely make decisions by himself; he cannot get enough information digested within his own head to be the integrator and sole decision maker. Instead, he finds himself increasingly having to manage the *process* of decision making, bringing the right people together around the right questions or problems, stimulating open discussion, ensuring that all relevant information surfaces and is critically assessed, managing the emotional ups and downs of his prima donnas, and ensuring that, out of all this human and interpersonal process, a good decision will result.

As I have watched processes like these in management groups, I have been struck by the fact that the decision emerges out of the interplay. It is hard to pin down who had the idea and who made the decision. The general manager in this setting is accountable for the decision, but rarely would I describe the process as one where he or she actually made the decision, except in the sense of recognizing when the right answer was achieved, ratifying that answer, announcing it, and following up on its implementation.

If the managerial *job* is increasingly moving in the direction I have indicated, managers of the future will have to be much more skilled in how to:

1. Select and train their subordinates.
2. Design and run meetings and groups.
3. Deal with conflict between strong individuals and groups.
4. Influence and negotiate from a low power base.
5. Integrate the efforts of diverse technical specialists.

If the above image of what is happening to organizations has any generality, it will force the field of human resource management increasingly to center stage. The more complex organizations become, the more they will be vulnerable to human error. They will not necessarily employ more people, but they will employ more sophisticated highly trained people, both in managerial and in individual-contributor staff roles. The price of low motivation, turnover, poor productivity, sabotage, and intraorganizational conflict will be higher in such an organization. Therefore it will become a matter of economic necessity to improve human resource planning and development systems.

Changing Social Values

A second reason why human resource planning and development will become more central and important is that changing social values regarding the role of work will make it more complicated to manage people. Several kinds of research findings and observations illustrate this point.

First, my own longitudinal research of a panel of Sloan School graduates of the 1960s strongly suggests that we have put much too much emphasis on the traditional success syndrome of "climbing the corporate ladder."[5] Some alumni indeed want to rise to high-level general-manager positions, but many others want to exercise their particular technical or functional competence and rise only to levels of functional management or senior staff roles with minimal managerial responsibility. Some want security, others are seeking nonorganizational careers as teachers or consultants, while a few are becoming entrepreneurs. I have called these patterns of motivation, talent, and values "career anchors" and believe that they serve to stabilize and constrain the career in predictable ways. The implication is obvious—organizations must develop multiple ladders and multiple reward systems to deal with different types of people.[6]

Second, studies of young people entering organizations in the last several decades suggest that work and career are not so central a life preoccupation as they once were. Perhaps because of a prolonged period of economic affluence, people see more options for themselves and are increasingly exercising those options. In particular, one sees more concern with a balanced life in which work, family, and self-development play more equal roles.[7]

Third, closely linked to the above trend is the increase in the number of women in organizations, which will have its major impact through the increase of dual-career families. As opportunities for women increase, we will see more new life-styles in young couples that will affect the organization's options as to moving people geographically, joint employment, joint career management, family support, etc.[8]

Fourth, research evidence is beginning to show that personal growth and development is a life-long process and that predictable issues and crises come up in every decade of our lives. Organizations will have to be much more aware of what these issues are, how work and family interact, and how to manage people at different ages. The current "hot button" is mid-career crisis, but the more research we do the more we find developmental crises at all ages and stages.[9]

An excellent summary of what is happening in the world of values, technology, and management is provided in a recent text by Elmer Burack:

The leading edge of change in the future will include the new technologies of information, production, and management, interlaced with considerable social dislocation and shifts in manpower inputs. These developments are without precedent in our industrial history.

Technological and social changes have created a need for more education, training, and skill at all managerial and support levels. The lowering of barriers to employment based on sex and race introduces new kinds of manpower problems for management officials. Seniority is coming to mean relatively less in relation to the comprehension of problems, processes, and approaches. The newer manpower elements and work technologies have shifted institutional arrangements: The locus of decision making is altered, role relationships among workers and supervisors are changed (often becoming more collegial), and the need to respond to changing routines has become commonplace. . . .

These shifts have been supported by more demanding customer requirements, increasing government surveillance (from product quality to antipollution measures), and more widespread use of computers, shifting power bases to the holders of specialized knowledge skills.[10]

In order for human resource planning and development (HRPD) systems to become more responsive and capable of handling such growing complexity, they must contain all the necessary components, must be based on correct assumptions, and must be adequately integrated.

Components of a Human Resource Planning and Development System

The major problem with existing HRPD systems is that they are fragmented, incomplete, and sometimes built on faulty assumptions about human or organizational growth.

Human growth takes place through successive encounters with one's environment. As the person encounters a new situation, he or she is forced to try new responses to deal with that situation. Learning takes place as a function of how those responses work out and the results they achieve. If they are successful in coping with the situation, the person enlarges his repertory of responses; if they are not successful the person must try alternate responses until the situation has been dealt with. If none of the active coping responses work, the person sometimes retreats from the new situation, or denies there is a problem to be solved. These responses are defensive and growth limiting.

For growth to occur, people basically need two things: *new challenges* that are within the range of their coping responses, and *knowledge of results*—information on how their responses to the challenge have worked out. If the tasks and challenges are too easy or too hard, the person will be demotivated and cease to grow. If the information is not available on how well the person's responses are working, the person cannot grow in a systematic, valid direction but is forced into guessing or trying to infer information from ambiguous signals.

Organizational growth similarly takes place through successful coping with the internal and external environment.[11] But since the organization is a complex system of human, material, financial, and informational resources, one must consider how each of those areas can be properly managed toward organizational effectiveness. In this article I will deal only with the human resources.

In order for the organization to have the capacity to perform effectively over a period of time it must be able to plan for, recruit, manage, develop, measure, dispose of, and replace human resources as warranted by the tasks to be done. The most important of these functions is the planning function, since task requirements are likely to change as the complexity and turbulence of the organization's environment increase. In other words, a key assumption underlying organizational growth is that the nature of jobs will change over time, which means that such changes must be continuously monitored in order to ensure that the right kinds of human resources can be recruited or developed to do those jobs. Many of the activities such as recruitment, selection, performance appraisal, and so on presume that some planning process has occurred that makes it possible to assess whether or not those activities are meeting organizational needs, quite apart from whether they are facilitating the individual's growth.

In an ideal HRPD system, one would seek to match the organization's needs for human resources with the individual's needs for personal career growth and development. One can then depict the basic system as involving both individual and organizational planning, and a series of matching activities designed to satisfy mutual needs. If we further assume that both individual and organizational needs change over time, we can depict this process as a developmental one, as in Figure 2.1.

In the right-hand column we show the basic stages of the individual career through the life cycle. While not everyone will go through these stages in the manner depicted, there is growing evidence that, for organizational careers in particular, these stages reasonably depict the movement of people through their adult lives.[12]

Given those developmental assumptions, the left-hand side of the diagram shows the organizational planning activities that must occur if human resources are to be managed in an optimal way, and if changing job requirements are to be properly assessed and continuously monitored. The middle column shows the various matching activities that have to occur at various career stages.

The components of an effective HRPD system now can be derived from the diagram. First, there have to be in the organization the overall planning components shown on the left-hand side of Figure 2.1. Second, there have to be components that ensure an adequate process of staffing the organization. Third, there have to be components that plan for and monitor growth

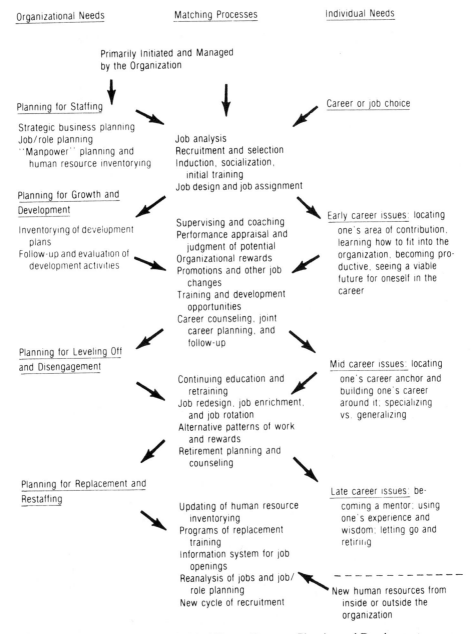

Organizational Needs	Matching Processes	Individual Needs

Primarily Initiated and Managed
by the Organization

Planning for Staffing

Strategic business planning
Job/role planning
"Manpower" planning and
 human resource inventorying

Job analysis
Recruitment and selection
Induction, socialization,
 initial training
Job design and job assignment

Career or job choice

Planning for Growth and
Development

Inventorying of development
 plans
Follow-up and evaluation of
 development activities

Supervising and coaching
Performance appraisal and
 judgment of potential
Organizational rewards
Promotions and other job
 changes
Training and development
 opportunities
Career counseling, joint
 career planning, and
 follow-up

Early career issues: locating
 one's area of contribution,
 learning how to fit into the
 organization, becoming productive, seeing a viable
 future for oneself in the
 career

Planning for Leveling Off
and Disengagement

Continuing education and
 retraining
Job redesign, job enrichment,
 and job rotation
Alternative patterns of work
 and rewards
Retirement planning and
 counseling

Mid career issues: locating
 one's career anchor and
 building one's career
 around it; specializing
 vs. generalizing

Planning for Replacement and
Restaffing

Updating of human resource
 inventorying
Programs of replacement
 training
Information system for job
 openings
Reanalysis of jobs and job/
 role planning
New cycle of recruitment

Late career issues: be-
 coming a mentor; using
 one's experience and
 wisdom; letting go and
 retiring

New human resources from
 inside or outside the
 organization

Figure 2.1 A Developmental Model of Human Resource Planning and Development

31

and development. Fourth, there have to be components that facilitate the actual process of the growth and development of the people who are brought into the organization; this growth and development must be organized to meet both the needs of the organization and the needs of the individuals within it. Fifth, there have to be components that deal with decreasing effectiveness, leveling off, obsolescence of skills, turnover, retirement, and other phenomena that reflect the need for either a new growth direction or a process of disengagement of the person from his or her job. Finally, there have to be components that ensure that, as some people move out of jobs, others are available to fill those jobs and, as new jobs arise, that people are available with the requisite skills to fill them.

In the remainder of this article I would like to comment on each of these six sets of components and indicate where and how they should be linked to each other.

Overall Planning Components

The function of these components is to ensure that the organization has an adequate basis for selecting its human resources and developing them toward the fulfillment of organizational goals.

Strategic Business Planning.   These activities are designed to determine the organization's goals, priorities, future directions, products, market growth rate, geographical location, and organization structure or design. This process should lead logically into the next two planning activities, but it is often disconnected from them, because it is located in a different part of the organization or is staffed by people with different orientations and backgrounds.

Job/Role Planning.   These activities are designed to determine what actually needs to be done at every level of the organization (up through top management) to fulfill the organization's goals and tasks. This activity can be thought of as a dynamic kind of job analysis, where a continual review is made of the skills, knowledge, values, etc., currently needed in the organization and that will be needed in the future. The focus is on the predictable consequences of the strategic planning for managerial roles, specialist roles, and skill mixes that may be needed to get the mission accomplished. If the organization already has a satisfactory system of job descriptions, this activity would concern itself with how those jobs will evolve and change, and what new jobs or roles will evolve in the future.[13]

This component is often missing completely in organizations or is carried out only for lower level jobs. From a planning point of view it is probably most important for the highest level jobs—how the nature of general and functional management will change as the organization faces new technologies, new social values, and new environmental conditions.

"Manpower Planning" and Human Resource Inventorying. These activities draw on the job/role descriptions generated in job/role planning and assess the capabilities of the present human resources against those plans or requirements. These activities may be focused on the numbers of people in given categories and are often designed to ensure that under given assumptions of growth there will be an adequate supply of people in those categories. Or the process may focus more on how to ensure that certain scarce skills that will be needed will in fact be available, leading to more sophisticated programs of recruitment or human resource development. For example, the inventorying process at high levels may reveal the need for a new type of general manager with broad integrative capacities which may further reveal the need to start a development program to ensure that such managers will be available five to ten years down the road.

These first three component activities are all geared to identifying the organization's needs in the human resource area. They are difficult to do, and tools are only now beginning to be developed for job/role planning.[14] In most organizations I have dealt with, the three areas, if they exist at all, are not linked to each other organizationally. Strategic planning is likely to exist in the Office of the President. Job/role planning is likely to be an offshoot of some management-development activities in Personnel. And human resource inventorying is likely to be a specialized subsection within Personnel. Typically, no one is accountable for bringing these activities together, even on an ad hoc basis.

This situation reflects an erroneous assumption about growth and development: The assumption is, if the organization develops its *present* human resources, it will be able to fill whatever job demands may arise in the future. Thus we do find in organizations elaborate human resource planning systems, but they plan for the present people in the organization, not for the organization per se. If there are no major changes in job requirements as the organization grows and develops, this system will work. But if jobs themselves change, it is no longer safe to assume that today's human resources, with development plans based on *today's* job requirements, will produce the people needed in some future situation. Therefore, I am asserting that more job/role planning must be done, independent of the present people in the organization.

The subsequent components to be discussed, which focus on the matching of individual and organizational needs, all assume that some sort of basic planning activities such as those described have been carried out. They may not be very formal, or they may be highly decentralized (e.g., every supervisor who has an open slot might make his own decision of what sort of person to hire based on his private assumptions about strategic business planning and job/role planning). Obviously, the more turbulent the environment, the greater the vulnerability of the organization if it does not centralize and coordinate its various planning activities—and generate its HRPD system from those plans.

Staffing Processes

The function of these processes is to ensure that the organization acquires the human resources necessary to fulfill its goals.

Job Analysis. If the organizational planning has been done adequately, the next component of the HRPD system is to specify what jobs need to be filled and what skills, etc., are needed to do those jobs. Some organizations go through this process very formally, others do it in an informal unprogrammed manner, but in some form it must occur in order to specify what kind of recruitment to undertake and how to select people from among the recruits.

Recruitment and Selection. This activity involves the actual process of going out to find people to fulfill jobs and developing systems for deciding which of those people to hire. These components may be very formal, including testing, assessment, and other aids to the selection process. If this component is seen as part of a total HRPD system, it will alert management to the fact that the recruitment-selection system communicates to future employees something about the nature of the organization and its approach to people. All too often this component sends incorrect messages or turns off future employees or builds incorrect stereotypes that make subsequent supervision more difficult.[15]

Induction, Socialization, and Initial Training. Once the employee has been hired, there ensues a period during which he or she learns the ropes, learns how to get along in the organization, how to work, how to fit in, how to master the particulars of the job, and so on. Once again, it is important that these activities are seen as part of a total process with long-range consequences for the attitudes of the employee.[16] The goal should be to facilitate the employee's becoming a productive and useful member of the organization both in the short run and in terms of long-range potential.

Job Design and Job Assignment.   One of the most crucial components of staffing is the actual design of the job given to the new employee and the manner in which the assignment is made. The issue is how to provide *optimal challenge,* a set of activities neither too hard nor too easy for the new employee, and neither too meaningless nor too risky from the point of view of the organization. If the job is too easy or too meaningless, the employee may become demotivated; if the job is too hard and/or involves too much responsibility and risk from the point of view of the organization, the employee may become too anxious, frustrated, or angry to perform at an optimal level. Some organizations have set up training programs for supervisors to help them to design optimally challenging work assignments.[17]

These four components are geared to ensuring that the work of the organization will be performed. They tend to be processes that have to be performed by line managers and personnel staff specialists together. Line managers have the basic information about jobs and skill requirements; personnel specialists have the interviewing, recruiting, and assessment skills to aid in the selection process. In an optimal system these functions will be closely coordinated, particularly to ensure that the recruiting process provides to the employee accurate information about the nature of the organization and the actual work that he or she will be doing in it. Recruiters also need good information on the long-range human resource plans, so that these can be taken into account in the selection of new employees.

Development Planning

It is not enough to get good human resources in the door. Some planning activities have to concern themselves with how employees who may be spending thirty to forty years of their total life in a given organization will make a contribution for all of that time, will remain motivated and productive, and will maintain a reasonable level of job satisfaction.

Inventorying of Development Plans.   Whether or not the process is highly formalized, there is in most organizations some effort to plan for the growth and development of all employees. The planning component that is often missing is some kind of pulling together of this information into a centralized inventory that permits coordination and evaluation of the development activities. Individual supervisors may have clear ideas of what they will do with and for their subordinates, but this information may never be collected, making it impossible to determine whether the individual plans of supervisors are connected in any way. Whether it is done by department, division, or total company, some effort to collect such information and to think through its implications is of great value to furthering the total development of employees at all levels.

Follow-up and Evaluation of Development Activities.   I have observed two symptoms of insufficient planning in this area: One, development plans are made for individual employees, are written down, but are never implemented; and two, if they are implemented they are never evaluated either in relation to the individual's own needs for growth or in relation to the organization's needs for new skills. Some system should exist to ensure that plans are implemented and that activities are evaluated against both individual and organizational goals.

Career Development Processes

This label is deliberately broad to cover all of the major processes of managing human resources during their period of growth and peak productivity, a period that may be several decades in length. These processes must match the organization's needs for work with the individual's needs for a productive and satisfying work career. The system must provide for some kind of forward movement for the employee through some succession of jobs, whether these involve promotion, lateral movement to new functions, or simply new assignments within a given area.[18] The system must be based both on the organization's need to fill jobs as they open up and on employees' needs to have some sense of progress in their working lives.

Supervision and Coaching.   By far the most important component in this area is the actual process of supervising, guiding, coaching, and monitoring. It is in this context that the work assignment and feedback processes that make learning possible occur, and it is the boss who plays the key role in molding the employee to the organization. There is considerable evidence that the first boss is especially crucial in giving new employees a good start in their careers,[19] and that training of supervisors in how to handle new employees is a valuable organizational investment.

Performance Appraisal and Judgment of Potential.   This component is part of the general process of supervision but stands out as such an important part of that process that it must be treated separately. In most organizations there is some effort to standardize and formalize a process of appraisal above and beyond the normal performance feedback which is expected on a day-to-day basis. Such systems serve a number of functions—to justify salary increases, promotions, and other formal organizational actions with respect to the employee; to provide information for human resource inventories or at least written records of past accomplishments for the employee's personnel folder; and to provide a basis for annual or semiannual formal reviews between boss and subordinate to supplement day-to-day feedback and to facilitate information exchange for career planning and counseling. In some organizations so little day-to-day feedback occurs that the *formal* system bears the burden of providing the employees with knowledge of how they are doing and what they can look forward to. Since knowledge of results, of how one is doing, is a crucial component of any developmental process, it is important for organizations to monitor how well and how frequently feedback is actually given.

One of the major dilemmas in this area is whether to have a single system that provides both feedback for the growth and development of the employee and information for the organization's planning systems. The dilemma arises because the information that the planning system requires (e.g., "how much potential does this employee have to rise in the organization?") may be the kind of information that neither the boss nor the planner wants to share with the employee. The more potent and more accurate the information, the less likely it is to be fed back to the employee in anything other than very vague terms.

On the other hand, the detailed work-oriented, day-to-day feedback the employee needs for growth and development may be too cumbersome to record as part of a selection-oriented appraisal system. If hundreds of employees are to be compared, there is strong pressure in the system toward more general kinds of judgments, traits, rankings, numerical estimates of ultimate potential, and the like. One way of resolving this dilemma is to develop two separate systems—one oriented toward performance improvement and the growth of the employee, and the other one oriented toward a more global assessment of the employee for future planning purposes involving judgments not shared with him or her except in general terms.

A second dilemma arises around the identification of the employee's "development needs" and how that information is linked to other development activities. If the development needs are stated in relation to the planning system, the employee may never get the feedback of what his needs may have been perceived to be, and, worse, no one may implement any program to deal with those needs if the planning system is not well linked with line management.

Two further problems arise from this potential lack of linkage. One, if individuals do not get good feedback around developmental needs, they remain uninvolved in their own development and potentially become complacent. We pay lip service to the statement that only the individual can develop himself or herself, but then deprive the individual of the very information that would make sensible self-development possible. Two, the development needs as stated for the various employees in the organization may have nothing to do with the organization's needs for certain kinds of human resources in the future. All too often, a complete lack of linkage between the strategic or business planning function and the human resource development function results in willy-nilly individual development based on today's needs and individual managers' notions of what will be needed in the future.

Organizational Rewards—Pay, Benefits, Perquisites, Promotion, and Recognition. Entire books have been written about the problems and subtleties in linking organizational rewards to the other components of a HRPD system to ensure both short-run and long-run human effectiveness. For purposes of this short article, I wish to point out only one major issue: how to ensure that organizational rewards are linked both to the needs of the individual and to the needs of the organization for effective performance and development of potential. All too often the reward system is responsive neither to the individual employee nor to the organization, being driven more by criteria of elegance, consistency, and what other organizations are doing. If linkage is to be established, line managers must actively work with compensation experts to develop a joint philosophy and set of goals based on an understanding of what the organization is trying to reward and what employee needs actually are. As organizational careers become more varied and as social values surrounding work change, reward systems will probably have to become much more flexible both in time (people at different career stages may need different things) and by type of career (functional specialists may need different things than general managers).

Promotions and Other Job Changes.   There is ample evidence that what keeps human growth and effectiveness going is continuing optimal challenge.[20] Such challenge can be provided for some members of the organization through promotion to more responsible jobs. For most members of the organization the promotion opportunities are limited, however, because the pyramid narrows at the top. An effective HRPD system will, therefore, concentrate on developing career paths, systems of job rotation, changing assignments, temporary assignments, and other lateral job moves that ensure continuing growth of all human resources.

One of the key characteristics of an optimally challenging job is that it both draws on the person's abilities and skills and that it has opportunities for "closure." The employee must be in the job long enough to get involved and to see the results of his or her efforts. Systems of rotation that move the person too rapidly either prevent initial involvement (as in the rotational training program), or prevent closure by transferring the person to a new job before the effects of his or her decisions can be assessed. I have heard many "fast track" executives complain that their self-confidence was low, because they could never really see the results of their efforts. Too often we move people too fast to fill slots and thereby undermine their development.

Organizational planning systems that generate slots to be filled must be coordinated with development planning systems that concern themselves with the optimal growth of the human resources. Sometimes it is better for the organization in the long run not to fill an empty slot in order to keep a manager in another job where he or she is just beginning to develop. One way of ensuring such linkage is to monitor these processes by means of a "development committee" composed of both line managers and personnel specialists. Here, the needs of the organization and the needs of the people can be balanced against each other in the context of the long-range goals of the organization.

Training and Development Opportunities.   Most organizations recognize that periods of formal training, sabbaticals, executive development programs outside of the company, and other educational activities are necessary in the total process of human growth and development. The important point about these activities is that they should be carefully linked both to the needs of the individual and to the needs of the organization. The individual should want to go to the program, because he or she can see how the educational activity fits into the total career. The organization should send the person because the training fits into some concept of future career development. It should not be undertaken simply as a generalized "good thing," or because other companies are doing it. As much as possible the training and educational activities should be tied to job/role planning. For example, many companies began to use university executive-development programs, because of an explicit recognition that future managers would require a broader perspective on various problems and that such "broadening" could best be achieved in the university programs.

Career Counseling, Joint Career Planning, Follow-up, and Evaluation.   Inasmuch as growth and development only come from within the individual himself or herself, it is important that the organization provide some means for individual employees at all levels to become more proactive about their careers and some mechanisms for joint dialogue, counseling, and career planning.[21] This process should ideally be linked to performance appraisal, because it is in that context that the boss can review with the subordinate the future potential, development needs, strengths, weaknesses, career options, etc. The boss is often not trained in counseling, but does possess some of the key information the employee needs to initiate career planning. More formal counseling could then be supplied by the personnel development staff or outside the organization altogether.

The important point to recognize is that employees cannot manage their own growth development without information on how their own needs, talents, values, and plans mesh with the opportunity structure of the organization. Even though the organization may have only imperfect, uncertain information about the future, the individual is better off knowing that than making erroneous assumptions about the future based on no information at all. It is true that the organization cannot make commitments, nor should it unless required to by legislation or contract. But the sharing of information, if properly done, is not the same as making commitments or setting up false expectations.

If the organization can open up the communication channel between employees, their bosses, and whoever is managing the human resource system, the groundwork is laid for realistic individual-development planning. Whatever is decided about training, next steps, special assignments, rotation, etc., should be jointly decided by the individual and the appropriate organizational resource (probably the supervisor and someone from personnel specializing in career development). Each step must fit into the employee's life plan and must be tied into organizational needs. The organization should be neither a humanistic charity nor an indoctrination center. Instead, it should be a vehicle for meeting both the needs of society and of individuals.

Whatever is decided should not merely be written down but executed. If there are implementation problems, the development plan should be renegotiated. Whatever developmental actions are taken, it is essential that they be followed up and evaluated both by the person and by the organization to determine what, if anything, was achieved. It is shocking to discover how many companies invest in major activities such as university executive development programs and never determine for themselves how effective those programs were or what was accomplished in them. In some instances, they make no plans to talk to the individual before or after the program, so that it is not even possible to determine what the activity meant to the participant, or what might be an appropriate next assignment for him or her following the program.

I can summarize the above analysis best by emphasizing the two places where I feel there is the most fragmentation and violation of growth assumptions. First, too many of the activities occur without the involvement of the person who is "being developed" and therefore may well end up being self-defeating. This is particularly true of job assignments and performance appraisal where too little involvement and feedback occur. Second, too much of the human resource system functions as a personnel *selection* system unconnected to either the needs of the organization or the needs of the individual. All too often it is only a system for short-run replacement of people in standard type jobs. The key planning functions are not linked in solidly and hence do not influence the system to the degree they should.

Planning for and Managing Disengagement

The planning and management processes reviewed below are counterparts of ones that have already been discussed but are focused on different problems: the late career, loss of motivation, obsolescence, and ultimately retirement. Organizations must recognize that there are various options available to deal with this range of problems beyond the obvious ones of either terminating the employee or engaging in elaborate measures to "remotivate" people who may have lost work involvement.[22]

Continuing Education and Retraining. These activities have their greatest potential if the employee is motivated and if there is some clear connection between what is to be learned and what the employee's current or future job assignments require in the way of skills. More and more organizations are finding out that it is better to provide challenging work first and only then the training to perform that work once the employee sees the need for it. Obviously for this linkage to work well continuous dialogue is needed between employees and their managers. For those employees who have leveled off, have lost work involvement, but are still doing high quality work, other solutions are applicable.

Job Redesign, Job Enrichment, and Job Rotation. This section is an extension of the arguments made earlier on job changes in general applied to the particular problems of leveled-off employees. In some recent research, it has been suggested that job enrichment and other efforts to redesign work to increase motivation and performance may work only during the first few years on a job.[23] Beyond that the employee becomes "unresponsive" to the job characteristics themselves and pays more attention to surrounding factors such as the nature of supervision, relationships with coworkers, pay, and other extrinsic characteristics. In other words, before organizations attempt to "cure" leveled-off employees by remotivating them through job redesign or rotation, they should examine whether those employees are still in a responsive mode or not. On the other hand, one can argue that there is nothing wrong with less motivated, less involved employees so long as the quality of what they are doing meets the organizational standards.[24]

Alternative Patterns of Work and Rewards.   Because of the changing needs and values of employees in recent decades, more and more organizations have begun to experiment with alternative work patterns, such as flexible working hours, part-time work, sabbaticals or other longer periods of time off, several people filling one job, dual employment of spouses with more extensive childcare programs, etc. Some are experimenting also with flexible reward systems in which employees can choose between a raise, some time off, special retirement, medical or insurance benefits, and other efforts to make multiple career ladders a viable reality. These programs apply to employees at all career stages, but are especially relevant to people in mid- and late-career stages whose perceptions of their career and life goals may be undergoing important changes.

None of those innovations should be attempted without first clearly establishing a HRPD system that takes care of the organization's needs as well as the needs of employees and links them to each other. There can be little growth and development for employees at any level in a sick and stagnant organization. It is in the best interests of both the individual and the organization to have a healthy organization that can provide opportunities for growth.

Retirement Planning and Counseling.   As part of any effective HRPD system, there must be a clear planning function that forecasts who will retire and that feeds this information into both the replacement staffing system and the counseling functions, so that the employees who will be retiring can be prepared for this often traumatic career stage. Employees need counseling not only with the mechanical and financial aspects of retirement, but also to prepare them psychologically for the time when they will no longer have a clear organizational base or job as part of their identity. For some people it may make sense to spread the period of retirement over a number of years by using part-time work or special assignments to help both the individual and the organization to get benefits from this period.

The counseling function here probably involves special skills and must be provided by specialists. However, the line manager continues to play a key role as a provider of job challenge, feedback, and information about what is ahead for any given employee. Seminars for line managers on how to handle the special problems of pre-retirement employees would probably be of great value as part of their managerial training.

Planning for and Managing Replacement and Restaffing

With this step the HRPD cycle closes back upon itself. This function must be concerned with such issues as:

1. Updating the human resource inventory as retirements or terminations occur.
2. Instituting special programs of orientation or training for new incumbents to specific jobs as those jobs open up.
3. Managing the information system on what jobs are available and determining how to match this information to the human resources available in order to determine whether to replace from within the organization or to go outside with a new recruiting program.
4. Continuously reanalyzing jobs to ensure that the new incumbent is properly prepared for what the job now requires and will require in the future.

How these processes are managed links to the other parts of the system through the implicit messages that are sent to employees. For example, a company that decides to post publicly all of its unfilled jobs is clearly sending a message that it expects internal recruitment and supports self-development activities. A company that manages restaffing in a very secret manner may well get across a message that employees might as well be complacent and passive about their careers, because they cannot influence them anyway.

Summary and Conclusions

I have tried to argue in this article that human resource planning and development is becoming an increasingly important function in organizations, that this function consists of multiple components, and that these components must be managed *both* by line managers and staff specialists. I have tried to show that the various planning activities are closely linked to the actual processes of supervision, job assignment, training, etc., and that those processes must be designed to match the needs of the organization with the needs of the employees throughout their evolving careers, whether or not those careers involve hierarchical promotions. I have also argued that the various components are linked to each other and must be seen as a total system if it is to be effective. The total system must be managed as a system to ensure coordination between the planning functions and the implementation functions.

I hope it is clear from what has been said above that an effective human resource planning and development system is integral to the functioning of the organization and must, therefore, be a central concern of line management. Many of the activities require specialist help, but the accountabilities must rest squarely with line supervisors and top management. It is they who control the opportunities and the rewards. It is the job-assignment system and the feedback that employees get that is the ultimate raw material for growth and development. Whoever designs and manages the system, it will not help the organization to become more effective unless that system is *owned* by line management.

3

Toward a "Truly" Scientific Management: The Concept of Organization Health

Warren G. Bennis

MUGGERIDGE: Now, Charles, you, because you're a scientist . . . you have this idea, as I understand from your writings, that one of the failings of our sort of society, is that the people who exercise authority, we'll say Parliament and so on, are singularly unversed in scientific matters.

SNOW: Yes, I think this is a terrible weakness of the whole of Western society, and one that we're not going to get out of without immense trouble and pain.

MUGGERIDGE: Do you mean by that, for instance, an M.P. would be a better M.P. if he knew a bit about science?

SNOW: I think some M.P.'s ought to know a bit about science. They'd be better M.P.'s in the area where scientific insight becomes important. And there are quite a number of such areas [52].

Extolling science has become something of a national and international pastime that typically stops short of the truly radical reforms in social organization that scientific revolution implies. Knowing a "bit about science" is a familiar and increasingly popular examplar of this, which C.P. Snow treats in his *Two Cultures* [69]. But if culture is anything it is a way of life, the way real people live and grow, the way ideals and moral imperatives are transmitted and infused. Culture is more *value* than knowledge. Dr. Bronowski, who shares with Snow the view that "humanists" tend to be ignorant of and removed from science, understands more than Snow seems to that a fundamental unification of cultural outlook is what is required [18]. The connective tissue required, then, is cultural, social, institutional, not grafted-on evening courses on science.

From *Sloan Management Review*, Fall 1962, Vol. 4, No. 1. Reprinted with permission.

In this connection, and closer to some of the general aims of this article, Nevitt Sanford has said:

The ethical systems of other professions, such as business or the military, have become models for whole societies. Why should not the practice of science become such a model? After we have shown, as we can, that joy and beauty have their places in this system. At any rate, anyone who takes it upon himself to be a scientist, and succeeds in living up to its requirements, may be willing for his behavior to become a universal norm [61].

This foreshadows the general theme of this article: the recognition that the *institution* of science can and should provide a viable model for other institutions not solely concerned with developing knowledge. To demonstrate this proposition, I first discuss the criterion problem in relation to organizations.[1] I then attempt to show that the usual criteria for evaluating organizational effectiveness, "enhancement of satisfaction on the part of industry's participants and improvement of effectiveness of performance" [36], are inadequate, incorrect, or both as valid indicators of organizational "health." (For the moment let us use the term *health* in the same vague way as *effectiveness*. Organizational health is defined later.) Next I suggest that an alternative set of criteria, extracted from the normative and value processes of science, provides a more realistic basis for evaluating organizational performance. These criteria are related to those of positive mental health, for it will be argued that there is a profound kinship between the mores of science and the criteria of health for an individual. From this confluence I fashion a set of psychologically based criteria for examining organizational health. Finally, I discuss some of the consequences of these effectiveness criteria for organizational theory and practice.

The Search for Effectiveness Criteria

There is hardly a term in current psychological thought as vague, elusive, and ambiguous as the term *mental health*. That it means many things to many people is bad enough. That many people use it without even attempting to specify the idiosyncratic meaning the term has for them makes the situation worse . . . for those who wish to introduce concern with mental health into systematic psychological theory and research.—M. Jahoda [34].

. . . no one can say with any degree of certainty by what standards an executive ought to appraise the performance of his organization. And it is questionable whether the time will ever arrive when there will be any pattern answers to such a question—so much does the setting of an organization and its own goal orientation affect the whole process of appraisal.—J. M. Pfiffner and F. P. Sherwood [57].

Raising the problem of criteria, the standards for judging the "goodness" of an organization, seldom fails to generate controversy and despair. Establishing criteria for an organization (or, for that matter, education, marriage, psychotherapy, etc.) accentuates questions of value, choice, normality, and all the hidden assumptions that are used to form judgments of operation. Often, as Jahoda has said in relation to mental-health criteria, the problem "seems so difficult that one is almost tempted to claim the privilege of ignorance" [34].

However, as tempting as ignorance can be, researchers on organizations—particularly industrial organizations—have struggled heroically to identify and measure a number of dimensions associated with organizational effectiveness [74]. Generally, these dimensions have been of two kinds: those dealing with some index of organizational performance, such as profit, cost, rates of productivity, or individual output, and those associated with the human resources, such as morale, motivation, mental health, job commitment, cohesiveness, or attitudes toward employer or company. In short, as Katzell pointed out in his 1957 review of industrial psychology, investigations in this area typically employ measures of *performance* and *satisfaction* [36]. In fact, it is possible to construct a simple twofold table that adequately accounts for most of the research on organizations that has been undertaken to date, as shown in Table 3.1. On one axis are located the criteria variables: organizational efficiency (the ethic of work performance) and member satisfaction (the ethic of "health"). On the other axis are located the two main independent variables employed, human and rationalized procedures. In other words, it is possible to summarize most of the research literature in the organizational area by locating the major independent variables (technological or human) on one axis and the dependent variables (efficiency or health) on the other.

Table 3.1   Major Variables Employed in the Study of Organizational Behavior

		Criteria Variables	
		Organizational Efficiency	Satisfaction or Health
Independent Variables	Technology (Rationalized Procedures)	Management science: Systems research, operations research, decision processes, etc.	Human engineering
	Human Factors	Personnel psychology, training, and other personnel functions	Industrial social psychology and sociology

This classification is necessarily crude and perhaps a little puzzling, principally for the reason that research on organizations lacks sufficient information concerning the empirical correlation between the two dependent variables, organizational efficiency and health factors. For a time it seemed (or was hoped) that personal satisfaction and efficiency were positively related, that as satisfaction increased so did performance. This alleged correlation allowed the "human relations" school and the industrial engineers (Taylorism being one example[2]) to proceed coterminously without necessarily recognizing the tension between "happy workers" and "high performance."

As Likert put it:

It is not sufficient merely to measure morale and the attitudes of employees toward the organization, their supervision, and their work. Favorable attitudes and excellent morale do not necessarily assure high motivation, high performance, and an effective human organization. A good deal of research indicates that this relationship is much too simple [41].

Indeed, today we are not clear about the relation of performance to satisfaction, or even whether there is any interdependence between them. Likert and his associates have found organizations with all the logical possibilities—high morale with low productivity, low productivity with low morale, etc. Argyris's work [2,4], with a popular assist from William H. Whyte, Jr., [76], clouds the picture even further by postulating the inevitability of conflict between human need-satisfaction and organizational performance (as formal organizations are presently conceived). This creates, as Mason Haire has recognized [31], a calculus of values: How much satisfaction or health is to be yielded for how many units of performance?

Generally speaking, this is the state of affairs: two criteria, crudely measured, ambiguous in meaning, questionable in utility, and fraught with value connotations [35]. In view of these difficulties, a number of other, more promising, approaches have been suggested. The most notable of these are the criterion of multiple goals, the criterion of the situation, and the criterion of system characteristics.

The Criterion of Multiple Goals

This approach rests on the assumption that "organizations have more than a single goal and that the interaction of goals will produce a different value framework in different organizations" [57]. Likert, who is a proponent of the multiple criterion approach, claims that very few organizations, if any, obtain measurements that clearly reflect the quality and capacity of the organization's human resources. This situation is due primarily to the shadow of traditional theory, which tends to overlook the human and motivational variables; and the relatively new developments in social science that only now permit measurements of this type. Likert goes on to enumerate twelve criteria, covering such dimensions as loyalty and identification with the institution and its objectives, degree of confidence and trust, adequacy and efficiency of communication, amount and quality of teamwork, etc. [41]. By and large, Likert's criteria are psychologically based and substantially enrich the impoverished state of effectiveness criteria.[3]

The Criterion of the Situation

This approach is based on the reasoning that organizations differ with respect to goals, and that they can be analytically distinguished in terms of goal orientation. As Parsons pointed out: "As a formal analytical point of reference, *primacy of orientation to the attainment of a specific goal is used as the defining characteristic of an organization* which distinguishes it from other types of social systems" [55].

In an earlier article by Bennis [9], a framework was presented for characterizing four different types of organizations based on a specific criterion variable. These "pure" types are rarely observed empirically, but they serve to sharpen the difference among formally organized activities. Table 3.2

Table 3.2   Typology of Organization*

Type of Organization	Major Function	Examples	Effectiveness Criterion
Habit	Replicating standard and uniform products	Highly mechanized factories, etc.	Number of products
Problem-solving	Creating new ideas	Research organizations; design and engineering divisions; consulting organizations, etc.	Number of ideas
Indoctrination	Changing people's habits, attitudes, intellect, behavior (physical and mental)	Universities, prisons, hospitals, etc.	Number of "clients" leaving
Service	Distributing services either directly to consumer or to above types	Military, government, advertising, taxi companies, etc.	Extent of services performed

*From W. G. Bennis, "Leadership Theory and Administrative Behavior: The Problem of Authority," *Administrative Science Quarterly,* December 1959, p. 297.

represents an example of developing effectiveness variables on the basis of organizational parameters.

The Criterion of System Characteristics

This approach, most cogently advanced by sociologists, is based on a structural-functional analysis. Selznick, one of its chief proponents, characterizes the approach in the following way:

> Structural-functional analysis relates contemporary and variable behavior to a presumptively stable system of needs and mechanisms. This means that a given empirical system is deemed to have basic needs, essentially related to self-maintenance; the system develops repetitive means of self defense; and day-to-day activity is interpreted in terms of the function served by that activity for the maintenance and defense of the system [62].

Derivable from this system model are basic needs or institutional imperatives that have to be met if the organism is to survive and "grow." Selznick, for example, lists five: the security of the organization as a whole in relation to social forces in its environment; the stability of the lines of authority and communication; the stability of informal relations within the organization; the continuity of policy and of the sources of its determination; and a homogeneity of outlook with respect to the meaning and role of the organization [62].

Caplow, starting from the fundamental postulate that organizations tend to maintain themselves in continuous operation, identifies three criteria of organizational success: the performance of objective functions, the minimization of spontaneous conflict, and the maximization of satisfaction for individuals. [22] Obviously, with the exception of the second criterion, these resemble the old favorites, performance and satisfaction.

The preceding summaries do not do full justice to the nuances in these three approaches or the enormous creative effort that went into their development. Nor do they include the ideas of many thoughtful practitioners.[4] Despite these limitations, the discussion of multiple criteria, situational parameters, and system characteristics represents the main attempts to solve the criterion problem.[5]

Inadequacy of Criterion Variables for the Modern Organization

> One thing that is new is the prevalence of newness, the changing scale and scope of change itself, so that the world alters as we walk on it, so that the years of man's life measure not some small growth or rearrangement or moderation of what he learned in childhood, but a great upheaval. . . . To assail the changes that have unmoored us from the past is futile, and in a deep sense, I think, it is wicked. We need to recognize the change and learn what resources we have.—Robert Oppenheimer [53].

The history of other animal species shows that the most successful in the struggle for survival have been those which were most adaptable to changes in their world.
—J. Bronowski [17].

The present ways of thinking about and measuring organizational effectiveness are seriously inadequate and often misleading. These criteria are insensitive to the important needs of the organization and out of joint with the emerging view of contemporary organization that is held by many organizational theorists and practitioners. The present techniques of evaluation provide static indicators of certain output characteristics (i.e., performance and satisfaction) without illuminating the processes by which the organization searches for, adapts to, and solves its changing goals [56]. However, it is these *dynamic* processes of problem-solving that provide the critical dimensions of organizational health, and without knowledge of them output measurements are woefully inadequate.[6]

This rather severe charge is based upon the belief that the main challenge confronting the modern organization (and society) is that of coping with external stress and change. This point hardly needs elaboration or defense. Ecclesiastes glumly pointed out that men persist in disordering their settled ways and beliefs by seeking out many inventions. The recent work in the field of organizational behavior reflects this need and interest; it is virtually a catalogue of the problems in organizational change.[7] In a 1961 monograph on managing major change in organizations, Mann and Neff stated the issue this way: "Among the most conspicuous values in American culture of the twentieth century are progress, efficiency, science and rationality, achievement and success. These values have helped to produce a highly dynamic society—a society in which the predominant characteristic is *change* [45]. Kahn, Mann, and Seashore, when discussing a criterion variable, "the ability of the organization to change appropriately in response to some objective requirement for change," remarked: "Although we are convinced of the theoretical importance of this criterion, which we have called organizational flexibility, we have thus far been unable to solve the operational problems involved in its use" [35].

The basic flaw in the present effectiveness criteria is their inattention to the problem of adapting to change. To illuminate some of the consequences of this omission, let us turn to one rather simple example. The example is drawn from an area of research that started at the Massachusetts Institute of Technology about 1949 on the effects of certain organizational patterns (communication networks) on problem-solving by groups [38]. Two of these networks, the Wheel and the Circle, are shown in Figure 3.1.

The results of these experiments showed that an organization with a structure like the Wheel can solve simple tasks (e.g., identification of the color of

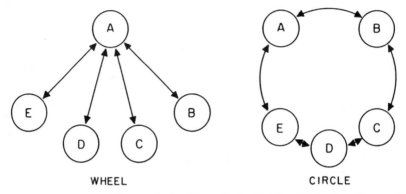

WHEEL   **CIRCLE**

Figure 3.1 Two Types of Communication Networks for Problem Solving by a Group of Five Persons

a marble that is common to all five group members) more rapidly, more clearly, and more efficiently than an organization like the Circle. Thus the Wheel arrangement is plainly superior in terms of the usual criteria employed to evaluate effectiveness. However, if we consider two other criteria of organizational effectiveness that are relevant to the concern with change-flexibility and creativity, we discover two interesting phenomena. First, the rapid acceptance of a new idea is more likely in the Circle than in the Wheel. The man in the middle of the Wheel is apt to discard an idea on the grounds that he is too busy or the idea is impractical. Second, when the task is changed, for example by going from "pure" color marbles to unusual color marbles (such as ginger-ale color or blue-green), the Circle organization is better able to adapt to this change by developing a new code [68].

As Leavitt pointed out:

. . . by certain industrial engineering-type criteria (speed, clarity of organization and job descriptions, parsimonious use of paper, etc.), the highly structured, highly routinized, noninvolving centralized net seems to work best. But if our criteria of effectiveness are more ephemeral, more general (like acceptance of creativity, flexibility in dealing with novel problems, generally high morale and loyalty), then the more egalitarian or decentralized type of net seems to work better [39].

If we view organizations as adaptive, problem-solving, organic structures, then inferences about effectiveness have to be made not from static measures of output, though these may be helpful, but on the basis of the processes through which the organization approaches problems. In other words, no single measurement of organizational efficiency or satisfaction—no single time-slice of organizational performance—can provide valid indicators of organizational health. An organization may be essentially healthy, despite measurements that reveal that its performance and satisfaction measurements are lower than last month's. It can be unhealthy even if its performance and efficiency figures are higher than last month's. Unhealthy and healthy, that is, in relation to the ability to cope with change, with the future. Discussing the neurotic processes, Kubie makes the same point:

> There is not a single thing which a human being can do or feel, or think, whether it is eating or sleeping or drinking or fighting or killing or hating or loving or grieving or exulting or working or playing or painting or inventing, which cannot be either sick or well. . . . The measure of health is flexibility, the freedom to learn through experience, the freedom to change with changing internal and external circumstances, to be influenced by reasonable argument, admonitions, exhortations, and the appeal to emotions; the freedom to respond appropriately to the stimulus of reward and punishment, and especially the freedom to cease when sated. The essence of normality is flexibility in all of these vital ways [37].

Any moment of behavior is unhealthy if the processes that set it in motion predetermine its automatic repetition, regardless of the environmental stimuli or consequences of the act. For example, it is plausible that lowering efficiency in order to adjust to some product change may be quite appropriate when market demands are considered. It is equally plausible that morale, or whatever measure is used to gauge the human factor, may also plummet during this period. In fact, maintaining the same level of efficiency and morale in new circumstances may be dysfunctional for the health of the organization.

Let me review the argument thus far. The main challenge confronting today's organization, whether it is a hospital or a business enterprise, is that of responding to changing conditions and adapting to external stress. The salience of change is forced on organizations because of the growing interdependence between their changing boundary conditions and society (a point that will be elaborated later) and the increasing reliance on scientific knowledge. The traditional ways that are employed to measure organizational effectiveness do not adequately reflect the true determinants of organizational health and success. Rather, these criteria yield static time-slices of performance and satisfaction, which may be irrelevant or misleading. These static, discrete measurements do not provide viable measures of health, for they tell us nothing about the processes by which the organization copes with its problems. Therefore, different effectiveness criteria have to be identified, criteria that reveal the processes of problem-solving. This point is corroborated by some recent works on organizational theory. Consider, for example, these remarks by Wilfred Brown, Chairman and Managing Director of the Glacier Metal Company:

Effective organization is a function of the work to be done and the resources and techniques available to do it. The changes in methods of production bring about changes in the number of work roles, in the distribution of work between roles and in their relationship to one another. Failure to make explicit acknowledgment of this relationship between work and organization gives rise to nonvalid assumptions (e.g., that optimum organization is a function of the personalities involved, that it is a matter connected with the personal style and arbitrary decision of the chief executive, that there are choices between centralized and decentralized types of organization, etc.). Our observations lead us to accept that optimum organization must be derived from an analysis of the work to be done and the techniques and resources available [19].

The work of Emery and Trist, which has influenced the thinking of Brown, stressed the "socio-technical system," based on Bertalanffy's "open system" theorizing [13]. They conclude that "the primary task of managing an enterprise as a whole is to relate the total system to its environment, and not internal regulation per se" [24]. And further that:

If management is to control internal growth and development it must in the first instance control the "boundary conditions"—the forms of exchange between the enterprise and the environment. . . . The strategic objective should be to place the enterprise in a position in its environment where it has some assured conditions for growth—unlike war the best position is not necessarily that of unchallenged monopoly. Achieving this position would be the primary task or overriding mission of the enterprise [24].

In reference to management development, A. T. M. Wilson, former Director of Tavistock Institute, pointed out:

One general point of high relevance can be seen in these discussions of the firm as an institution. The tasks of the higher level managers center on problems in which there is a continuously high level of uncertainty; complex value decisions are inevitably involved; and this has a direct bearing on the requirements of personality for top-level management [77].

And H. J. Leavitt said on the same subject:

Management development programs need, I submit, to be oriented much more toward the future, toward change, toward differences from current forms of practice and behavior. . . . We ought to allocate more of the effort of our programs to making our student a more competent analyst. We ought, in other words, to try to teach them to think a little more like scientists, and indeed to know a good deal more about the culture and methods of scientists [39].

What relevance have these quotations[8] to the main theme of this essay? Note, first of all, that these theorists all view the organization (or institution) as an adaptive structure actively encountering many different environments, both internal and external, in their productive efforts. Note also the key terms: change, uncertainty, future, task, mission, work to be done, available resources, exchanges between the enterprise and environment. There is no dialogue here on the relation between "productivity" and "satisfaction," no fruitless arguments between the "human relationists" and scientific management advocates. Indeed, it seems that it is no longer adequate to perceive organization as an analogue to the machine, as Max Weber indicated: "[Bureaucracy is like] a modern judge who is a vending machine into which the pleadings are inserted together with the fee and which then disgorges the judgment together with its reasons mechanically derived from the code." [8] Nor is it reasonable to view the organization solely in terms of the sociopsychological characteristics of the persons involved at work, a viewpoint that has been so fashionable of late.[9] Rather, the approach that should be taken is that of these quoted writers: Organizations are to be viewed as "open systems" defined by their primary task or mission and encountering boundary conditions that are rapidly changing their characteristics.[10] Given this rough definition, we must locate some effectiveness criteria and the institutional prerequisites that provide the conditions for the attainment of this criteria.

The Spirit of Inquiry as a Model for Organization

Findings are science's short-range benefits, but the method of inquiry is its long-range value. I have said that the invention of organization was Man's first most important achievement; I now add that the development of inquiry will be his second. Both of these inventions change the species and are necessary for its survival. But both must become a part of the nature of Man himself, not just given house room in certain groups. Organization is by now a part of every man, but inquiry is not. The significant product of science and education will be the incorporation within the human animal of the capability and habit of inquiry.—H. Thelen [70].

Whether our work is art or science or the daily work of society, it is only the form in which we explore our experience which is different; the need to explore remains the same. This is why, at bottom, the society of scientists is more important than their discoveries. What science has to teach us here is not its techniques but its spirit; the irresistible need to explore.—J. Bronowski [18].

It has been asserted throughout this article that organizations must be viewed as adaptive, problem-solving systems operating and embedded in complicated and rapidly changing environments. If this view is valid, then it is fair to postulate that the methodological rules by which the organization approaches its task and "exchanges with its environments" are the critical determinants of organizational effectiveness. These methodological rules or operating procedures bear a close resemblance to the rules of inquiry, or scientific investigation. Therefore, the rules and norms of science may provide a valuable, possibly necessary model for organizational behavior.

First, it should be stated what is meant and what is not meant by "science" in this context. It is not the findings of science, the vast array of data that scientists produce. Nor is it a barren operationalism—what some people refer to as "scientism"—or the gadgetry utilized for routine laboratory work. Rather it is what may be called the scientific "temper" or "spirit." It is this "spirit of inquiry," which stems from the value position of science, that such authors as Dewey, Bronowski, Geiger, and Sanford have emphasized must be considered if our world is to survive. This position says essentially that the roles of scientist and citizen cannot be sharply separated. As Waddington put it:

> The true influence of science is an attitude of mind, a general method of thinking about and investigating problems. It can, and I think it will, spread gradually throughout the social consciousness without any very sharp break with the attitudes of the past. But the problems for which it is wanted face us already; and the sooner the scientific method of handling them becomes more generally understood and adopted, the better it will be [72].

Now it is necessary to look a bit more closely at what is meant by the "scientific attitude." This complex includes many elements, only two of which are considered here. The first may be called the hypothetical spirit, the feeling for tentativeness and caution, the respect for probable error. As Geiger says: "The hypothetical spirit is the unique contribution scientific method can offer to human culture; it certainly is the only prophylactic against the authoritarian mystique so symptomatic of modern nerve failure" [28].

The second ingredient is experimentalism, the willingness to expose ideas to empirical testing, to procedures, to action. The hypothetical stance without experimentalism would soon develop into a rather arid scholasticism. Experimentalism without the corrective of the hypothetical imagination would bring about a radical "dustbowl" empiricism lacking both significant insight and underlying structures capable of generalization. These two features, plus the corrective of criticism, is what is meant by the methodological rules of science; it is the spirit of inquiry, a love of truth relentlessly pursued, that ultimately creates the objectivity and intelligent action associated with science.

But the scientific attitude of which I speak can most easily flourish under specific conditions usually associated with the social organization of the scientific enterprise. A number of social scientists, inspired by the work of Parsons [54] and Merton [49,50] have examined the society of scientific enterprise [5,21,47,60]. What they have said is important for the argument presented here. Only when the social conditions of science are realized can the scientific attitude exist. As Sanford pointed out:

Science flourishes under that type of democracy that accents freedom of opinion and dissent, and respect for the individual. It is against all forms of totalitarianism, of mechanization and regimentation. . . . In the historical development of the ends that are treasured in Western societies there is reason to believe that science has had a determining role. Bronowski again: Men have asked for freedom, justice and respect precisely as science has spread among them [61].

Or as Parsons states:

Science is intimately integrated with the whole social structure and cultural tradition. They mutually support one another—only in certain types of society can science flourish and conversely without a continuous and healthy development and application of science such a society cannot function properly [5].

What are the conditions that comprise the ethos of science? Barber identifies five that are appropriate to this discussion: rationality, universalism, individualism, communality, and disinterestedness [6]. A brief word about each of these is in order. The goal of science is understanding, understanding in as abstract and general a fashion as possible. Universalism, as used here, means that all men have morally equal claims to discover and to understand. Individualism, according to Barber, expresses itself in science as antiauthoritarianism; no authority but the authority of science need be accepted or trusted. Communality is close to the Utopian communist slogan: "From each according to his abilities, to each according to his needs." This simply means that all scientific peers have the right to share in existing knowledge; withholding knowledge and secrecy are cardinal sins. The last element, disinterestedness, is to be contrasted with the self-interest usually associated with organizational and economic life. Disinterestedness in science requires that role incumbents serve others and gain gratification from the pursuit of truth itself. These five conditions comprise the moral imperatives of the social organization of science. They are, of course, derived from an "ideal type" of system, an empirically imaginable possibility but a rare phenomenon. Nevertheless, insofar as they are imperatives, they do in fact determine significantly the behavior of scientific organization.

There are two points to be made in connection with this model of organization. The first was made earlier but may require reiteration: The spirit of inquiry can flourish only in an environment where there is a commitment toward the five institutional imperatives. The second point is that what is now called the "human relations school"[11] has been preoccupied primarily with the study of those factors that this article has identified as the institutional imperatives of the science organization. In fact, only if we look at the human-relations approach from this perspective do we obtain a valid view of their work. For example, a great deal of work in human relations has focused on "communication," "participation," and "decision-making" [11 and 43]. Overgeneralizing a bit, we can say that most of the studies have been (from a *moral* point of view) predicated on and lean toward the social organization of science as has been outlined here. Note, for instance, that many studies have shown that increased participation, better communication (keeping workers "informed"), more "self-control," and decreased authoritarianism are desirable ends. Because of their emphasis on these factors, the researchers and theoreticians associated with human-relations research have sometimes been perceived as "soft-headed," unrealistic, too academic, and even Utopian. In some cases, the social scientists themselves have invited these criticisms by being mainly interested in demonstrating that these participative beliefs would lead to heightened morale and, on occasion, to increased efficiency. So they have been accused by many writers as advocates of "happiness" or a moo-cow psychology.[12]

These are invalid criticisms, mainly because the issue is being fought on the wrong grounds. One of the troubles is that the social scientists have not foreseen the full implications of their studies. Rather than debating the viability of sociopsychological variables in terms of the traditional effectiveness variables, which at this point is highly problematical, they should be saying that the only way in which organizations can develop a scientific attitude is by providing conditions where such an attitude can flourish. In short, the norms of science are both compatible and remarkably homogeneous with those of a liberal democracy. We argue, then, that the way in which organizations can master their dilemmas and solve their problems is by developing a spirit of inquiry. This can flourish only under the social conditions associated with the scientific enterprise (i.e., democratic ideals). Thus it is *necessary* to emphasize the "human side of enterprise," that is, institutional conditions of science, if organizations are expected to maintain mastery over their environment.[13]

Now, assuming that the social conditions of science have been met, let us return to the designated task of identifying those organizational criteria that are associated with the scientific attitude.

The Criteria of Science and Mental Health Applied to Organizations

Perhaps no other area of human functioning has more frequently been selected as a criterion for mental health than the individual's reality orientation and his efforts at mastering the environment.—M. Jahoda [34].

I now propose that we gather the various kinds of behavior just mentioned, all of which have to do with effective interaction with the environment, under the general heading of competence.—Robert White [75].

All aspects of the enterprise must be subordinated to . . . its *primary task*. It is not only industrial enterprises, however, which must remain loyal to their primary tasks. This is so of all human groups, for these are all compelled, in order to maintain themselves in existence, to undertake some form of appropriate action in relation to their environment. . . . An organism, whether individual or social, must do work in order to keep itself related to its external environment, that is, to meet reality."—Eric Trist [19].

These three quotations provide the framework for the following analysis. They express what has been the major concern throughout this article: that, when organizations are considered as "open systems," adaptive structures coping with various environments, the most significant characteristic for understanding effectiveness is competence, mastery, or as the term has been used in this essay, problem-solving. It has been shown that competence can be gained only through certain adaptations of science: its attitude and social conditions. It is now possible to go a step further by underlining what the above quotations reveal, that the criteria of science bear a close kinship to the characteristics of what mental-health specialists and psychiatrists call "health."

There is an interesting historical parallel between the development of criteria for the evaluation of mental health and the evolution of standards for evaluating organizational health. Mastery, competence, and adaptive, problem-solving abilities are words relatively new to both fields. In the area of organizational behavior these words are replacing the old terms "satisfaction" and "work competence." Similarly, an important change has taken place in the mental-health field, which has had some of the same problems in determining adequate criteria. Rather than viewing health exclusively in terms of some highly inferential intrapsychic reconstitutions, these specialists are stressing "adaptive mechanisms" and "conflict-free," relatively autonomous ego-functioning, independent of id energies. The studies of White [75], Rapaport [58], Erikson [25], Hartmann [33], and other so-called ego-psychologists all point in this direction.

The main reason for the confluence of organizational behavior and mental health is basically quite simple. Both the norms of science and the methodology of psychotherapeutic work have the same goal and methodology: to perceive reality, both internal and external; and to examine unflinchingly the positions of these realities in order to act intelligently. It is the belief here that what a patient takes away and can employ *after* treatment is the methodology of science, the ability to look facts in the face, to use the hypothetical and experimental methods—the spirit of inquiry—in understanding experience.

Sanford has said of Freud's psychoanalytic method of investigation and treatment:

> (This method is in my view, Freud's greatest, and it will be his most lasting contribution.) By the method I mean the whole contractual arrangement according to which both the therapist and patient become investigators, and both objects of careful observation and study; in which the therapist can ask the patient to face the truth because he, the therapist, is willing to try to face it in himself; in which investigation and treatment are inseparable aspects of the same humanistic enterprise [61].

And in Freud's own words, "Finally, we must not forget that the relationship between analyst and patient is based on a love of truth, that is, on the acknowledgment of reality, and that it precludes any kind of sham or deception" [26].

It is now possible to postulate the criteria for organizational health. These are based on a definition by Marie Jahoda, according to which a healthy personality "actively masters his environment, shows a certain unit of personality, and is able to perceive the world and himself correctly" [25]. Let us take each of these elements and extrapolate it into organizational criteria.

1. "Actively Masters His Environment": Adaptability

In terms of this article, this characteristic coincides with problem-solving ability, which in turn depends upon the organization's flexibility. Earlier it was pointed out that flexibility is the freedom to learn through experience, to change with changing internal and external circumstances. Another way of putting it, in terms of organizational functioning, is to say that it is "learning how to learn." This is equivalent to Bateson's notion of "deutero-learning," the progressive change in rate of simple learning [7].

2. "Certain Unit of Personality": The Problem of Identity

In order for an organization to develop adaptability, it needs to know who it is and what it is to do; that is, it has to have some clearly defined identity.[14] The problem of identity, which is central to much of the contemporary literature in the mental-health field, can in organizations be examined in at least two ways: by determining to what extent the organizational goals are understood and accepted by the personnel; and by ascertaining to what extent the organization is perceived veridically by the personnel.

As to the problem of goals, Selznick has pointed out:

The aims of large organizations are often very broad. A certain vagueness must be accepted because it is difficult to foresee whether more specific goals will be realistic or wise. This situation presents the leader with one of his most difficult but indispensable tasks. *He must specify and recast the general aims of his organization so as to adapt them, without serious corruption, to the requirements of institutional survival.* This is what we mean by the definition of institutional mission and role [63].

The same point is made by Simon, Smithburg, and Thompson: "No knowledge of administrative techniques . . . can relieve the administrator from the task of moral choice—choice as to organizational goals and methods and choice as to his treatment of the other human beings in his organization" [67].

In addition to the clear definition of mission, which is the responsibility of the leader to communicate, there also has to be a working consensus on the organization of work. Wilfred Brown's definition of work is extremely useful in this connection. He enumerates four concepts of organization: the *manifest* organization, the one that is seen on the "organization chart" and is formally displayed; the *assumed* organization, the one that individuals perceive as the organization; the *extant* organization, the situation as revealed through systematic investigation by, say, a student of organizations; and the *requisite* organization, or the situation as it would be if it were "in accord with the real properties of the field in which it exists."

"The ideal situation," Brown goes on to say, "is that in which the manifest, the assumed, the extant, and the requisite are as closely as possible in line with each other" [19]. Wherever these four organizational concepts are in contradiction, we find a case of what Erikson calls "identity diffusion" [25]. Certainly this phenomenon is a familiar one to students and executives of organizations. Indeed, the great attention paid to the "informal group" and its discrepancy with the formal (difference between the manifest and the assumed organizations or between the manifest and the extant) testifies to this.

Another useful analogy to the mental-health field shows up in this discussion. Many psychotherapeutic schools base their notions of health on the degree to which the individual brings into harmony the various "selves" that make up his or her personality. According to Fromm-Reichmann, "The successfully treated mental patient, as he then knows himself, will be much the same person as he is known to others" [27].

Virtually the same criterion is used here for organizational health, i.e., the degree to which the organization maintains harmony and knowledge about and among the manifest, assumed, extant, and requisite situations. This point should be clarified. It is not necessary to organizational health that all four concepts of organization be identical. Rather, all four types should be recognized and allowance made for all the tensions attendant upon their imbalance. It is doubtful that there will always be total congruence in organizations. The important factor is recognition; the executive function is to strive toward congruence insofar as it is possible.

3. "Is Able to Perceive the World and Himself Correctly": Reality-Testing

If the conditions for requisite organizations are to be met, the organization must develop adequate techniques for determining the "real properties" of the field in which it exists. The field contains two main boundaries, the internal organization and the boundaries relevant to the organization. March and Simon, in their cognitive view of organization, place great emphasis on adequate "search behavior." Ineffective search behavior—cycling and stereotypy—are regarded as "neurotic" [46].

However, it is preferable here to think about inadequate search behavior in terms of perception that is free from need-distortion [36]. Abraham Maslow places this in perspective:

> Recently Money-Kyrle, an English psychoanalyst, has indicated that he believes it possible to call a neurotic person not only *relatively* inefficient, simply because he does not perceive the real world as accurately or as efficiently as does the healthy person. The neurotic is not only emotionally sick—he is cognitively *wrong* [34]. The requisite organization requires reality-testing, within the limits of rationality, for successful mastery over the relevant environments.[15]

In summary, then, I am saying that the basic features of organization rely on adequate methods for solving problems. These methods stem from the elements of what has been called the scientific attitude. From these ingredients have been fashioned three criteria or organizational mechanisms, which fulfill the prerequisites of health. These criteria are in accord with what mental-health specialists call health in the individual.

Undeniably, some qualifications have to be made. The mensuration problem has not been faced, nor have the concrete details for organizational practice been fully developed. Nonetheless, it has been asserted that the processes of problem-solving—of adaptability—stand out as the single most important determinant of organizational health and that this adaptability depends on a valid identity and valid reality-testing.[16]

Some Implications of the Science Model for Organizational Behavior

There is one human characteristic which today can find a mode of expression in nationalism and war, and which, it may seem would have to be completely denied in a scientific society. That is the tendency to find some dogma to which can be attached complete belief, forthright and unquestioning. That men do experience a need for certainty of such a kind can scarcely be doubted. . . . Is science, for all its logical consistency, in a position to satisfy this primary need of man?—C. H. Waddington [72].

We are not yet emotionally an adaptive society, though we try systematically to develop forces that tend to make us one. We encourage the search for new inventions; we keep the mind stimulated, bright, and free to seek out fresh means of transport, communication, and energy; yet we remain, in part, appalled by the consequences of our ingenuity and, too frequently, try to find security through the shoring up of ancient and irrelevant conventions, the extension of purely physical safeguards, or the delivery of decisions we ourselves should make into the keeping of superior authority like the state. These solutions are not necessarily unnatural or wrong, but historically they have not been enough, and I suspect they will never be enough to give us the serenity and competence we seek. [I suspect] . . . we may find at least part of our salvation in identifying ourselves with the adaptive process and thus share . . . some of the joy, exuberance, satisfaction and security . . . to meet the changing time.—E. Morison [51].

The use of the model of science as a form for the modern organization implies some profound reforms in current practice, reforms that may appear to some as too adventurous or Utopian. This criticism is difficult to deny, particularly since not all the consequences can be clearly seen at this time. However, let us examine a few consequences that do stand out rather sharply.

1. The Problem of Commitment and Loyalty

Although the viewpoint does have its critics, such as William H. Whyte, Jr., most administrators desire to develop high commitment and loyalty to the organization. Can the scientific attitude, with its ascetic simplicity and acceptance of risk and uncertainty, substitute for loyalty to the organization and its purpose? Can science, as Waddington wonders, provide the belief in an illusion that organizational loyalty is thought to provide? The answer to this is a tentative yes and no. Substituting the scientific attitude for loyalty would be difficult for those people to whom the commitment to truth, to the pursuit of knowledge, is both far too abstract and far too threatening. For some, the "escape from freedom" is a necessity and the uncertain nature of the scientific attitude difficult to accept. However, it is likely that even these individuals would be influenced by the adoption of the science model by the organization. Loyalty to the organization per se would be transformed into loyalty and commitment directed to the spirit of inquiry. What effect would this have on commitment?

Gouldner, in another context, has supplied an important clue. He pointed to a difference between individuals in terms of two organizational roles, "locals and cosmopolitans" [30]. The cosmopolitan derives his rewards from inward standards of excellence, internalized and reinforced through professional (usually scientific) identification. On the other hand, the local (what Marvick calls the "bureaucratic orientation") [48] derives his rewards from manipulating power within the hierarchy. The locals are considered to be better organization men than the cosmopolitans. Loyalty within the scientific organizational conditions specified here would be directed not to particular ends or products or to work groups but to identification with the adaptive process of the organization.

2. Recruitment and Training for the Spirit of Inquiry

There are some indications that the problems of recruitment and training for the social organization of science are not so difficult as has been expected. For one thing, as Bruner has shown [20], today's school children are getting more and better science teaching. It is to be hoped that they will learn as much about the attitude of science as they will about its glamour and techniques. In addition, more and more research-trained individuals are entering organizations.[17] As McGregor points out: "Creative intellectual effort by a wide range of professional specialists will be as essential to tomorrow's manager as instruments and an elaborate air traffic control system are to today's jet pilot" [44]. Individuals trained in scientific methodology can easily adapt to, in fact will probably demand, more and more freedom for intellectual inquiry. If McGregor's and Leavitt and Whisler's [40] prognostications are correct, as they seem to be, then there is practically no choice but to prepare a social milieu in which the adaptive, problem-solving processes can flourish.

As to training, only a brief word needs to be said. The training program of the National Training Laboratories [16] and the work of Blake [13], Blansfield [15], and Shepard [65] are based rather specifically on developing better diagnosticians of human behavior. It is apparent from such training studies that the organization of tomorrow, heavily influenced by the growth of science and technology and manned by an increasing number of professionals, appears to have the necessary requirements for constructing organizations based on inquiry.

3. Intergroup Competition

Blake and Mouton, guided partly by the work of the Sherifs [66], have disclosed for examination one of organization's most troublesome problems, intergroup conflict and collaboration. These chronic conflicts probably dissipate more energy and money than any other single organizational disease. Intergroup conflict, with its "win-lose" orientation, its dysfunctional loyalty (to the group or product, not to the truth), its cognitive distortions of the outsider (the "enemy"), and its inability to reach what has been called "creative synthesis," effectively disrupts the commitment to truth. By means of a laboratory approach Blake and Mouton have managed to break

. . . the mental assumptions underlying win-lose conflict. Factually based mutual problem identification, fluidity in initial stages of solution, proposing rather than fixed position taking, free and frequent interchange between representatives and their constitutent groups and focusing on communalities as well as differences as the basis for achieving agreement and so on, are but a few of the ways which have been experimentally demonstrated to increase the likelihood of arriving at mutually acceptable solutions under conditions of collaboration between groups [14].

What the authors do not explicitly say but only imply is that the structure of their experimental laboratory approach is based on the methods of inquiry that have been advocated in this article. Theirs is an action-research model, in which the subjects are the inquirers who learn to collect, use, and generalize from data in order to understand organizational conflict. Rational problem-solving is the only prophylaxis presently known to rid organizations of persistent intergroup conflict.

Loyalty, recruitment and training, and intergroup hostility are by no means all the organizational consequences that this article suggests. The distribution of power, the problems of group cohesiveness,[18] the required organizational fluidity for arranging task groups on a rational basis, and the change in organizational roles and status all have to be considered. More time and energy than are now available are needed before these problems can be met squarely.

However, one thing is certain: Whatever energy, competence, and time are required, it will be necessary to think generally along the directions outlined here. Truth is a cruel master, and the reforms that have been mentioned or implied may not be altogether pleasant to behold. The light of truth has a corrosive effect on vested interests, outmoded technologies, and rigid, stereotypic patterns of behavior. Moreover, if this scientific ethos is ever realized, the remnants of what is now known as morale and efficiency may be buried. For the spirit of inquiry implies a confrontation of truth that may not be "satisfying" and a deferral of gratification that may not, in the short run, be "efficient." However, this is the challenge that must be met if organizations are to cope more successfully within their increasingly complicated environments.

PART II

Development of Human Resources

4

From Confusion to Fusion: Integrating Our Educational and Managerial Efforts

Richard Beckhard

This article was presented as the Fourth Douglas McGregor Memorial Lecture in honor of the late Douglas McGregor, Alfred P. Sloan Professor of Management at the Massachusetts Institute of Technology.

The potential for integration of human efforts within the firm, within educational institutions, and between the firm and educational system is suggested by the author, who points out that many of our current efforts, while related in purpose, are unconnected, in fact. Forces impeding integration of efforts in firms and educational institutions are discussed. Some collaborative efforts that have yielded substantial benefits are described. In particular, the article suggests means of improving effectiveness through collaboration among staff groups in the firm, among departments in the business school, and between faculty and practicing managers. *SMR*.

A major dilemma, one we cannot afford to ignore, faces all of us, whether we are managers of economic enterprises or educational enterprises, or managers of our own learning. The dilemma is: How can we optimally integrate the technical and human resources and energy that we manage toward achieving the organization's mission, be it profit or learning, and at the same time so manage the working arrangements and role relationships that people's needs for self worth, growth, and satisfaction are significantly met in our organizations? Never before has there been such a need for those of us who are responsible for the firm and those of us who are responsible for producing knowledge and teaching it, to be in touch with the times, to be in touch with the students, to be in touch with the employees, and to be in touch with each other.

From *Sloan Management Review*, Fall 1968, Vol. 10, No. 1. Reprinted with permission.

"Connections" as a Common Theme

When I began to prepare for this event, one of the first things I did was to reread the three previous McGregor lectures. I was struck, as I had not been when I listened to the individual lectures and read the papers separately, by the strong common theme running through all three. Each writer makes a major point of the need for connection, the need for finding ways to integrate the efforts of all of us in our work.

Professor Warren Bennis, at the convocation three years ago, pointed out the need for new organization forms and values that will have to emerge in order to connect with the technologies of the future. He identified the dominant characteristics of the new environment: interdependence rather than competition, turbulence rather than steadiness, and large-scale rather than small-scale enterprise. A year later Professor Mason Haire looked critically and creatively at the lack of connection between the efforts of many behavioral scientists to understand organizations and the efforts of many managers to improve them. He pointed out that both groups are moving along parallel courses, but too little joint effort is being made to find mechanisms for examining and analyzing their common goals, and for setting priorities in working toward them. Last year, Professor Edgar Schein spoke on the lack of connection between what the product of the business school, the graduate, takes from the school in terms of values, ideas, and expectations, and what he actually finds as values, norms, and behavior in the environment of the firm. He pointed out some of the costs of this lack of connection in terms of the large number of students who move to a second firm within the first year or two after leaving school.

In another context, John Paul Jones of Federated Stores, and formerly of Union Carbide, prepared a paper entitled "What's Happened to the Cognitive Dialogue?" for the McGregor conference on organization development, held here last year. He mournfully noted the reduction in discussion and collaboration between behavioral scientists in the university and the men who are particularly concerned with the application of this knowledge in organizations. He related this to Douglas McGregor's unique efforts to establish and maintain this dialogue by having a foot in both camps.

Today, I want to add my thoughts to this recurring theme.

Opportunities for Integration

My work in both the university and the firm is committed toward building more connections between the production of behavioral science knowledge and its use in organizations. From this bias, I would like to discuss what I see as the prime needs and opportunities for more collaboration and integration of the efforts of all of us here, managers, specialists, faculty, and students. My starting point is based on two premises:

1. We must develop new models to help students acquire knowledge and application principles, help students apply their learning in a work setting, and enable students to transmit their expertise effectively to operating groups.
2. Development of these models will require more collaboration, more joint efforts among the producers and transmitters of knowledge, the specialists in the organization, and the managers who ultimately utilize this knowledge.

With these premises, I would like to identify three areas where I feel major efforts to find better connections are needed, and look briefly at some of the forces in these environments that tend to impede better integration of effort. I will then discuss some examples in the university, in the firm, and in joint projects that illustrate the direction I believe our efforts must take.

Three areas that I believe provide substantial opportunity for better integration are:

1. The academic disciplines taught in our graduate schools.
2. The activities of specialists in the firm.
3. Collaborative efforts among faculty members, managers of organizations, and students which connect the development of the student with the development of the manager and/or specialist.

Causes of Disconnections

Let me examine briefly some of the conditions in the environments of the university and of the firm, and in the relationship between the two, that foster disconnection.

In the Schools

One major problem in the transmission of new knowledge in the behavioral sciences, the management sciences, marketing, and finance, is that information itself is increasing so rapidly. Many faculty members who are producing new knowledge, and teaching it in the classroom, are so heavily committed to the transmission of their own information that they have little time or energy for looking at how it integrates with data from another field. As a result, the application of this knowledge to the operating organizational situation tends to become exclusively the concern of the student.

For example, it is not unusual for a graduate student or a Sloan Fellow to go to one class at 10:00 in the morning and be told that the way to organizational effectiveness and economic health is to develop rational decision-making models and better simulation. At 11:00, the same student might well go to another class and be told that the key to organizational health, effectiveness, growth, and even survival, is a deeper attention to human needs, to developing collaboration, trust, and open communication. The source of each input, the instructor, has no responsibility for integrating the knowledge he presents with knowledge presented to the student from the other source. The student must decide where, if at all, these two inputs come together and how much to accept of each input, and then integrate the learning in himself in order to apply it to managerial performance.

It might be useful to look at some of the root causes for this type of disconnection.

1. One of the realities of the university is that people are hired to study and teach a specialization. Most faculty members are not generalists; they are interested in, concerned about, and rewarded for contributions made to their particular field of knowledge.
2. Many people teaching in a graduate school are more concerned with furthering the production of knowledge in the area of their particular interest than with transmitting it. For these faculty members, research is likely to be more rewarding than teaching.
3. Status in the profession and approval by colleagues in one's own field is often more important to the faculty member than institutional approval.
4. The reward system of many schools and universities tends to encourage research more than teaching. "Publish or perish" is a common phrase.
5. The norms associated with academic freedom have in some cases produced a form of anarchy. *Collaboration* in teaching is a relatively new phenomenon.
6. The complexity of coordinating a curriculum makes it an extremely difficult business to build collaborative teaching arrangements from an economic, cost-effectiveness point of view, as well as from the point of view of managing the competing demands on the time of the various teaching personnel.

To summarize, there are strong traditions, norms, and habits all tending to maintain *separation* in the transmission of different fields of knowledge. Conscious efforts, a real desire to collaborate, and a great deal of work will be required to move toward more connected and integrated efforts in teaching.

In the Specialties in the Firm

Most firms today have specialists in such functions as operations research, management services, and methods improvement, all utilizing the management sciences, and specialists in human resources management, management development, and organization development, utilizing the behavioral sciences. Each specialist is expected by his organization to perform his specialty and to see that his technology is used effectively in the organization—in short, to do his thing. Generally speaking, these specialists do not mix. The personnel department or management-development department is often separated in location, and usually separated in reporting line, from the departments of management services and operations research. The industrial-engineering department probably has relatively little connection with the industrial-relations department when it comes to effecting changes in the organization. There is little tendency for specialists to be held jointly accountable for efforts toward organizational improvement.

Perhaps one of the most important causes for this lack of collaboration is the increasing complexity of the problems facing managers in organizations. The result is a need for more and more specialists to deal with the individual aspects. A second cause is the extensive resistance to change encountered in the line organization. Specialists must spend large amounts of their energy getting acceptance from their line "clients," which leaves them little energy, frequently, to worry about collaboration with other specialists. Third, the reward system in many organizations reinforces noncollaboration. The specialist scores his points from the application of his technology; he does not get any rewards for collaborating effectively with other specialists. This condition is less widespread in organizations than in schools, but nonetheless it is a serious factor. A fourth cause is the lack of interpersonal skills and team orientation among specialists. It is still true, unfortunately, that a good part of the education and training of most specialists is in the technical aspects of the specialty. All too little attention is paid to the application aspects. Very little time is spent, either in the business school or in the organization, on exposure to such subjects as "How to Introduce a Technology into a System," "How to Help People Learn," "How to Reduce Resistance to Change," "How to Improve One's Consulting Effectiveness."

Summing up, the causes of disconnection in organizations include the reward systems, the need for introducing one's own technology, the lack of interpersonal competence, and the increasing complexity of technologies.

Between Managers and Faculties

Let me now look at the third area: the relationship between managers in the firm and faculties in the school. There are large areas of disconnection between those of us who are preparing the student for a career and those of us who are managing his career. Most of us express common concern for the application of what a student learns in the school to his work on the job. But how frequently do the managers and the faculty members get together to discuss or work on this common concern? And how often do we include the student, the real connector?

In addition, I believe there are many unused opportunities that we should consider in helping managements of firms tune into the new knowledge and developments emerging in our schools. Conversely, I think we need to de-velop new mechanisms for keeping the faculty of the school better informed on how effectively the knowledge they are teaching is being applied. Unfor-tunately, the job of educating the student is still left pretty much to the school, while the job of using the technology remains the province of the firm.

Too little dialogue exists between manager and faculty about what is useful and practical in a curriculum and what kinds of knowledge are lacking in the graduate from the manager's point of view. Too little dialogue exists between faculty and manager on how to reduce the discrepancy between what the *faculty* tells the student he can contribute to the firm, what the *recruiter* tells the student the firm is looking for, and what the student actually *finds* when he enters the firm. This is a dramatic example of com-mon concern in which there is very little connection of our efforts.

Specifically, I believe there is:

1. A lack of feedback to the school about the product, that is, the student, from the management of the firm.
2. Insufficient focus in the school curriculum on the application of concepts.
3. Too little managerial dialogue between managers and faculty. Considera-ble technical dialogue does take place between specialists from the same discipline. One finds the faculty in computer technology in the business school maintaining contact with specialists in computer technology in the firm. Similarly, the behavioral scientists in the university talk to the organization development people in the firm. But there is very little discussion of the student as a person and of the connection between his development in the school and his utilization and continued development in the field.

Conditions for Facilitating Connections

To achieve real integration of effort, a number of forces in each environment must be changed. I want to turn now to some of the conditions that can facilitate this effort and to identify some programs and projects in each of these environments.

In the Schools

The conditions needed to facilitate the integration of knowledge transmission in the school include:

1. Growing faculty interest in experimenting with teaching methods.
2. Some high priority commitment on the part of faculties to connecting various areas of special knowledge toward the solution of management problems.
3. Institutional rewards for collaborative teaching and research.
4. More research on the management of education and of technology.

These changes could take many forms. We might need more vertical curricula dealing with such subjects or problem areas as "The Human Side of Marketing" or "The Human and Technical Aspects of Introducing a Computer." We could introduce courses in subjects such as team effectiveness, with inputs on rationalizing the decision making as well as inputs on increasing and improving working relationships within a team.

It is encouraging to note that at the Sloan School major efforts are under way toward these types of connection. There has been a complete revision of the undergraduate curriculum in industrial management to build more integration into the entire program. The master's curriculum has undergone considerable change in the direction of better integration, with a focus on the total environment and how the various disciplines relate to it. This year, a new course, "Information and Decision Systems," integrates the efforts of a number of faculty from the disciplines of information systems, marketing, production, and finance.

In the field of management of technology, Professor Donald Marquis joins his behavioral-science orientation with Professor Edward Roberts's quantitative orientation to form an integrated research and teaching program that deals with the field from the point of view of the end use.

In the research area, an in-depth study of the management of education is under way, involving Professors Amstutz, Kolb, Morton, Schein, White, and Zannetos of the Sloan faculty. This significant paragraph appears in the introduction to their plan: "Although, for operational efficiency, our proposed research efforts are presented in the form of individual projects, we plan, whenever appropriate, to work as a team. We realize the *interdependence of our activities* and the necessity for establishing sequencing priorities. Through constant interactions we hope to achieve efficiency by utilizing common data and for greater impact than we would as individuals." The statement represents the kind of collaboration I believe is necessary to achieve our joint ends.

In the Specialties in the Firm

Moving on to the firm, I think we must look for new ways of connecting the efforts of the many specialists who are trying to help the organization adapt to the changing environment. For example, it may well become the practice to gather management services, operations research, manpower planning, organization development, and career planning under one umbrella—organization improvement—and to have this cluster of functions report directly to the top of the organization.

It will be necessary, I am convinced, to examine the ways in which staff members are rewarded and to develop mechanisms that assure that points are achieved for joint efforts as well as for the introduction of individual technologies.

I suspect there is a need for broader education of specialists in related fields of management and science. It would seem important for the specialist in management sciences or computer technology to be familiar with the behavioral area in order to deal with such matters as "how to introduce change," "how to get collaboration," and the like. The behaviorally oriented specialist, on the other hand, needs to have more orientation to computer technology, information systems, decision making, and marketing strategies.

Let me describe briefly a few organization attempts to move toward new models of collaboration and to improve integration of the specialist resources in an organization.

In a large consumer goods company there have been, for a number of years, massive efforts to move the organization toward better integration of its various services. The operating field units, and there are many all over the country, are supported by several central staff organizations. These include an industrial-relations division concerned with labor relations, employee relations, training, and compensation, and an industrial-engineering division concerned with operations research, methods improvement, and information systems. The industrial-relations people had one set of treatments and cures for the ills of the organization, and the industrial-engineering people had another set. The two central staffs were rewarded by the organization for the quantity as well as the quality of satisfied customers, and therefore competed heavily in the field for customers, with relatively little communication between the two staffs. The field people, aware of the competition, had their own favorites and chose, more or less, on a friendship basis.

The personnel in field operations had a feeling of distance from and disgust with the central staffs. Their general attitude was, "We're supporting heavy overhead and not getting that much help."

As part of a general organization development effort, those of us working with the organization became aware of this condition, as did one of the key line managers. He was deeply concerned about the lack of communication and the inefficient use of the highly competent staff capabilities. He set about to change the condition.

A meeting was held with the various plant managers in which they identified their concerns about the service, or lack of it, that they were getting from the central groups, as a basis for dialogue with the staffs. At the same time the two central office staffs held a series of joint meetings at which they discussed their relationships, their past practices, their current modes of operation, and their feelings about each other and about the field groups. The staff groups also examined ways by which collaborative efforts on field problems could be initiated and competitive efforts to sell their particular services reduced. Following these activities, a series of meetings was convened with representatives of management from the field units and key personnel from the two central staffs to look at the total problem. Their mission was to develop mechanisms for improving the situation. Out of these meetings emerged a model which operates today. In the central office staff there is a group comprised of former specialists who are assigned on an individual basis to certain field locations to function as "account executives." Although these people still have a technical specialty, in most cases employee relations, their mission is to work with their own specific field "clients" in assessing needs for organizational and operations improvement, and to coordinate and manage the resources from all the specialist functions necessary to meet the field's needs. In other words, it is the account executive's mission to assure a team effort on the field organization's problems and to eliminate the selling of technology A or technology B, or staff group A or staff group B.

This model has been extended to some other staff services in the organization. Field people report considerably improved service from the central headquarters. Some significant new applications of technology have occurred. New information systems have been introduced. There are positive signs in terms of improved productivity data, as well as a significant improvement in morale.

A second example involves a large chemical company. For a number of years the field people had used the consulting services of a management-methods group, and in recent years, of an organization-development group as well. Many of the customers found the efforts of these two services to be confusing and, in some cases, contradictory.

When the leaders of the two staff groups became aware of the problem, they got together, as in the previous illustration, and worked out a procedure followed throughout the organization today. If either department receives a call for help from a line organization, it is standard practice, at the initial diagnosis stage, to bring in the other department. This joining of efforts has not only alleviated the problem but also produced a much higher quality of service and some very creative solutions to line problems.

A third situation deals with the introduction of a new technology. A computer was being introduced into the trust operations of a large bank. A staff of methods specialists was attached to the various units that would receive the computer. There was a great deal of resistance among some parts of the organization to the change.

In conjunction with the personnel people in the bank and a behavioral consultant, a program was planned for dealing with the human aspects of the change, as well as the introduction of the new technology. An analysis of the attitudes of those who would receive the computer was made. An experimental program was set up with the group that was seen as potentially the most difficult.

A team development project was started in which a group, composed of the nine people in the work group, plus the three people from the methods staff who were assigned to that group, became a learning team with the mission of examining the problems of introducing the change and working out the management of the change. Following a brief human relations seminar, the team held three off-site meetings, each two and one half days in duration. At these meetings, the members examined their own functioning and relationships and then built a plan for the introduction of the computer and a number of other improvements in their operations.

Research conducted on this experiment yielded significant data. Productivity in the experimental group went up, whereas the two control groups in the trust division did not show positive change. Personnel data, such as absence due to tardiness, showed improvement in the experimental group and not in the control groups. Finally, the computer was introduced with considerably less difficulty in the experimental group than in the control groups.

A number of things learned from this experiment have since been applied throughout the organization. Behavioral and management-science specialists now collaborate on the introduction of any technical change.

Between Managers and Faculty

I would like to move now to the area of collaboration between managers and faculty, and to describe a few exciting efforts toward collaboration in this area.

Last year, we started an experimental program at the Sloan School for our master's students which we call the *Organization Development Track*. This is one of several programs designed to allow a person working toward a master's degree in industrial management to focus his electives toward some special area—in this case, with the end of becoming a change specialist or organization-development specialist. The program is designed to ensure that the student will have a continuing learning experience and continuity in his or her exposure to knowledge and the application of that knowledge, both in the classroom and in operating organizations.

In the first semester, the student takes a basic course in social psychology. Between the first and second semesters, he or she participates in a one-week human relations laboratory. The student then joins a seminar in the second semester that deals with the issues of organizational behavior, change, and development. This is a laboratory course in which the student works as a member of a team on a number of real organization cases. In addition to faculty instructors, several managers from organizations bring cases to the course for diagnosis and planning.

During the summer between his first and second years, the student works in a firm on a specific project in organization development. Last summer, for example, one of our students worked at Procter & Gamble, doing a review and historical study of a planned-change effort in the opening of a major new plant. His study became the briefing document for a new division manager moving into the area. Another student was at TRW, in Cleveland, working on a team-development program in the equipment division with a series of middle managers engaged in major change efforts in their organizations. A third worked at Polaroid in organization-development projects. In all cases, the students were connected to both the supervisors in the firm and faculty from the school, and their summer work resulted in a follow-up program in the firm, as well as in the school.

This fall, the same students are engaged in an organization-development practicum that Professor Kolb and I conduct. The students, in conjunction with faculty and supervisors from the firms, use the summer cases and experience as a basis for further study. They also work in teams on additional field problems. In the second semester, they will write their theses in organization development or planned change. Their first postgraduate job will be in the organization development field. It is the intention of the faculty of the school to provide continued liaison with the students and with their managers in the firm for at least the first year of their employment.

Although it is too early to be sure of the results, the summer experience and reports from the students and firms indicate that this type of connection is having high payout.

There are some interesting experiments in new models of hiring both a teacher and a series of students as consultants to an organization. Given the competition for time of people in the university to do consulting, this type of effort holds high attraction.

Another model can be illustrated with Case Western Reserve University's organization-behavior intern program. In this program, doctoral students spend from six months to a year working as interns in organizations before completing their theses. In each case, the student becomes a connecting link. He or she brings to the organization current information on the state of the art but is, at the same time, inexperienced. The student is assigned to people who have considerable experience, some knowledge of the field, and an awareness of the need for much more. The student functions as a "trainer of trainers," but is also in training. Organizations have reported very effective results, and students have reported significant learnings.

At a policy-sciences program at the State University of New York at Buffalo, each student has a personal program that includes a core curriculum and an internship. The faculty includes representatives of a series of disciplines within the university and an adjunct faculty from the organizations in which the students have their internships. There is, for example, an internship with Jonas Salk on science policy, with Mayor Lindsay's office on city administration, with the director of the Buffalo Model Cities Program, and with TRW Systems. This program has its total focus on the problem area. Both the work on the campus and the work in the field are integrated around the student and his connection to the problem area.

A fifth and very exciting program is one currently taking place in Colombia, South America. The Universidad del Valle in Cali, with some guidance from MIT and Georgia Tech, has set up in its business school a total collaborative effort with the organization and enterprise leaders in that geographic area. The advisers to the school are the leaders of business in the Couca Valley area, and the students at the school are these same business leaders and their subordinates. They have developed an eighteen-month program attended by the top managements of the public and private enterprises in the area, three days a week from 7:30 to 10:30 in the morning. They have also, in the last couple of years, instituted a twelve-month master's program for high-potential people in their organizations. In both courses, there is a continuing connection between the faculty and the students, both in the classroom and in the organizations. Faculty members consult with "students" on their projects in the organizations. Student projects are an important part of the curriculum. This joint effort is making a significant difference both in the operating effectiveness of the organizations in that community and in the development of the whole region. The university provides the connection between the knowledge needed for development and the problems in the organizations.

A similar program has recently been extended to Bogota, Colombia. Forty-one men, including three cabinet ministers, thirty-five of the top business leaders of the nation, and three top labor leaders, have constituted themselves into a student body for the purpose of acquiring knowledge about management and behavioral sciences, economics, finance, and marketing, and developing projects to apply this knowledge in their organizations and institutions. Professor Michael Brower and I have already participated in this program, and next spring Professor Zenon Zannetos will spend several weeks there.

In each of these cases, imaginative efforts and a sense of common purpose have produced significant results.

The Challenge Ahead

I have tried to examine three major areas of opportunity for developing further connections and collaborative efforts in the integration of knowledge transmission in the business school, in the utilization of specialties in the firm, and in the development of more collaborative efforts between managers in the firm and faculties in the business school.

It seems to me that the challenges facing all of us are to recognize the inevitability of increased complexity and continued change and to mobilize our joint efforts for coordinating and integrating the specialties that we represent. We must, in my opinion, organize to fight the creation of a new "establishment of specialists" and replace it with "teams of capabilities" who work together to alleviate organizational problems.

We must work to change the reward system, so that it recognizes collaboration between specialists. We must attack, head on, the difficulties of curriculum coordination in the business school and of reorganizing staff functions in the firm. We must provide continuous field-work activities for graduate students and use these students to help keep technology updated in the firm. We must have more dialogue between the manager-user and the faculty educator on the curriculum in the school and the transition to the firm.

The legacy that Douglas McGregor left all of us is his dedication to collaborative inquiry and problem solving. He lived to find out about and to improve man's and organization's conditions. He acted out his commitment by working both in the firm and in the classroom and by bringing the members of the faculty and the leaders of the firm into closer collaboration. I believe we can extend this effort to more faculty, to more managers in the firm, and to the student. It is this joint effort that offers the brightest hope for achievement of our individual and shared goals.

5

Organizational Socialization and the Profession of Management

Edgar H. Schein

This article was presented as the 1967 Douglas McGregor Memorial Lecture in honor of the late Douglas McGregor, Alfred P. Sloan Professor of Management at the Massachusetts Institute of Technology.

It examines the process of organizational socialization—the process by which a new member learns and adapts to the value system, the norms, and the required behavior patterns of an organization, society, or group. It indicates the power of the organizational socialization process and goes on to point out the dangers of either nonconformity or overconformity to the individual and to the organization. Finally, it presents the relationship between organizational socialization and professional socialization and discusses the impact on this relationship of changes in the practices of both business schools and business organizations. *SMR.*

There are few times in one's professional life when one has an opportunity, indeed something of a mandate, to pull together one's thoughts about an area of study and to communicate these to others.

I can define my topic best by reviewing briefly the issues upon which I have focused my research over the last several years. In one way or another I have been trying to understand what happens to an individual when he enters and accepts membership in an organization. My interest was originally kindled by studies of the civilian and military prisoners of the Communists during the Korean War. I thought I could discern parallels between the kind of indoctrination to which these prisoners were subjected and some of the indoctrination that goes on in American corporations when college and business-school graduates first go to work for them. My research efforts came to be devoted to learning what sorts of attitudes and values students

From *Sloan Management Review,* Winter 1968, Vol. 9, No. 2. Reprinted with permission.

had when they left school, and what happened to these attitudes and values in the first few years of work. To this end I followed several panels of graduates of the Sloan School into their early career.

When these studies were well under way, it suddenly became quite apparent to me that, if I wanted to study the impact of an organization on the attitudes and values of its members, I might as well start closer to home. We have a school through which we put some 200 students per year—undergraduates, regular master's students, Sloan Fellows, and Senior Executives. Studies of our own students and faculty revealed that not only did the student groups differ from each other in various attitude areas, but that they also differed from the faculty.

For example, if one takes a scale built up of items that deal with the relations of government and business, one finds that the senior executives in our program are consistently against any form of government intervention, the Sloans are not so extreme, the master's students are roughly in the middle, and the faculty are in favor of such intervention. A similar line-up of attitudes can be found with respect to labor-management relations, and with respect to cynicism about how one gets ahead in industry. In case you did not guess, the senior executives are least cynical and the faculty are most cynical.

We also found that student attitudes change in many areas during school, and that they change away from business attitudes toward the faculty position. However, a recent study of Sloan Fellows, conducted after their graduation, indicated that most of the changes toward the faculty had reversed themselves to a considerable degree within one year, a finding not unfamiliar to us in studies of training programs of all sorts.

The different positions of different groups at different stages of their managerial career and the observed changes during school clearly indicate that attitudes and values change several times during the managerial career. It is the process that brings about these changes that I would like to focus on today—a process sociologists call "occupational socialization," but that I prefer to call "organizational socialization" in order to keep our focus clearly on the setting in which the process occurs.

Organizational socialization is the process of "learning the ropes," the process of being indoctrinated and trained, the process of being taught what is important in an organization or some subunit thereof. This process occurs in school. It occurs again, and perhaps most dramatically, when the graduate enters an organization on his first job. It occurs again when he switches within the organization from one department to another, or from one rank level to another. It occurs all over again if he leaves one organization and enters another. And it occurs again when he goes back to school, and again when he returns to the organization after school.

Indeed, the process is so ubiquitous, and we go through it so often during our total career, that it is all too easy to overlook it. Yet it is a process that can make or break a career, and that can make or break organizational systems of manpower planning. The speed and effectiveness of socialization determine employee loyalty, commitment, productivity, and turnover. The basic stability and effectiveness of organizations therefore depends upon their ability to socialize new members.

Let us see whether we can bring the process of socialization to life by describing how it occurs. I hope to show you the power of this process, particularly as it occurs within industrial organizations. Having done this, I would like to explore a major dilemma that I see at the interface between organizations and graduate management schools. Schools socialize their students toward a concept of a profession; organizations socialize their new members to be effective members. Do the two processes of socialization supplement each other or conflict? If they conflict, what can we do about it in organizations and in the schools?

Some Basic Elements of Organizational Socialization

The term *socialization* has a fairly clear meaning in sociology, but it has been a difficult one to assimilate in the behavioral sciences and in management. To many of my colleagues it implies unnecessary jargon, and to many of my business acquaintances it implies the teaching of socialism—a kiss of death for the concept right there. Yet the concept is useful, because it focuses clearly on the interaction between a stable social system and the new members who enter it. The concept refers to the process by which a new member learns the value system, the norms, and the required behavior patterns of the society, organization, or group that he is entering. It does not include all learning. It includes only the learning of those values, norms, and behavior patterns that, from the organization's point of view or group's point of view, it is necessary for any new member to learn. This learning is defined as the price of membership.

What are such values, norms, and behavior patterns all about? Usually they involve:

1. The basic *goals* of the organization.
2. The preferred *means* by which these goals should be attained.
3. The basic *responsibilities* of the member in the role granted to him by the organization.
4. The *behavior patterns* required for effective performance in the role.

5. A set of rules or principles that pertain to the *maintenance of the identity and integrity* of the organization.

The new member must learn not to drive Chevrolets if he is working for Ford, not to criticize the organization in public, not to wear the wrong kind of clothes or be seen in the wrong kinds of places. If the organization is a school, beyond learning the content of what is taught, the student must accept the value of education, he must try to learn without cheating, he must accept the authority of the faculty and behave appropriately to the student role. He must not be rude in the classroom or openly disrespectful to the professor.

By what processes does the novice learn the required values and norms? The answer to this question depends in part upon the degree of prior socialization. If the novice has correctly anticipated the norms of the organization he is joining, the socialization process merely involves a reaffirmation of these norms through various communication channels, the personal example of key people in the organization, and direct instructions from supervisors, trainers, and informal coaches.

If, however, the novice comes to the organization with values and behavior patterns that are in varying degrees out of line with those expected by the organization, then the socialization process first involves a destructive or unfreezing phase. This phase serves the function of detaching the person from his former values, of proving to him that his present self is worthless from the point of view of the organization and that he must redefine himself in terms of the new roles he is to be granted.

The extremes of this process can be seen in initiation rites or novitiates for religious orders. When the novice enters his training period, his old self is symbolically destroyed by loss of clothing, name, often his hair, titles, and other self-defining equipment. These are replaced with uniforms, new names and titles, and other self-defining equipment consonant with the new role for which he is being trained.

It may be comforting to think of such activities as being characteristic only of primitive tribes or total institutions: military basic-training camps, academies, and religious orders. But even a little examination of areas closer to home will reveal the same processes both in our graduate schools and in the business organizations to which our graduates go.

Perhaps the commonest version of the process in school is the imposition of a tight schedule, of an impossibly heavy reading program, and of the assignment of problems that are likely to be too difficult for the student to solve. Whether these techniques are deliberate or not, they serve effectively to remind the student that he is not so smart or capable as he may have thought he was, and therefore, that there are still things to be learned. As our Sloan Fellows tell us every year, the first summer in the program pretty well destroys many aspects of their self-image. Homework in statistics appears to enjoy a unique status comparable to having one's head shaved and clothes burned.

Studies of medical schools and our own observations of the Sloan program suggest that the work overload on students leads to the development of a peer culture, a kind of banding together of the students as a defense against the threatening faculty and as a problem-solving device to develop norms of what and how to study. If the group solutions that are developed support the organizational norms, the peer group becomes an effective instrument of socialization. However, from the school's point of view, there is the risk that peer-group norms will set up counter-socializing forces and sow the seeds of sabotage, rebellion, or revolution. The positive gains of a supportive peer group generally make it worthwhile to run the risks of rebellion, however, which in turn usually motivates the organization to encourage or actually to facilitate peer-group formation.

Many of our Sloan Fellow alumni tell us that one of the most powerful features of the Sloan program is the fact that a group of some forty men and women share the same fate of being put through a very tough educational regimen. The peer-group ties formed during the year have proven to be one of the most durable end-results of the educational program and, of course, are one of the key supports to maintaining some of the values and attitudes learned in school. The power this kind of socializing force can have can be appreciated best by pondering a statement many alumni have made: Prior to the program, they identified themselves primarily with their company; following the program, they identified themselves primarily with the other Sloan Fellows. Such identification has lasted, as far as we can tell, for the rest of their career.

Let me next illustrate the industrial counterpart of these processes. Many of my panel members, when interviewed about the first six months in their new jobs, told stories of what we finally labeled as "upending experiences." Upending experiences are deliberately planned or accidentally created circumstances that dramatically and unequivocally upset or disconfirm some of the major assumptions new employees hold about themselves, their companies, or their jobs.

One class of such experiences if to receive assignments so easy or so trivial that they carry the clear message that the new employee is not worthy of being given anything important to do. Another class of such experiences is at the other extreme—assignments so difficult that failure is a certainty, thus proving unequivocally to the new employees that they may not be so smart as they thought they were. Giving work clearly for practice only, asking for reports that are then unread or not acted upon, and protracted periods of training during which the new employee observes others work all have an upending effect.

The most vivid example came from an engineering company where a supervisor had a conscious and deliberate strategy for dealing with what he considered to be unwarranted arrogance on the part of newly hired engineers. He asked each new engineer to examine and diagnose a particular complex circuit, which happened to violate a number of textbook principles but actually worked very well. The new employee would usually announce with confidence, even after an invitation to double-check, that the circuit could not possibly work. At this point the manager would demonstrate the circuit, tell the new engineer that the company had been selling it for several years without customer complaint, and demand that he or she figure out why it did work. None of the engineers was able to do it, but all of them were thoroughly chastened and came to the manager anxious to learn where their knowledge was inadequate and needed supplementing. According to this manager, it was much easier from this point on to establish a good give-and-take relationship with his new engineer.

It should be noted that the success of such socializing techniques depends upon two factors that are not always under the control of the organization. The first is the initial motivation of the entrant to join the organization. If his motivation is high, as in the case of a fraternity pledge, he will tolerate all kinds of uncomfortable socialization experiences, even to the extremes of Hell week. If his motivation for membership is low, he may well decide to leave the organization rather than tolerate uncomfortable initiation rites. If he leaves, the socialization process has obviously failed.

The second factor is the degree to which the organization can hold the new member captive during the period of socialization. His motivation is obviously one element here, but one finds organizations using other forces as well. In the case of military basic training, there are legal forces to remain. In the case of schools, one must pay one's tuition in advance—in other words, invest in the system materially, so that leaving becomes expensive. In the case of religious orders, one must make strong initial psychological commitments in the form of vows and the severing of relationships outside the order.

In the case of business organizations, the pressures are more subtle but nevertheless identifiable. A new member is encouraged to get financially committed by joining pension plans, stock-option plans, and/or house-purchasing plans that would mean material loss if he or she decided to leave. Even more subtle is the reminder by the boss that it takes a year or so to learn any new business; therefore, if you leave, you will have to start all over again. Why not stick it out in the hope that things will look rosier once the initiation period is over?

Several of my panel members told me that at the end of a year at work they were quite dissatisfied, but were not sure they should leave, because they had invested a year of learning in that company. Usually their boss encouraged them to think about staying. Whether or not such pressures will work depends, of course, on the labor market and other factors not under the control of the organization.

Let me summarize thus far. Organizations socialize their new members by creating a series of events that serve the function of undoing old values, so that the person will be prepared to learn the new values. This process of undoing or unfreezing is often unpleasant and therefore requires either strong motivation to endure it or strong organizational forces to make the person endure it. The formation of a peer group of novices is often a solution to the problem of defense against the powerful organization, and at the same time can strongly enhance the socialization process if peer-group norms support organizational norms.

Let us look next at the positive side of the socialization process. Given some readiness to learn, how does the novice acquire his or her new learning? The answer is, from multiple sources: the official literature of the organization; the example set by key models in the organization; the instructions given directly by trainer, coach, or boss; the example of peers who have been in the organization longer; the rewards and punishments that result from the new employee's efforts at problem solving and experimenting with new values and new behavior.

The instructions and guidelines given by senior members of the organization are probably one of the most potent sources. I can illustrate this point best by recalling several incidents from my own socialization into the Sloan School back in 1956. I came here at the invitation of Doug McGregor from a research job. I had no prior teaching experience or knowledge of organizational or managerial matters. Contrary to my expectations, I was told by Doug that knowledge of organizational psychology and management was not important, but that some interest in learning about these matters was.

The first socializing incident occurred in an initial interview with Elting Morison, who was then on our faculty. He said in a completely blunt manner that, if I knew what I wanted to do and could go ahead on my own, the Sloan School would be a great place to be. If I wasn't sure and would look to others for guidance, I shouldn't bother to come.

The second incident occurred in a conversation with our then dean, Penn Brooks, a few weeks before the opening of the semester. We were discussing what and how I might teach. Penn said to me that he basically wanted each of his faculty members to find his own approach to management education. I could do whatever I wanted, so long as I did not imitate our sister school up the river. Case-discussion leaders need not apply, was the clear message.

The third incident (I was a slow learner) occurred a few days later when I was planning my subject in social psychology for our master's students. I was quite nervous about it and unsure of what to include. I went to Doug and innocently asked him to lend me outlines of previous versions of the subject, which had been taught by Alex Bavelas, or at least to give me some advice on what to include and exclude. Doug was very nice and very patient, but also quite firm in his refusal to give me either outlines or advice. He thought there was really no need to rely on history, and expressed confidence that I could probably make up my own mind. I suffered that term but learned a good deal about the value system of the Sloan School, as well as how to organize a subject. I was, in fact, so well socialized by these early experiences that nowadays no one can get me to coordinate anything with anybody else.

Similar kinds of lessons can be learned during the course of training programs, in orientation sessions, and through company literature. But the more subtle values of the organization, which may not even be well understood by the senior people, are often communicated through helpful peers communicating how the boss wants things done, how higher management feels about things, the kinds of things that are considered heroic in the organization, the kinds of things that are taboo.

Of course, on occasion the values of the immediate group into which a new person is hired are partially out of line with the value system of the organization as a whole. If this is the case, the new person will learn the immediate group's values much more quickly than those of the total organization, often to the chagrin of the higher levels of management. This is best exemplified at the level of hourly workers, where fellow employees have much more socializing power than the boss.

An interesting managerial example of this conflict was provided by one recent graduate who was hired into a group whose purpose was to develop cost-reduction systems for a large manufacturing operation. His colleagues on the job, however, showed him how to pad his expense account whenever they traveled together. The end result of this kind of conflict was to accept neither the cost-reduction values of the company nor the cost-inflation values of the peer group. The man left the company in disgust to start up some businesses of his own.

One of the important functions of organizational socialization is to build commitment and loyalty to the organization. How is this accomplished? One mechanism is to invest much effort and time in the new member and thereby build up expectations of being repaid by loyalty, hard work, and rapid learning. Another mechanism is to get the new member to make a series of small behavioral commitments that can be justified by him only through the acceptance and incorporation of company values. He then becomes his own agent of socialization. Both mechanisms involve the subtle manipulation of guilt.

To illustrate the first mechanism, one of our graduates went to a public-relations firms that made it clear to him that he had sufficient knowledge and skill to advance, but that his values and attitudes would have to be evaluated for a couple of years before he would be fully accepted. During the first several months he was frequently invited to join high-ranking members of the organization at their luncheon meetings in order to learn more about how they thought about things. He was so flattered by the amount of time they spent on him that he worked extra hard to learn their values and became highly committed to the organization. He said that he would have felt guilty at the thought of not learning or of leaving the company. Sending people to expensive training programs, giving them extra perquisites, indeed the whole philosophy of paternalism, is built on the assumption that if you invest in the employee he will repay the company with loyalty and hard work. He would feel guilty if he did not.

The second mechanism, that of getting behavioral commitments, was most beautifully illustrated during the Korean conflict in Communist techniques of coercive persuasion. The Communists made tremendous efforts to elicit a public confession from a prisoner. One of the key functions of such a public confession, even if the prisoner knew he was making a false confession, was that it committed him publicly. Once he made this commitment, he found himself under strong internal and external pressure to justify why he had confessed. For many people it proved easier to justify the confession by coming to believe in their own crimes than to have to face the fact that they were too weak to withstand the captor's pressure.

In organizations, a similar effect can be achieved by promoting a rebellious person into a position of responsibility. The same values that the new member may have criticized and jeered at from his position at the bottom of the hierarchy suddenly look different when he has subordinates of his own whose commitment he must obtain.

Many of my panel members had very strong moral and ethical standards when they first went to work, and these stood up quite well during their first year at work even in the face of less ethical practices by their peers and superiors. But they reported with considerable shock that they adopted some of the practices they had condemned in their bosses once they had themselves been promoted and faced the pressures of the new position. As one man put it very poignantly, "My ethical standards changed so gradually over the first five years of work that I hardly noticed it, but it was a great shock to suddenly realize what my feelings had been five years ago and how much they had changed."

Another version of obtaining commitment is to gain the new member's acceptance of very general ideals like "one must work for the good of the company," or "one must meet the competition." Whenever any counterorganizational behavior occurs one can then point out that the ideal is being violated. The engineer who does not come to work on time is reminded that his behavior indicates a lack of concern for the good of the company. The employee who wears the wrong kind of clothes, lives in the wrong neighborhood, or associates with the wrong people can be reminded that he is hurting the company image.

One of my panel members on a product-research assignment discovered that an additive approved by the Food and Drug Administration might in fact be harmful to consumers. He was strongly encouraged to forget about it. His boss told him that it was the F.D.A.'s problem. If the company worried about things like that it might force prices up and thus make it tough to meet the competition.

Many of the upending experiences that new members of organizations endure are justified to them by the unarguable ideal that they should learn how the company really works before expecting a position of real responsibility. Once the new man accepts this ideal, it serves to justify all kinds of training and quantities of menial work that others who have been around longer are unwilling to do themselves. This practice is known as "learning the business from the ground up," or "I had to do it when I first joined the company, so now it's someone else's turn." There are clear elements of hazing involved not too different from those associated with fraternity initiations and other rites of passage.

The final mechanism to be noted in a socialization process is the transition to full-fledged member. The purpose of such transitional events is to help the new member incorporate his new values, attitudes, and norms into his identity so that they become part of him, not merely something to which he pays lip service. Initiation rites which involve severe tests of the novice serve to prove to him that he is capable of fulfilling the new role—that he now is a man, no longer merely a boy.

Organizations usually signal this transition by giving the new employee some important responsibility or a position of power which, if mishandled or misused, could genuinely hurt the organization. With this transition often comes titles, symbols of status, extra rights or prerogatives, sharing of confidential information or other things that in one way or another indicate that the new member has earned the trust of the organization. Although such events may not always be visible to the outside observer, they are felt strongly by the new member. He knows when he has finally "been accepted," and feels it when he becomes "identified with the company."

So much for examples of the process of socialization. Let us now look at some of the dilemmas and conflicts that arise within it.

Failures of Socialization—Nonconformity and Overconformity

Most organizations attach differing amounts of importance to different norms and values. Some are *pivotal*. Any member of a business organization who does not believe in the value of getting a job done will not survive long. Other pivotal values in most business organizations might be belief in a reasonable profit, belief in the free-enterprise system and competition, belief in a hierarchy of authority as a good way to get things done, and so on.

Other values or norms are what may be called *relevant*. These are norms that it is not absolutely necessary to accept as the price of membership, but that are considered desirable and good to accept. Many pertain to standards of dress and decorum, not being publicly disloyal to the company, living in the right neighborhood, and belonging to the right political party and clubs. In some organizations some of these norms may be pivotal. Organizations vary in this regard. You all know the stereotype of IBM as a company that requires male employees to wear white shirts and hats. In some parts of IBM such values are indeed pivotal; in other parts they are only relevant, and in some parts they are quite peripheral. The point is that not all norms to which the new member is exposed are equally important for the organization.

The socialization process operates across the whole range of norms, but the amount of reward and punishment for compliance or noncompliance will vary with the importance of the norm. This variation allows the new member some degrees of freedom in terms of how far to conform and allows the organization some degrees of freedom in how much conformity to demand. The new employee can accept none of the values, or only the pivotal values, and carefully remain independent on all those areas not seen as pivotal, or he or she can accept the whole range of values and norms. Some can tune in so completely on what they see to be the way others are handling themselves that they become carbon copies and sometimes caricatures of them.

These basic responses to socialization can be labeled as follows:

Type 1 *Rebellion*. Rejection of all values and norms.

Type 2 *Creative individualism*. Acceptance only of pivotal values and norms; rejection of all others.

Type 3 *Conformity*. Acceptance of all values and norms.

Most analyses of conformity deal only with types 1 and 3, failing to note that both can be viewed as socialization failures. The rebellious individual either is expelled from the organization or turns his energies toward defeating its goals. The conforming individual curbs his creativity and thereby moves the organization toward a sterile form of bureaucracy. The trick for most organizations is to create the type 2 response—acceptance of pivotal values and norms, but rejection of all others, a response I like to call "creative individualism."

To remain creatively individualistic in an organization is particularly difficult because of the constant resocialization pressures that come with promotion or lateral transfer. Every time the employee learns part of the value system of the particular group to which he is assigned, he may be laying the groundwork for conflict when he is transferred. The engineer has difficulty accepting the values of the sales department, the staff man has difficulty accepting the pressured ways of the production department, and the line manager has difficulties accepting the service and helping ethic of a staff group. With each transfer, the forces are great toward either conforming or rebelling. It is difficult to keep focused on what is pivotal and retain one's basic individualism.

Professional Socialization and Organizational Socialization

The issue of how to maintain individualism in the face of organizational socialization brings us to the final and most problematical area of concern. In the traditional professions like medicine, law, and teaching, individualism is supported by a set of professional attitudes that serve to immunize the person against some of the forces of the organization. The questions now to be considered are (1) Is management a profession? (2) If so, do professional attitudes develop in managers? and (3) If so, do these support or conflict with organizational norms and values?

Professionalism can be defined by a number of characteristics:

1. Professional decisions are made by means of general principles, theories, or propositions independent of the particular case under consideration. For management this would mean that there are certain principles of how to handle people, money, information, etc., independent of any particu-

lar company. The fact that we can and do teach general subjects in these areas would support management's claim as a profession.

2. Professional decisions imply knowledge in a specific area in which the person is expert, not a generalized body of wisdom. The professional is an expert only in his profession, not an expert at everything. He has no license to be a "wise man." Does management fit this criterion? I will let you decide.

3. The professional's relations with his clients are objective and independent of particular sentiments about them. The doctor or lawyer makes his decisions independent of his liking or disliking his patients or clients. On this criterion we have a real difficulty, since, in the first place, it is very difficult to specify an appropriate single client for a manager, and, in the second place, it is not at all clear that decisions can or should be made independent of sentiments. What is objectively best for the stockholder may conflict with what is best for the enterprise, which, in turn, may conflict with what is best for the consumer.

4. A professional achieves his status by accomplishment, not by inherent qualities such as birth order, his relationship to people in power, his race, religion, or color. Industry is increasingly moving toward an acceptance of this principle for managerial selection, but in practice the process of organizational socialization may undermine it by rewarding the conformist and rejecting the individualist whose professional orientation may make him look disloyal to the organization.

5. A professional's decisions are assumed to be on behalf of the client and to be independent of self-interest. Clearly this principle is at best equivocal in manager-customer relations, though again one senses that industry is moving closer to accepting the idea.

6. The professional typically relates to a voluntary association of fellow professionals and accepts only the authority of these colleagues as a sanction on his own behavior. The manager is least like the professional in this regard, in that he is expected to accept a principle of hierarchical authority. The dilemma is best illustrated by the example of our Sloan Fellow alumni who, after the program, related themselves more to other Sloans than to their company hierarchy. By this criterion they had become truly professionalized.

7. A professional has sometimes been called someone who knows better what is good for his client than the client. The professional's expertness puts the client into a very vulnerable position. This vulnerability has necessitated the development of strong professional codes and ethics that serve to protect the client. Such codes are enforced through the colleague

peer group. One sees relatively few attempts to develop codes of ethics for managers or systems of enforcement.

On several bases, then, management is a profession, but on several others it is clearly not yet a profession.

This long description of a professional was motivated by the need to make a crucial point. I believe that management education, particularly in a graduate school like the Sloan School, is increasingly attempting to train professionals and in this process is socializing the students to a set of professional values that are, in fact, in severe and direct conflict with typical organizational values.

For example, I see us teaching general principles in the behavioral sciences, economics, and quantitative methods. Our applied subjects like marketing, operations management, and finance are also taught as bodies of knowledge governed by general principles that are applicable to a wide variety of situations. Our students are given very broad concepts that apply to the corporation as a whole, and they are taught to see the relationship between the corporation, the community, and the society. They are taught to value the long-range health and survival of economic institutions, not the short-range profit of a particular company. They come to appreciate the necessary interrelationships between government, labor, and management rather than to define these as mutually warring camps. They are taught to look at organizations from the perspective of high-ranking management, to solve the basic problems of the enterprise rather than the day-to-day practical problems of staff or line management. Finally, they are taught an ethic of pure rationality and emotional neutrality: analyze the problem and make the decisions independent of feelings about people, the product, the company, or the community. All of these are essentially professional values.

Organizations value many of the same things, in principle. But what is valued in principle by the higher ranking and senior people in the organization often is neither supported by their own behavior, nor even valued lower down in the organization. In fact, the value system graduates encounter on their first job is in many respects diametrically opposed to the professional values taught in school. The graduate is immediately expected to develop loyalty and concern for a particular company with all of its particular idiosyncrasies. He is expected to recognize the limitation of his general knowledge and to develop the sort of ad hoc wisdom the school has taught him to avoid. He is expected to look to his boss for evaluation, rather than to some group of colleagues outside the company.

Professional training tells him that knowledge is power, but the graduate now must learn that knowledge by itself is nothing. It is the ability to sell knowledge to other people that is power. Only by being able to sell an application of knowledge to a highly specific, local situation can the graduate obtain respect for what he knows. Where his education has taught the graduate principles of how to manage others and to take the corporate point of view, his organizational socialization tries to teach him how to be a good subordinate, how to be influenced, and how to sell ideas from a position of low power.

On the one hand, the organization via its recruiters and senior people tells the graduate that it is counting on him to bring fresh points of view and new techniques to bear on its problems. On the other hand, the man's first boss and peers try to socialize him into their traditional mold.

A man is hired to introduce linear programming into a production department, but once he is there he is told to lay off because if he succeeds he will make the old supervisors and engineers look bad. Another man is hired for his financial-analysis skills but is not permitted access to data worth analyzing because the company does not trust him to keep them confidential. A third man is hired into a large group responsible for developing cost-reduction programs in a large defense industry, and is told to ignore the fact that the group is overstaffed, inefficient, and willing to pad its expense accounts. A fourth man, hired for his energy and capability, put it this way as an explanation of why he quit to go into private consulting: "They were quite pleased with work that required only two hours per day; I wasn't."

In my panel of 1962 graduates, 73 percent have already left their first job and many are on their third or fourth. In the class of 1963, the percentage is 67, and in the class of 1964, the percentage is 50. Apparently, most of our graduates are unwilling to be socialized into organizations whose values are incompatible with the ones we teach. Yet these organizations are precisely the ones who may need creative individualists most.

What seems to happen in the early stages of the managerial career is either a kind of postponement of professional socialization while organizational socialization takes precedence, or a rebelling by the graduate against organizational socialization. The young man who submits must first learn to be a good apprentice, a good staff man, a good junior analyst, and perhaps a good low-level administrator. He must prove his loyalty to the company by accepting this career path with good graces, before he is trusted enough to be given a position of power. If he has not lost his education by then, he can begin to apply some general principles when he achieves such a position of power.

The businessman wants the school to provide both the professional education and the humility that would make organizational socialization smoother. He is not aware that teaching management concepts of the future precludes justifying the practices of today. Some professional schools clearly do set out to train for the needs of the profession as it is designed today. The Sloan School appears to me to reject this concept. Instead, we have a faculty that is looking at the professional manager of five, ten, or twenty years from now and that is training its graduates in management techniques it believes are coming in the future.

Symptomatic of this approach is the fact that in many of our subjects we are highly critical of the management practices of today, and we are highly committed to reeducating managers who come back to study at MIT. We get across in a dozen different ways the belief that most organizations of today are obsolete, conservative, constipated, and ignorant of their own problems. Furthermore, I believe that this point of view is what society and the business community demand of a good professional school.

It would be no solution to abandon our own vision of the manager of the future, and I doubt that those of you in the audience from business and industry would really want us to do this. What you probably want is to have your cake and eat it too—you want us to teach our students the management concepts of tomorrow, and you want us to teach them how to put these concepts into deep freeze while they learn the business of today. Then when they have proven themselves worthy of advancement and have achieved a position of some influence, they should magically resurrect their education and put it to work.

Unfortunately, socialization processes are usually too powerful to permit that solution. If you succeed in socializing your young graduates to your organizations, you will probably also succeed in proving to them that their education was pretty worthless and might as well be put on a permanent rather than temporary shelf. We have research evidence that many well-educated graduates do learn to be complacent and to play the organizational game. It is not at all clear whether they later ever resurrect their educational arsenal.

What Is to Be Done about This Situation?

I think we need to accept, at the outset, the reality of organizational socialization phenomena. As my colleague, Leo Moore, so aptly put it, organizations like to put their fingerprints on people, and they have every right to do so. By the same token, graduate schools of business have a right and an obligation to pursue professional socialization to the best of their ability. We must find a way to ameliorate the conflicts at the interface, without, however, concluding that either schools or organizations are to blame and should stop what they are doing.

What the Schools Can Do

The schools, our school in particular, can do several concrete things to help the situation. First, we can insert into our total curriculum more apprenticeship experience to bring the realities of organizational life home to the student earlier. But such apprenticeship experiences will not become educational unless we combine them with a second idea, that of providing a practicum on how to change organizations. Such a practicum should draw on each of the course specialties and should be specifically designed to teach a student how to translate his professional knowledge into viable action programs at whatever level of the organization he is working.

Ten years ago we would not have known how to do this. Today there is no excuse for not doing it. Whether the field is operations research, sophisticated quantitative marketing, industrial dynamics, organizational psychology or whatever, we must give our students experience in trying to implement their new ideas, and we must teach them how to make the implementation effective. In effect, we must teach our students to become change-agents, whatever their disciplinary specialty turns out to be. We must teach them how to influence their organizations from low positions of power without sacrificing their professional values in the process. We must teach them how to remain creative individualists in the face of strong organizational socialization pressures.

Combined with these two things, we need to do a third thing. We need to become more involved in the student's efforts at career planning, and we need to coordinate our activities more closely with the company recruiters and the university placement officers. At the present I suspect that most of our faculty is quite indifferent to the student's struggles to find the right kind of a job. I suspect that this indifference leaves the door wide open to faulty selection on the part of the student, which can only lead, in the end, to an undermining of the education into which we pour so much effort. We need to work harder to ensure that our graduates get jobs in which they can further the values and methods we inculcate.

What the Companies Can Do

Companies can do at least two things. First, they can make a genuine effort to become aware of and understand their own organizational socialization practices. I fear very few higher level executives know what is going on at the bottom of their organization, where all the high-priced talent they call for is actually employed. At the same time, I suspect that it is their own value system that ultimately determines the socialization activities that occur throughout all segments of the organization. Greater awareness and understanding of these practices should make possible more rational choices as to which practices to encourage and which to deemphasize. The focus should be on pivotal values only, not on peripheral or irrelevant ones.

Second, companies must come to appreciate the delicate problems that exist both for the graduate and for his first boss in the early years of the career when socialization pressures are at the maximum. If more companies appreciated the nature of this dilemma they would recognize the necessity of giving some training to the men who will be the first bosses of the graduates.

I have argued for such training for many years, but still find that most company effort goes into training the graduate rather than his boss. Yet it is the boss who really has the power to create the climate that will lead to rebellion, conformity, or creative individualism. If the companies care whether their new hires use one or the other of these adaptation strategies, they had better start looking at the behavior of the first boss and training him for what the company wants and hopes for. Too many bosses concentrate on teaching too many peripheral values and thus undermine the possibilities for creative individualism and organization improvement.

Conclusion

The essence of management is to understand the forces acting in a situation and to gain control over them. It is high time that some of our managerial knowledge and skill be focused on those forces in the organizational environment that derive from the fact that organizations are social systems that socialize their new members. If we do not learn to analyze and control the forces of organizational socialization, we are abdicating one of our primary managerial responsibilities. Let us not shrink away from a little bit of social engineering and management in this most important area of the human side of the enterprise.

6

The Problem of Moral Education for the Business Manager

Edgar H. Schein

The appropriate role of ethics in the corporation and the need for ethical training in business education remain topics of intense debate. This article examines executive morality by classifying the "clients" with whom managers interact—customers, stockholders, the community, subordinates, etc.—and exploring the ethical dimensions of each relationship. It goes on to question whether traditional business school education adequately prepares students to anticipate the moral dilemmas they may confront in their careers. *SMR.*

When we refer to the moral education of the business manager, we may have one of three different concepts in mind: education for general character, which would reflect itself in moral behavior in any occupation; morality in the *process* of education itself—that is, an educational process that *exemplifies* the moral values to be taught; and the teaching of a particular value system as part of the general preparation of a candidate for a particular occupational role.[1] This article will focus on the third of these concepts.

I have chosen this focus deliberately, in order to stimulate research on moral education in the business realm. Such research has been carried out in medicine, dentistry, and law, but is lacking in the business area. I suspect that one reason for this is the difficulty in elucidating what may be moral questions and moral solutions for business managers. My attempt here will be to provide some clarifying categories drawn from a sociopsychological frame of reference that, I hope, will make it possible to select research questions and testable hypotheses relevant to the moral problem, whether we are talking about the behavior of practicing managers or the teaching of management.

From *Sloan Management Review,* Fall 1966, Vol. 8, No. 1. Reprinted with permission.

Some Categories for Classifying Moral Values

Moral or ethical behavior and the values from which such behavior derives are often believed to be generalizable across all kinds of situations and all kinds of human relationships. Yet most research on such behavior consistently finds that people apply different standards to different situations. For example, killing is wrong, yet we may do it in wartime or in self-defense. Stealing is wrong, yet a prisoner of war may steal from his captor. Lying is wrong, yet we may and are supposed to lie if we must do so to protect someone's self-esteem. In the early 1960s, in cases of price-fixing in the electrical industry, it was argued by the defense that the forces at work in the particular situation offered the executives no choice but to collude, just as the soldier has no choice but to try to kill the enemy.

If we accept the argument that one must analyze values and moral standards in reference to *particular* situations or relationships, we can next ask: What kinds of categories would help us to classify such situations?

My major classifying principle will be to consider who is involved in the relationship. I shall ask: With respect to whom is the behavior being judged as moral or immoral? Following a detailed discussion of this classification, I will discuss briefly some additional issues, such as who benefits vs. who gets hurt, the closeness of the behavior to the consequences thereof, the reversibility of the behavior, the problem of intentions vs. effects, and sins of commission vs. sins of omission.

Who Is Involved? The Multiple Clients of the Manager

There are a number of ways of defining a professional. One of my favorites comes from the sociologist Everett Hughes, who has stated the simple proposition that a professional is someone who knows better what is good for his client than the client himself does.[2] This definition embodies the idea that the professional has had extensive training in knowledge and skills that he exercises on behalf of his clients.

If we examine this definition in reference to the well-established professions of medicine and law, we find that the value or moral issues of the profession tend to be defined around the relationship with the client. Both doctor and lawyer receive moral training in how to exercise responsibility in their relationship with clients, and in how to work for the client's welfare— even if this means the sacrifice of self-interest or the compromising of some other value. Doctors are expected to make economic sacrifices if the patient's welfare demands it, to ignore the welfare of their own family if midnight calls require their services, to lie to their patients about their conditions, and so on. Perhaps the best example comes from the prisoner-of-war camp where the doctor's oath required him to treat enemy officers in clear violation of the patriotic standards of the POWs who were witness to the behavior and who viewed it as traitorous.

If we accept this definition of professionalism—knowing better what is good for the client than the client himself—we may speculate that it is the *vulnerability of the client* which has necessitated the development of moral and ethical codes surrounding the relationship. The client must be protected from exploitation in a situation in which he is unable to protect himself because he lacks the relevant knowledge to do so.

In recent years we have tended to view the businessman and industrial manager as becoming increasingly professionalized. There is a broader base of technical knowledge and skills required to be a manager, a longer period of training for managerial responsibility, and a greater tendency for managers to be able to move from one type of organization to another, implying that managerial skills are quite general. If, then, the manager is becoming a professional, who is his client? With respect to whom is he exercising his expert knowledge and skills? Who needs protection against the possible misuse of these skills?

The Consumer as Client

Business generates products and services that are purchased by various types of consumers, thus raising the obvious possibility of exploitation of the consumer. Traditional economic theory minimized this problem by assuming that the marketplace was an automatic arbiter of prices and quality, hence the businessman enjoyed no special power relative to the consumer. *Caveat emptor,* let the buyer beware, was a not-so-gentle reminder to the consumer to exercise what power he had to prevent himself from being exploited. This assumption in turn legitimized any practice that any manager may have wished to engage in vis-à-vis the consumer, and thereby bypassed the moral issues altogether.

The point is well made by the story of the storekeeper whose son asked him what it meant to be in moral conflict. The father replied: "If a customer comes into the store and looks at some material, and asks how much it costs, and I tell him it is $1.00 per yard, and he asks for one yard, and pays me the dollar, and as he is leaving the store I discover that there are two one-dollar bills stuck together—then I face the moral conflict—do I tell my partner about it or just keep the extra dollar."

Many economists argue persuasively that the traditional economic assumptions have never been validated by experience; that the marketplace has not been able to curb the power of the businessman vis-à-vis the consumer; that the consumer has not been in a position to know what he was buying and hence was, in fact, in a relatively vulnerable position. Thus we have seen the development of formal codes, laws, and informal ethical standards pertaining to cleanliness in production processes, weights and measures in packaging, truthfulness in stating contents of products and in making advertising claims, rights of consumers to sue businesses for the return of their money if they have been cheated, and so on.

Clearly then, one whole area of values deals with the relationship between the manager and consumers, and one area of moral training for the individual manager concerns the development in him of a sense of responsibility to his customers. Whether graduate schools of management actually attempt to inculcate a sense of responsibility to the consumer is an important question for empirical research. Our own school, if it touches the area at all, does so implicitly. Courses in marketing tend to focus heavily on the technical issues, not on the moral ones. I would hypothesize that most of our faculty would assume that the requisite set of responsible feelings and values are already "built into" our students, hence do not have to be a subject of concern in graduate courses.

The Stockholder as Client

The consumer is a client of the manager only in a very limited sense. Most managers do not deal directly with customers, and only a small percentage of their decisions have anything to do with the final consumer relationship. Instead, one often hears the assertion that the manager's only responsibility is to the stockholder.

According to this concept, the manager is a person who uses his expert knowledge and skills to bring to fruition some ideas about how to build or develop a product or service for profit, to implement these ideas, and actually to generate a reasonable rate of return on the investment of the stockholders. The client-professional relationship is here defined as primarily an economic one, and the vulnerability of the client lies in the possibility that the manager may misuse, misallocate, steal, or otherwise mishandle the economic resources entrusted to him.

Deriving from this concept is a second area of potential moral training, having to do with embezzlement, misappropriation of funds, not taking advantage of inside financial information, nepotism, and a variety of other behaviors that have in common that they reduce the profitability of the enterprise and thus take advantage of the stockholders. The power of the stockholder to protect himself is greater than that of the consumer, however. He has a potential organization in the form of the annual meeting and his representative body, the Board of Directors. He can and often does demand more direct surveillance of the financial activities of the managers to supplement those of regulatory agencies such as the Security Exchange Commission.

The Community as Client

A third client of the manager is the community, viewed broadly as the individuals and other organizations who are in some way interdependent with the business enterprise. The individuals in the community who depend upon the company for jobs are vulnerable to discriminatory hiring policies, the suppliers are vulnerable to discrimination, exploitation, and bribery, and the community as a whole is highly vulnerable to economic loss if the business moves or conducts its affairs in such a way as to minimize the economic return to the community. The company can bring in its own labor force, refuse to buy supplies or raw materials from local vendors, fail to support community activities, and so on.

It is interesting to note that in this value area, as in the others, the legal sanctions tend to be applied where vulnerability is at a maximum, such as in the case of discriminatory hiring practices, or of minimum wages for employment.[3] The more difficult moral decisions occur, however, where ambiguity is greater, as in the process of defining the economic responsibilities of a company if it is the sole employer in a community.

A special case of the community as client results when businesses have overseas subsidiaries and the managers become not only representatives of the particular organization vis-à-vis the local foreign community, but become representatives of the United States as a nation with a certain kind of value system. In this situation it is often not clear who is more vulnerable—the local community, the business enterprise, or the United States in having its image tarnished. Do we expect the overseas manager to uphold the values of service and community development, the values of efficiency and economic growth for the business, the values of democracy and free enterprise, or the values of nationalism, patriotism, and allegiance to the United States? These values can and often do come into conflict with each other. What is best for the local community, for the business, and for the United States are often not the same things.

We have had to face this issue in the Sloan School when we were selecting candidates for our Fellows in Africa and Fellows in South America programs. In each case our graduate was expected to become an employee of the local government and to convince it that he could be trusted. He had to have a value system that would permit him to work on behalf of his employer, even if this meant short-run disregard of United States interests, as in the case of planning a local development program that might draw most of its financial and technical resources from the Soviet Union if these were more accessible than their U.S. equivalent. In our selection we were clear about one thing: We could not afford to send superpatriots or individuals whose prime motivation was to export their own concept of American values to another culture. Whether our Fellows faced such conflicts, and how they handled them if they did, constitutes an important research question that we are currently trying to answer.

The Enterprise as Client

A fourth client is the enterprise itself—the organization that employs the manager.[4] With the increasing tendency to analyze business organizations as complex social systems comes an increasing tendency for the manager to view himself as being basically responsible to the system as a whole. He is responsible for its efficiency, maintenance, effectiveness, and growth. He is expected to make decisions on behalf of these values even if they run counter to the short-run interests of consumers, stockholders, and the community.

The important value referent becomes the organization as a whole, and the assumption is made that in the long run what is good for the organization will be good for the consumer, the stockholder, and the community. Considerations of profit, consumer benefits, and community involvement are subordinated to the ethic or values of efficiency and growth, based on criteria of the "health" of the organizational system. What is required of the manager is commitment and dedication to organizational goals.

Thus, whether the manager decides to hire only certain kinds of employees at certain very low wages is based not on moral considerations in the usual sense, but on considerations of what is required to produce the product efficiently. I know of one industry that has solved this dilemma by moving to countries where labor was cheap and no legal sanctions existed concerning hiring practices.

Teaching the importance of commitment and loyalty to the enterprise as values may be particularly important because the enterprise, being an abstraction, is not in a good position to control such behavior. It is highly vulnerable to low commitment, indifference, disloyalty, apathy, sabotage, and treason. Business organizations cannot apply legal sanctions against such behaviors as easily as nations can and do through their governments. Businesses can only fire the apathetic person, but if apathy is widely spread through managerial ranks there may be a tendency not only to condone such behavior but to develop practices of concealing it from top management, the Board of Directors, and the stockholders.

Most of the technical courses in a business school probably take the values of enterprise efficiency and growth for granted. Organizational goals are accepted as given; the only problem is how best to achieve them. If ethical or moral dilemmas are involved in the choice of means, they are either ignored or settled by considering whether the means are in fact illegal. If the survival of the organization depends upon it, even illegal means are sometimes condoned with the argument that the law is not fair in the first place.

The Subordinate as Client

A fifth type of client of the business manager is his subordinate-employee. Many kinds of managerial behaviors labeled as immoral or unethical deal with aspects of the superior-subordinate relationship—starvation wages, excessive working hours, unsafe working conditions, withholding a promotion or raise to enforce subordination, and arbitrary layoffs. Employees as clients have been so vulnerable to these kinds of behavior on the part of their managers that they have had to band together and, through unions and the passage of protective legislation, reinforce their own position.

Thus, much behavior formerly labeled immoral is now defined as illegal, but the issue remains unsettled in that a more subtle counterpart of each of the above kinds of behaviors is possible. Bosses can still threaten their employees with the withholding of rewards or with subtle punishments; they can still exercise arbitrary and unfair authority; they can play favorites, fail to give credit where credit is due, persecute someone until he quits, steal their subordinates' suggestions, or fail to recommend their best subordinates for promotions.[5]

As one story puts the issue, a company wanted to institute a new benefit program more favorable to employees. All employees signed up except one older clerk who held up the entire proceedings by refusing to sign. His boss told him of the great benefits, but to no avail. The boss asked the vice-president to try, but no amount of persuasion could get the old employee to sign. After several more futile attempts to get the man to understand the benefits, the president himself was told about the case. The president called the old man in, sat him down at the desk, put the paper in front of him, and said, "Listen, you S.O.B. Sign that paper right now or you're fired." The old man signed. The president, somewhat puzzled, asked him why he signed so readily when others had had such difficulty getting him to sign. The old man said, "Well, sir, you were the first one who really explained the program to me."

The values implied by traditional management theory have always held that the boss is the boss and should do only that which is good for the enterprise. The argument has been that no special obligations or responsibilities accrue to workers and/or managerial subordinates beyond those specified by the contract or law. On the other hand, the human relations movement has usually been viewed as an attempt to reverse this trend and to argue that managers are responsible to their subordinates, should consider their needs, should treat them as human beings and not merely as interchangeable economic resources, and that they should do this because it is right in and of itself in a democratic society.

A third argument, which many human relationists/behavioral scientists claim for themselves, is that managers should consider the needs of their subordinates not because it is basically immoral not to do so, but because it will in fact lead to greater economic and productive efficiency on the part of the enterprise. Since commitment, loyalty, and energy are desirable in employees for good organizational performance, it is argued that these qualities are most easily obtainable by treating people fairly, by considering their needs, and by attempting to enhance rather than weaken their sense of individuality and contribution to the organization.

We have here an area where values and science overlap to an unknown degree, since the evidence is not yet clearcut whether in fact people will generally perform better if trusted and treated well, or whether this happens only under certain special conditions. If the latter is the more accurate statement of where our scientific knowledge lies, the manager is in the difficult position of having to be a diagnostician in an area where it is not at all clear whether the issues are scientific or moral ones.

What we then teach in a school of management may well be a function of whether the teacher is an economist who leans toward traditional assumptions about economic man or a behavioral scientist, who leans toward assumptions of a complex man capable of a variety of involvements in organizations.[6] In our school we teach both positions.

The Peer and/or Boss as Client

A sixth type of client for the manager is his peer and/or boss. I am assuming that the manager is by definition a part of an organized enterprise, and that any organized enterprise depends on the coordinated behavior of all its members. The nature of organized effort thus makes the members of the organization highly interdependent, and therefore highly vulnerable to certain kinds of behaviors vis-à-vis each other. For example, the boss is vulnerable to having his subordinates lie to him about what is going on in those portions of the organization that he cannot check on directly. Peers are vulnerable to having negative information about themselves passed on to their boss, which is one aspect of the set of activities generally referred to as "playing politics."

Where departments of a single organization are arrayed competitively with each other, the manager of each may be motivated to exaggerate the virtues of his own group and devalue the other group, and may implement the motive by falsifying figures, by failing to pass on key information, by subtle distortions, and the like. All the pathology of intergroup conflict in society and community can play itself out inside the organization, with managers being tempted into various kinds of questionable behavior in regard to their peers and superiors.

Part of the value dilemma in this area is that we do not have clear ethical or moral standards pertaining to collaboration-competition. Not only is it unclear in our society how far one should go in defining the game as being a competitive one, but it is not clear how far one can go in bending or breaking rules in the process of trying to win. We say that free enterprise is by definition a competitive game and that competition is good for all the various enterprises engaging in it, yet we find that competition breeds behavior that is clearly harmful, and against which society must protect itself. For example, for a company to win over a competitor may mean reducing its costs by cutting its labor force, compromising on quality of product, making untrue advertising claims, or sabotaging the competitor to the point where government intervention becomes necessary to redefine the rules of the game.

Most companies assume that the productivity of individuals as well as departments within their organization can be enhanced by having them compete with each other. Rarely do they observe until too late some of the costs of such competition—in the amount of distortion of information, hiding of failures, falsification of figures, empire building, and mutual mistrust among managers presumably working for the same enterprise. Are these managers immoral, or does competition stimulate certain kinds of behavior well within the rules of the *competitive* game? It is only in the context of persons attempting to work together that some of these behaviors look questionable.

I would state the hypothesis that most schools of management start with the values of individualism and competition, rarely examining the consequences of these values inside the enterprise. Group effort, collaboration, and cooperative coordination tend to be viewed as fuzzy inventions of the behavioral scientists, not as concepts to be taken seriously. The only group in our faculty that believes in the effectiveness of *group* incentives (which force cooperation among workers) is the labor-relations—organizational-psychology group. The economists, mathematicians, marketers, and others are clearly in favor of individual effort and individual incentives and, by implication, the ethic of competition.[7]

The Profession as Client

A final type of client can be thought of as the profession with which the person identifies and to which he belongs. To the extent that management has become a mature profession with clear standards, the individual manager can judge his own behavior against those standards, regardless of the requirements of the various other client systems. In a sense the manager then becomes his own client in that he protects his own self-esteem and his professional identity at the same time that he upholds the profession. However, the profession as client may not solve the problem of identifying moral standards in that the professional standard may merely be to try to serve the various other client systems as well as possible.

Summary and Implications

The various clients of the manager are represented in Figure 6.1. The manager as a professional has obligations and responsibilities to each of these clients. This very fact has a number of implications:

• The managerial role, in contrast to many other professional roles, tends to be defined in terms of a system of *multiple clients*. It is not yet clear in the profession which clients, if any, are to be considered the primary ones.
• Because the values which underlie the different manager-client relationships differ from each other, creating potential conflict situations, and because we have not yet defined primary client responsibilities for the managerial role, *we cannot specify a single set of values and moral behaviors for the manager*. The search for such a single value system is doomed to failure until we define to whom we ultimately want the manager to be responsible.
• The responsibilities with respect to one client system often require the compromising of responsibilities to another client system. Just as members of organizations have often been found to suffer from role conflict because of the multiple links they have to others, so they suffer from potential *value conflict* or *moral conflict* because of the conflicting responsibilities to different client systems.
• Because of the potential value conflicts which the manager faces, we cannot glibly label his behavior as moral or immoral in any particular

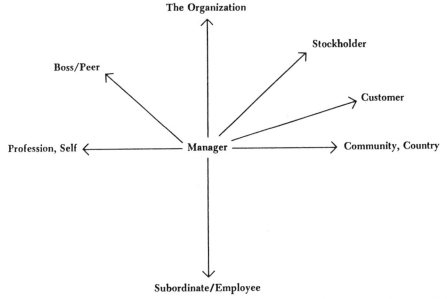

Figure 6.1 Various Client Systems Toward Which the Manager Has Responsibilities. Each Arrow Defines One Area of Values and Moral Behavior.

situation. We must know the *frame of reference* within which the behavior occurred in order to judge it. In other words we must know which of several values the individual was trying to implement before we praise or condemn him.

- By classifying types of behavior in terms of the client relationship involved, we can study empirically the kinds of values managers hold, and how these vary as a function of other variables such as rank, type of job in the organization, age, prior experience, and so on. It would be extremely valuable to know, for example, whether managers are more likely to view as immoral behavior that hurts a consumer rather than behavior that hurts a subordinate. At present we have no value theory able to make any predictions about this sort of question.

- The nearest thing to a superordinate value is the assertion that the manager is ultimately responsible to the enterprise. Much of the teaching in our school seems to be based on this premise, and most often when managers are under attack they seem to retreat to this as the ultimate defense: What is good for the company is ultimately good.

- If indeed we are moving toward an organizational ethic of the type implied above, it becomes essential to study carefully the implications of this "ultimate" value position. If managers are taught primarily to respond to the needs of the organization, will this undermine or subvert other important values, or are the needs of the organization indeed compatible with the needs of the consumer, the employee, and the community?

Who Gets Hurt and Who Benefits?

A second way of classifying moral value questions is according to the criterion of whether the immoral behavior involved is defined as immoral, because it unfairly benefits the person doing it, or because it unfairly hurts one or more others who are affected by it. To exemplify the distinction, discriminatory hiring practices or personal prejudice leading to unfair treatment of an employee are immoral, because they are unduly harmful to the recipient of the behavior. Embezzlement on a small scale, theft of company office supplies, financial gain due to inside information, accepting bribes or kickbacks from suppliers, etc., are immoral, because they are unduly beneficial to the person committing the deed. The latter type of behavior may in fact be doing no one any visible harm in the short run. But it implies that there are certain categories of rewards to which people are not entitled or certain means of obtaining benefits that are not sanctioned regardless of whether anyone else is harmed or not.

A closely related issue concerns whether the potential harm from an immoral action is directed at a particular individual or small group, or whether it is widely distributed among an anonymous mass. I would conjecture that we tend to label behavior as immoral much more readily if the harm is directed at particular persons.[8] Thus, to cheat a customer in a face-to-face relationship is considered more immoral than to cheat an anonymous mass of customers by mislabeling a package. To fire twenty particular men from a hundred-man work force is considered more immoral than to order an arbitrary 20 percent reduction in the labor force and draw names out of a hat. Stealing office supplies, tools, and materials from the "company" is not so immoral as stealing a single tool from a fellow worker that may make his job more difficult to perform.

The double standard we use in this regard is illustrated by the story of the man whose son came home from school complaining that a friend had taken his pencil. The father told his boy that it was probably accidental, not to worry about it, and gave him another pencil. The next day the boy reported that the friend had again taken his pencil. Once more the father played the issue down and gave his son another pencil. When the behavior was repeated a third and fourth day, the father finally got mad, called the friend's father and said, "Look, Fred, my boy tells me that your boy has been taking his pencils. I want you to see that this stops. It is the principle of the thing which is bothering me, not the pencils. I can get plenty of those at the office."

It is not clear whether the tendency to condone cheating or stealing with respect to a large anonymous mass like a company comes about because of the belief that the anonymous mass can somehow afford it, and that it is not really hurt, or whether it is simply easier to commit hurtful deeds when the hurt party is not there to reproach or induce guilt. The latter position would lead to the proposition that the greater the physical or psychological distance between the manager and the client, the easier it would be for him to commit irresponsible hurtful acts toward the client.

Some recent experiments by Milgram support the idea that morality is easier to give up as psychological distance builds up between the person hurting and the person hurt.[9] In Milgram's experiments, subjects are asked to give extremely painful electric shocks to a partner whenever he makes an incorrect response on a learning problem. In fact there is no partner, but the subject believes there is one. Not only did Milgram find that a surprisingly high number of people will give extreme shocks to partners in this situation if ordered to do so by the experimenter, but that they are more likely to do so if they cannot see, hear, or feel the reactions of the partner. In other words, fewer subjects will obey the experimenter if they can hear moans whenever they give a shock, and still fewer will obey if the "partner" holds hands with the subject and clenches the hand strongly every time the presumed shock is delivered. Apparently, we *do* find it easier to be cruel if we *don't* have to witness the effect of our cruelty.

If this phenomenon is general, one might suppose that the manager is most likely to be moral with his immediate subordinates, peers, and superiors, and least likely to be moral with customers (unless he is in sales), the community (unless he is in public relations), and stockholders (unless he is a large one himself or the treasurer who must report to them). It suggests also that one of the most effective means of curbing immoral behavior or training for morality is to maintain close contact between the manager and those clients toward whom one wants him to be particularly responsible. In conflict situations, one might predict that the person will choose behavior that will be least hurtful to those clients (including the person himself) who are psychologically closest to him.[10, 11]

A further hypothesis would be that we tend to view either self-enhancement or hurting as more immoral if the person is viewed to be acting on his own behalf rather than as an agent or representative of some group. One of the commonest defenses against charges of immoral behavior is that the person was only carrying out orders (as in the Milgram experiment and the Nuremberg trials) or was only representing the best interests of some other client system with which he is identified.[12]

If this last hypothesis is supportable, it has implications for the way in which we train members of any profession. To the extent that we teach them to identify with groups, to allow themselves to become representatives, and to develop loyalties, to that extent we are encouraging them to abdicate more personal concepts of responsibility. Perhaps one of the functions of professional associations is to "drain off" the belongingness needs of the individual professional lest he join a group that will bias his moral judgments.

Reversibility, Sins of Omission, and Intentions vs. Consequences

When we consider society's judgments with respect to certain categories of immoral behavior, it appears clear that not only is the amount of harm and the fairness of the deed considered, but that irreversible harms are more severely judged than reversible ones. Thus, killing is most severely punished because it is most harmful and totally irreversible. Rape, maiming, and other physical insults fall under this same umbrella. Do they have a counterpart in the realm of managerial behavior?

Blacklisting a fired employee and thus depriving him of a livelihood, driving someone out of business by unfair means, ruining a colleague's career by a whispering campaign that destroys his reputation, and stealing a patent all have a certain quality of irreversibility, but the judgment is not too easy to make in many cases. It is easier to identify the clearly reversible cases such as those that involve cheating a customer (wherein the customer can recover his money), fraud (wherein the injured party can sue for damages), or accepting a bribe (which the person can be forced to return).

The most difficult judgments arise in situations where it is not easy to determine what harm was done. Suppose a supervisor deliberately gives low ratings to an employee whom he dislikes even though the employee's performance is excellent. If the low ratings cause the employee to be passed over for promotion, he has clearly been harmed, but neither he nor the boss may know whether this has actually occurred. As was noted previously, employees in organizations do not have the protection of anything comparable to due process of law. The manager, especially, is highly vulnerable with respect to higher levels of management, and has few channels of appeal in most organizations. Hence, even if immoral behavior were reversible in principle, it often would not be in practice.

In discussion with Robert Kahn another dimension was identified that poses difficult judgment problems. This dimension concerns essentially the distinction between sins of commission vs. sins of omission. Most of my discussion so far has taken its examples from sins of commission—some clear behavior irresponsible with respect to some client. Yet many kinds of situations become unduly hurtful or beneficial only if the manager does *not* do certain things.

For example, the manager may not transmit his positive evaluation of a subordinate and thus undermine the subordinate's chance for promotion. He may fail to report to the production manager information received from customers pertaining to defects in a product, and thus make the production department more vulnerable to criticism. He may allow slipshod practices in the organization to continue rather than correct them, thus weakening the competitive position of the company. He may fail to report a potential problem in a product to the customer, thus endangering the customer. Failing to inform car buyers of possible safety hazards in certain models or failing to notify NASA of weak spots in a missile system would be extreme examples of this sort.[13]

How do we tend to judge this category of "sins of omission"? Two criteria that appear to be involved are the amount of potential harm that can result from the omission, and whether the manager knew that he was withholding behavior and knew of the potential consequences. In the case of commission, we generally hold the person responsible for the consequences whether or not he knew what he was doing. "Ignorance of the law is no excuse." But in the case of sins of omission, ignorance or good intentions appear to be sounder defenses. If this hypothesis is supportable, it suggests that specific training in thinking through the consequences both of acting and not acting becomes an important part of professional training, particularly for the manager.

It is my impression that such training is indeed heavily emphasized in graduate school. Without stating specific value criteria for the student, we emphasize being able to think through various courses of action and accurately assessing consequences in order that the person should learn how to implement those values that he holds.

Conclusion

I have tried to clarify the issue of moral education for the manager by pointing out the inherent difficulty of classifying for this emerging profession what is moral and what is not. Not only is it not clear to which client the manager is ultimately responsible, but it is difficult to judge the amount of benefit or harm, the effect of psychological distance from the client, intentions within a given frame of reference and the obligations of the manager to do more than avoid illegal or clearly immoral actions. All of these difficulties should make us cautious in glibly labeling particular managerial acts as moral or immoral.

On the other hand, the issue cannot be dismissed merely because it is difficult. We should vigorously pursue empirical research to clarify the conditions under which different kinds of behavior will in fact occur and how various groups in our society judge these behaviors. We should determine what kinds of value positions are held in our professional schools of management and how these jibe with values in business and in the larger community. And we should stimulate inquiry among students themselves to begin investigation of the educative process on the part of its recipients.

Until we have more data, we should attempt to discern what the trends are in our present educative process. I would like to conclude this article by pulling together some of these trends, as I see them from the perspective of our own Sloan School.

- Most faculty members tend to avoid the value issues, concentrating instead on what they call "analytical approaches" to problem solving. This means that goals are taken as given and the focus of the course is on how best to achieve the goals. The emphasis is on means and how to choose among competing means in terms of criteria of efficiency. A corollary emphasis is to "know the consequences of your own behavior" and choose means appropriately in terms of rationally assessed consequences.
- If the faculty member is pushed on the value issue or asked what are the ultimate goals toward which the means are to be used, he would most often choose the enterprise as the relevant client. The goals are to maximize the economic performance of the enterprise or to ensure the survival and growth of the enterprise as a social system. The values are efficiency and effectiveness. I am not aware that any course seriously questions whether any given enterprise should in fact exist or not. Such questions are treated as being outside the realm of most of our courses.
- If asked about other clients such as consumers, employees, and community, the faculty member would tend to respond that "other courses" worry about these unless it happens to fall squarely within his own area. Thus, obligations to employees are the concern of psychology or labor relations courses, not economics or mathematics. Within the area, emphasis on the pragmatic means tends to be maintained. Speaking for my own area of organizational psychology, I would tend to justify moral behavior toward employees, colleagues, and superiors on the pragmatic basis that such behavior ensures better organizational performance, thus seemingly removing the question from the moral realm.
- A recent survey of the beliefs and values of our faculty revealed that in a

number of areas there were considerable differences, as a function of teaching area. If these findings are reliable, they suggest that even though, as individual teachers, we may try to deemphasize the value questions, in fact we do feel differently about certain basic issues; and students probably are well aware of this. I have evidence also that students definitely are influenced by faculty beliefs and values. But, since we differ as a function of teaching area, we influence the student differentially as a function of the courses he takes.[14]

- If we have within the school a kind of pluralism with respect to values, the ultimate responsibility for value choice seems to fall to the student himself. Either we force him through a pattern of required courses exposing him to a variety of positions which he must then integrate, or we let him choose his own courses and thus force him to make value choices during the process of education itself, or some of both. In the Sloan School I believe we do both, but we do not provide a clear forum during the student's second year of education for integrating the diverse points of view or forcing an examination of value issues. The fact that such integrative courses have been difficult to design and to teach may well reflect the difficult value questions with which they would have to deal.

7

Strategic Selection: Matching Executives to Business Conditions

Marc Gerstein

Heather Reisman

Each business situation requires that executives have a specific set of management skills and characteristics to make the business successful. As businesses adapt their strategies and organizational structures to a changing environment, this set of managerial characteristics must also change: A company may discover its executives are not so suited to manage under the new conditions as they were under the old. The authors contend that executive selection should be linked to strategy, and they present a framework for assessing the managerial characteristics required by various strategic business situations. *SMR.*

Our first contact with selecting executives on the basis of strategic requirements occurred fourteen years ago while we were working on a consulting assignment for a major consumer-products company. Part of the assignment involved briefing a new plant manager on our study. He was replacing the individual who had built the 1,300-man plant from scratch over an eighteen-month period. Through the course of this study, we began to raise the question, Why was senior management making such a change, considering the incumbent had achieved one of the most trouble-free start-ups as well as the highest overall productivity in the division's history?

In preparing the briefing, we had an opportunity to put this question to a divisional senior manager. His answer was very simple: "Some people are better at starting things up, some are better at squeezing the most out of them once they are running, and some are better at fixing them when they

From *Sloan Management Review*, Winter 1983, Vol. 24, No. 2. Reprinted with permission.

go wrong. Right now, the start-up is completed, and it's time for a new man."

Of course, the concept of matching individuals with specific positional requirements has been around for many years for those manual or technical jobs where both the skills required for the job and the appropriate testing procedures for selecting the candidate are more or less straightforward. The application of this concept to managerial jobs has been slow, however, and slower still to executive positions. Our analysis suggests the following reasons for this lengthy delay:

Management Is Considered a "Mysterious" Act.   An untold number of executives feel that management, especially at senior levels, is mysterious and defies objective analysis. Certain critical elements, such as a manager's "style" and the degree to which he "fits in" with his colleagues, are too abstract to be measured and too sensitive to be identified explicitly. Rather, a manager just gets a *sense* of all these factors and makes decisions accordingly.

Promotion Is Considered a "Just Reward."   Although there is little question today that the nature of jobs changes as one moves up the ladder—"the best salesman does not necessarily make the best sales manager"—the pressure is, nevertheless, to reward performance with promotion. In most organizations, objective rewards are still largely hierarchically based, and many managers feel that they have very little choice but to promote their best performers, or they risk demoralizing them or losing them to competition.

Compatibility with People, Not Jobs.   There seems to be a pervasive desire for people to surround themselves with individuals of similar kind. Consequently, the selection process is often less one of matching candidates with job requirements, and more of matching candidates with selectors.

Lack of Skill.   Hiring subordinates is a skill an executive is expected to possess by virtue of his or her position. Consequently, executives are rarely trained in selection, and only a few executives are naturally gifted in this area. Furthermore, since selection is always time-consuming and often tedious, it may get short shrift, despite its importance.

Belief in the "Universal Manager."   For many years, executives believed that a good manager can handle any situation, irrespective of its idiosyncratic demands. Growth businesses and those that are more mature are seen as minor variations of a common theme, rather than as specialized business problems that create particular demands on the management in place. Consequently, senior executives have often tended to search for "universal managers" rather than those who are more specialized.[1] Furthermore, executives have not typically replaced managers as business conditions evolve, but they have waited until performance erodes markedly before acting in the belief that "good managers should be able to adapt."

Despite these forces, a number of firms have endeavored to bring increased order to executive selection and to tie selection decisions explicitly to the job requirements created by their firms' strategy. *Business Week* listed Chase Manhattan Bank, Heublein, Texas Instruments, Corning Glass, and General Electric among those companies engaged in linking executive selection with strategic requirements.[2]

Thus the purpose of this article is to describe the selection process and tools we have developed to help a number of firms that are committed to strategic selection. The reader will find that our concepts and procedures do not make the executive staffing process easier. In fact, they may make it more difficult. However, we believe that they do produce effective results. Our intended audience is, therefore, the senior executive or human resource manager who seeks to improve his or her corporation's executive-selection processes and who is willing, if necessary, to devote considerable resources toward this end.[3]

Weaknesses of Current Practices

During recent studies, we have identified several weaknesses in the current practices of staffing at the executive level.[4]

1. Use of Unclear Language. As participants in a large number of executive-staffing assignments, we have found that the language used to discuss job requirements and individual capabilities is extremely vague. While there is an abundant vocabulary, the words used are not precise. For example, a "simple" term such as *delegation* does not mean the same thing to everyone. Likewise, a "complex" concept such as *interpersonal influence* is even less universally defined.

Consequently, the specification of job requirements and the evaluation of personnel are hampered by a tremendous inefficiency in communication. Most of the time, however, vague and unclear language is not apparent or dismissed as mere "semantics" because the discussions tend to stay at a general level. However, if one probes for concrete illustrations of required on-the-job behavior, one often finds that executives do not necessarily have the same ideas in mind about what the job entails or which skills are critical for success.

2. *Inadequate Job Description.*   The job description is one of contemporary business's most common pieces of paperwork. Yet, we have found that managers consider job descriptions a "necessary evil," mostly useful for establishing salary levels. However, the reason that job descriptions are generally inadequate is that not enough time and resources are put into writing them, and the results show it.[5] Consequently, the selection committee often lacks a clear written focus for its deliberations and, in combination with imprecise language, is heavily hampered in its task.

3. *Enduring Belief in Universal Managers.*   As already mentioned, many executives believe there is an "ideal" managerial profile that is largely independent of the organizational role or business circumstance—the idea that "a manager is a manager," and a good one will do well in any situation. This belief is most significantly manifested in the unqualified use of results in previous positions as a predictor of a manager's future performance.[6]

4. *No Access to Relevant Behavioral Data.*   In evaluating candidates, executives generally have access only to the managerial behavior they observe first-hand. Many critical areas, such as the ability to delegate work and relate to one's peers, are not readily observable by superiors, and they must be assessed by specific techniques. In addition, certain skills required for a senior job may not be required in a more junior position, thus making data collection in these areas difficult. For example, strategy formulation may not be required in positions below the general management level, and the only "human resource management" required in many jobs is the occasional replacement of subordinates.

In combination, these four weaknesses lead to ineffectiveness in the executive staffing process, both in terms of hiring the wrong person or not using the existing personnel optimally. In contrast, the strategic selection system we have developed overcomes these weaknesses by providing: (1) a set of starting points to understand job demands in the context of generalized strategic requirements, thereby focusing clearly on job requirements under the actual conditions anticipated; (2) a concise format for documenting these job requirements in order to provide a vehicle for communication; (3) a carefully constructed "common language" for discussing and documenting the managerial aspects of jobs and individual capabilities; (4) the means to collect valid, behavioral data; and (5) a step-by-step guide to help organize the executive selection process.

Table 7.1 Characteristics of Various Strategic Situations

I. Start-up	High financial risk
	Limited management team cohesiveness
	No organization, systems, or procedures in place
	No operational experience base
	Endless workload: Multiple priorities
	Generally insufficient resources to satisfy all demands
	Limited relationship with suppliers, customers, and environment
II. Turnaround	Time pressure for "results": Need for rapid situational assessment and decision making
	Poor results, but business is worth saving
	Weak competitive position
	Eroded morale: Low-esteem/cohesion
	Inadequate systems: Possible weak or bureaucratic organizational infrastructure
	Strained and eroded relationships with suppliers, customers, and environment
	Lack of appropriate leadership: Period of neglect
	Limited resources: Skills shortages: Some incompetent personnel
III. Extract Profit/Rationalize Existing Business	"Controlled" financial risk
	Unattractive industry in long term: Possible need to invest selectively, but major new investments not likely to be worthwhile
	Internal organizational stability
	Moderate-to-high managerial/technical competence
	Adequate systems and administrative infrastructure
	Acceptable to excellent relationships with suppliers, customers, and environment

Components of the Strategic Selection System

In its current form, the strategic selection system contains four components. These components are strategy-related job requirements, a role-description format, the dimensions of senior-management effectiveness, and a set of assessment techniques.

Strategy-related job requirements consist of a set of "educated guesses" as to the business demands that various strategic situations create and the managerial requirements that these situations place on incumbent management (see Tables 7.1 and 7.2).[7] The role-description format presents a logic or structure for job descriptions oriented toward the facilitation of staffing and objective setting rather than toward compensation decisions. The dimensions of senior-management effectiveness comprise nineteen performance areas (with explicit definitions) that are used to characterize job requirements with individual capabilities or performances (see Appendix 1).

Table 7.1   *Continued*

IV. Dynamic Growth in Existing Business	Moderate-to-high financial risk
	New markets, products, technology
	Multiple demands and conflicting priorities
	Rapidly expanding organization in certain sectors
	Inadequate managerial/technical/financial resources to meet all demands
	Unequal growth across sectors of organization
	Likely shifting power bases as growth occurs
	Constant dilemma between doing current work and building support systems for the future
V. Redeployment of Efforts in Existing Business	Low-moderate, short-term risk–high long-term risk
	Resistance to change: Likely bureaucracy in some sections
	High mismatch between some organization skill sets, technology, people vs. needs created by redefined strategy
	Likelihood of lack of strategic planning for some historical period—highly operational orientation to executive team
VI. Liquidation/Divestiture of Poorly Performing Business	Weak competitive position, unattractive industry, or both
	Likely continuance of poor returns
	Possible morale problems and skills shortages
	Little opportunity for turnaround or redeployment due to unsatisfactory "payback"
	Need to cut losses and make tough decisions
VII. New Acquisitions	Acquisitions may be classified into one of the above situations. In addition, the following conditions characterize a recent acquisition situation:
	• Pressure on new management to "prove themselves"
	• Existing management ambivalent/defensive about change
	• Fundamental need to integrate acquired company with parent at some levels

Finally, the assessment techniques comprise various data-collection methods, particularly "behavioral interviewing," that shed maximum light on a candidate's capabilities vis-à-vis the dimensions of senior-management effectiveness (see Appendix 2).

All of the components and the manner in which they fit together are derived from a series of consulting projects and field studies of existing executive-selection systems. Together, these components enable the individual (or group) charged with an executive staffing assignment to identify specific job requirements based on strategic needs, to document these requirements in an efficient fashion, and to collect data on each candidate that are specifically related to the key managerial requirements of the job.

Strategy-related Job Requirements

The characteristics required of candidates in specific positions were derived by means of the logic displayed in Tables 7.1 and 7.2. First, a set of seven

Table 7.2 General Management Requirements for Various Strategic Situations

Situation	Major Job Thrusts	Specific Characteristics of Ideal Candidates
I. Start-up	Creating vision of business Establishing core technical and marketing expertise Building management team	Vision of finished business Hands-on orientation: A "doer" In-depth knowledge in critical technical areas Organizing ability Staffing skills Team-building capabilities High-energy level and stamina Personal magnetism: Charisma Broad knowledge of all key functions
II. Turnaround	Rapid, accurate problem diagnosis Fixing short-term and, ultimately, long-term problems	"Take charge" orientation: strong leader Strong analytical and diagnostic skills, especially financial Excellent business strategist High-energy level Risk taker Handles pressure well Good crisis-management skills Good negotiator
III. Extract Profit/Rationalize Existing Business	Efficiency Stability Succession Sensing signs of change	Technically knowledgeable: "Knows the business" Sensitive to changes: "Ear-to-the-ground" Anticipates problems: "Problem finder" Strong administrative skills Oriented to "systems" Strong "relationship orientation" Recognizes need for management succession and development Oriented to getting out the most: Efficiency, not growth

IV. Dynamic Growth in Existing Business	Increasing market share in key sectors Managing rapid change Building long-term health toward clear vision of the future	Excellent strategic and financial planning skills Clear vision of the future Ability to balance priorities, i.e., stability vs. growth Organizational and team-building skills Good crisis-management skills Moderate-high risk taker High-energy level Excellent staffing skills
V. Redeployment of Efforts in Existing Business	Establishing effectiveness in limited business sphere Managing change Supporting the "dispossessed"	Good politician/manager of change Highly persuasive: High "interpersonal influence" Moderate risk taker Highly supportive, sensitive to people: Not "bull in a china shop" Excellent "systems thinker": Understands how complex systems work Good organizing and executive staffing skills
VI. Liquidation/Divestiture of Poorly Performing Business	Cutting losses Making tough decisions Making best deal	"Callousness": Tough-minded, determined—willing to be the bad guy Highly analytical re: costs/benefits—does not easily accept current ways of doing things Risk taker Low-glory seeking: willing to do dirty jobs—does not want glamour Wants to be respected, not necessarily liked
VII. New Acquisitions	Integration Establishing sources of information and control	Analytical ability Relationship-building skills Interpersonal influence Good communication skills Personal magnetism—some basis to establish "instant credibility"

"pure" strategic situations were identified on the basis of discussions with operating executives, case examples, and the strategy literature. These strategic situations are: start-up; turnaround; extract profit/rationalize an existing business; dynamic growth in an existing business; redeployment of efforts in an existing business; liquidation/divestiture; and new acquisitions.[8] Second, a set of characteristics associated with each strategic situation was developed, again based on the literature, case examples, and discussions with senior executives.

Logically stemming from the strategic situations and their associated characteristics are sets of major job thrusts and ultimately, the specific characteristics of ideal candidates (see Table 7.2). These characteristics were developed on the basis of a large number of executive selections with the help of Personnel Decisions, Inc., a firm specializing in management assessment. General management requirements for various strategic situations are presented in Table 7.2.[9]

It should be noted, however, that actual situations rarely fit precisely with the generalized strategic situations. Often, some combination or modification of strategic situations will exist. For example, a senior executive of a Mexican holding company described one of his operating divisions as "preturnaround"—in other words, an operating division that is still functioning but is on the verge of rapid deterioration. This situation combined elements of redeployment of efforts and turnaround. Likewise, the condition demanded that the incumbent general manager have a combination of specific characteristics required by each of these strategic situations (see Table 7.2).

In practice, these managerial characteristics must be augmented by specifying the required industry knowledge, political skills, and personality characteristics that the particular organizational circumstances demand of an incumbent manager. Once these characteristics have been identified, a proper role description can be prepared.

Role Description

A role description is an expanded job description containing the following four elements:

1. A basic-function statement summarizing the job's overall purpose and thrust, which are conceived in the context of the strategic situation clarified above.
2. A description of the position's technical and managerial responsibilities (i.e., the key activities the incumbent is expected to perform in order to fulfill the elements in the basic function).
3. A description of the key organizational and outside relationships necessary to support the above.

4. Candidate requirements: a synthesis of the characteristics identified under strategy-related job requirements.

In addition to its value as a selection tool, the role description is extremely valuable to brief the new incumbent of his or her responsibilities and to establish job objectives for later performance appraisal.[10]

Dimensions of Senior-Management Effectiveness

The dimensions of senior-management effectiveness provide a vehicle through which the managerial requirements of various jobs and candidate capabilities may be delineated (see Appendix 1). These dimensions were developed with the aid of Personnel Decisions, Inc., on the basis of a large number of management assessments, the management-assessment literature, and many discussions with senior executives.[11]

Subsequently, the dimensions were refined and tested through the creation, validation, and rating of hundreds of "behavioral incidents."[12] (A behavioral incident is a description of a real life story that is written by a manager, then professionally edited, and finally rated by a large number of executives to determine its "fit" with a specific dimension and the performance level portrayed by its main character.)

The development of the dimensions and their associated behavior scales took two years and considerable management time and energy.[13] However, these tools provide an extremely reliable and concrete system for evaluating and comparing managerial behavior, even when the managers who are contrasted are not known equally well by all evaluators.

Assessment Techniques: Behavioral Interviewing and Assessment Center Testing

Two data-collection–assessment techniques are employed in the context of our selection system to furnish valid data on identified job requirements. The first, behavioral interviewing, is a method to extract highly specific information on the candidate's past behavior from the candidate himself or herself and from those individuals with whom he or she has worked.[14]

Specifically, behavioral interviewing elicits descriptions of past experiences (of much the same nature as the behavioral incidents mentioned above) from those individuals interviewed. These "story-telling" interviews produce detailed, richly textured information concerning specific skill areas required on the job. This information can then be easily evaluated by a trained interviewer and the selection committee. Unlike more conventional interviews, information furnished during behavioral interviews is very difficult to exaggerate or fake. The only drawbacks to this technique are: (1)

considerable interviewing time is required, usually three to four hours at a minimum; and (2) as in any interview, articulate interviewees have some advantage over similarly capable but less self-expressive individuals.

To provide a sense of the methodology, a set of sample questions from our behavioral interviewing primer, a companion document to the dimensions of senior-management effectiveness, is presented in Appendix 2. In practice, these questions serve as a jumping-off point for a series of "probes," which is a way of obtaining a complete description of the candidate's behavior that can be identified under circumstances similar to those he or she will be facing. The basic premise of this assessment technique is that the "best predictor of future behavior is past behavior under similar circumstances."

The second data-collection technique we employ is the assessment-center testing, a version of which has been developed (again with Personnel Decisions, Inc.) to specifically illuminate performance in senior-management skill areas.[15] A full-length center runs for four days and consists of a series of integrated simulation exercises and ability tests.[16] Unlike many other assessment centers, this particular center focuses on the circumstances and prospects of a single company, General Cosmetics, Inc., which forms the backdrop for all of the exercises. The single-company context provides a vehicle to assess the candidate's information processing and associative skills over four days.

The advantage of assessment centers, of course, is that they provide a consistent setting for comparisons across candidates: assessors are able to observe how a large number of candidates handle a standardized set of situations and stimuli. Thus, they are able to develop a clearer picture of the range of typical responses, and a better sense of the unacceptable, acceptable, or outstanding behaviors than is otherwise possible when evaluating an actual working environment.

In combination, behavioral interviewing and assessment-center testing provide the selection committee with valid, highly reliable information concerning identified job requirements. When integrated with an assessment of key technical capabilities and personality characteristics, the assessment committee can make a secure prediction of the likely "fit" between the candidate and the job for which he or she is being considered.

The System in General Use

It should be noted that the executive-staffing process is not a mechanical one. On the contrary, executive selection always requires considerable knowledge and judgment on the part of the parties involved. The tools and procedures we offer merely structure the thought and decision process in order to leave the members of the selection team free to focus on that which only they can provide: business strategy and candidate evaluation. In this light, our overall process for matching executive requirements to strategic needs progresses straightforwardly, although somewhat more slowly than conventional staffing processes.

Step 1: Specification of Business Condition and Strategic Direction

This step requires a "good sense" of both the current business and its desired future, although not necessarily a detailed strategic plan. Management's objective in this step is to broadly outline the current situation and the business's "strategic posture" over an appropriate planning horizon. (Toward this end, the categories in Table 7.1 may prove a helpful starting point.)

Two related examples illustrate contrasting strategic situations. A financial-services company contains two operating divisions, a consumer-finance company and a medium-sized insurance company. The consumer-finance division, one of the best run companies in the industry, was faced with the need to consolidate its operations, trim operating costs, and generally adapt to the changing character of the marketplace and the "interest rate squeeze."

The insurance division, on the other hand, faced enormous growth opportunities as a result of the changing character of the consumer, new delivery systems, changing regulations, and a set of constraints encumbering the industry giants, which delayed their adaptation to these conditions.

Clearly, the requirements placed on the chief executives of these two divisions were very different. In simplest terms, the CEO of the consumer-finance division needed to "extract profit/rationalize" his business, while the CEO of the other division was clearly mandated to achieve "dynamic growth."

Step 2: Confirmation or Modification of Organization Structure

The notion that structure is a vehicle for strategy implementation is gaining wide support. Consequently, our strategic selection process examines the appropriateness of the current structure and the need for its modification prior to the specification of job requirements. Obviously, major reorganizations have direct impact on the nature of the jobs within them.[17] However, equally important are the "minor" modifications that contemporary organizations make to their structures through the creation of various "overlays" to facilitate integration and communication.

For example, as part of a strategy-formulation process undertaken by the insurance division mentioned above, a large number of data-processing and administrative projects were created within its operations department. As a result, the job of the vice-president of operations changed dramatically from routine day-to-day responsibilities to project-oriented responsibilities. This, in turn, required greater group management, interpersonal influence, and large systems skills—in short, a very different capability mix than it did in the past.

It is easy to overlook the impact on job requirements of such changes, and doing so may underemphasize the importance of particular management skills (such as those mentioned), which are far more significant in these organizational arrangements than in the classical functional form.

As structures are changed or important task forces or committees are created to implement required work, it is important that the impact of these changes be reflected in a job's definition and in its skills requirements. In Step 3, these changes are documented, so that they become a formal aspect of the job itself.

Step 3: Development of Role Descriptions for Each Key Job in the Structure

While the staffing of positions in stable circumstances focuses almost exclusively on vacant positions, staffing in the context of a change in business strategy involves an examination of the fit between all members of the executive team (and perhaps others as well) and the situational requirements of their jobs.

For example, in another financial-services company, a change in strategy from a "me-too" marketer to an aggressive developer of new products totally changed every role on the senior-management team. The vice-president of marketing needed to behave more innovatively and aggressively; the vice-president of operations needed to create a more flexible department by upgrading his technology and reorganizing the work; the investment function required much sharper management to produce the yields required for more aggressive pricing; and personnel, previously merely an administrative activity, became a critical component in the facilitation of the many changes required to support the new strategy.

Unfortunately, the notion that strategy may dramatically redefine existing jobs is often inconsistent with the de facto job tenure that exists inside many firms, a problem exacerbated by the retention of many of the same titles after a reorganization, despite altered strategy, structure, and positional requirements.

Our approach suggests the articulation of full role descriptions for each key position in the structure, with an emphasis on analyzing the *differences* between required managerial behavior in the context of the new strategy/ structure and that of the old.[18] As a first pass for this task, we suggest preparing descriptions for ideal candidates, rather than basing the descriptions on the incumbents (or readily available personnel). Adjustments, if appropriate, should be made later in the process when the tradeoffs can be seen in a fuller context.

Step 4: Assessment of Key Personnel

In the context of a change in strategy, structure, or both, the traditional matches between individuals and positions may no longer be appropriate. Our suggestion is to assess the management skills of each member of the management team, but to delay overlaying this information onto the job requirements created in Step 3. Rather, we ask senior management to compare managers' capabilities to one another's on a dimension-by-dimension basis, so that the *relative* strengths and weaknesses of the members of the management team become clear.[19] The steps we suggest in the assessment process are as follows:

- Use the role description as a foundation, specify the knowledge, ability, and attitude areas that require assessment.
- Develop a plan to collect this information, based both on the individual being assessed and the organizational circumstances. Clearly, inside versus outside candidates, or better known candidates versus lesser known ones, will require different data-collection approaches.
- Collect the required information using interviews, observations, and discussions with third parties; examine tangible outputs, such as records, reports, and other documentation; use assessment centers and psychological tests, if appropriate.
- Synthesize this information into a narrative report covering each of the required areas.
- Reflect this information in dimension-by-dimension ratings on standardized dimensions for comparison purposes.

The output of this process is a set of comparative ratings among individuals for all critical areas. This output contrasts with that produced during the traditional selection process, which is typically a set of person-job comparisons. Comparative data are of considerably greater utility in optimizing the use of available staff in the matching process described below in Step 5.

Step 5: Matching Individuals with Positions

The objectives of the job/person matching processes are twofold. First, we must try to match positional requirements with the skills and aspirations of individuals. This is known as traditional selection logic. Second, we must try to assess the quality of the overall team produced by this one-at-a-time selection process. Often, it is some combination of job/person matching and "team balancing" that produces the most viable working organization.[20] The steps are as follows:

- Identify the *feasible* positions for each candidate.
- Evaluate each candidate's current capabilities against the job requirements of each feasible position. (This will create a matrix of candidates against jobs.)
- Produce two sets of ranks: (1) a list of best candidates for each job; (2) a list of "best-fit" jobs for each candidate. Synthesize this information with any relevant data on individual preferences, organizational constraints, and career plans into a set of optimum matches (or matches and unfillable positions, if the assessment process identifies some major weaknesses).[21]

Step 6: Implementation

The complexity of implementing a change in strategy, structure, and staff obviously depends on the extent of the changes involved. It is important to recognize that the staffing decisions deriving from changes in strategy and structure are not routine replacements. Rather, they tend to induce a ripple effect—a wave of change stemming from the new orientation. Consequently, implementation may be a highly complex undertaking involving the orchestration of multiple structural changes, staffing replacements, and follow-up actions.

In this light, the following outline is offered as a simplified logic for the personnel and structural aspects of these changes. However, it is not intended to be a detailed road map, since each case is likely to be different and all cases are somewhat complex. The steps are:

- Itemize the proposed staffing changes.
- Develop a logical sequence of structural and staffing changes into an implementation timetable.
- Formulate a plan to announce these changes in the most functional manner. Typically, individuals are informed before groups are, but all announcements should take place rapidly to avoid miscommunications and the "rumor mill."[22]
- Formulate training/development plans and line-up consulting support for those areas in which individuals are weak relative to the requirements of

their job. (Clearly, even the best matches will rarely fully meet all important criteria.)

- Provide outplacement resources for any individuals relieved of responsibilities.
- Communicate new responsibilities to individuals, possibly as part of a larger reorganization or planning exercise.
- Develop a process for establishing "job contracts," performance objectives, and development plans between individuals and their supervisors.
- Facilitate the provision of all needed educational and consulting resources to individuals and groups associated with new strategy/structure. (Identifying the need for resources at the time of a staffing change or confirmation usually produces less defensiveness than delaying this information until the first performance review.)
- Identify specific steps to help build cohesion and clarify interdependencies within work groups that have had changes in roles or membership.

Comments from the Field

When strategies change and structures are modified, especially after a period of relative organizational stability, it is likely that it will be impossible to use all the pieces from the old puzzle to construct the new one, or to easily find all the pieces one needs. Let us discuss two areas of difficulty.

First, managers inevitably ask what tradeoffs should be made, since it is unusual to find individuals with all the required skills for each job. Unfortunately, the only answer is: "It depends." Overall, linking staffing to strategy requires a good sense of which requirements are essential and which requirements are peripheral to performance in each role. Furthermore, one must know how important each role is to the functioning of the total structure. This "systems perspective" on the staffing question is in sharp contrast to traditional approaches, which often view the importance of a job solely as a function of its level and managerial skills as largely undifferentiated.

In dealing with essential skills and key roles, we feel that training the manager who has potential to grow is better than trying to compensate for his or her weaknesses.[23] However, strategies often fail and structures collapse because of inadequate skills. Thus, we feel that management should be acutely sensitive to the need for individuals with the proper skills in critical positions, and they should make careful assessments of development potential and training requirements prior to final staffing decisions.

Second, despite their participation in extensive discussions of strategy, organization design, and staffing, we have found that a number of executives are still unprepared for the human consequences of major organization change. Our suggestion, drawn from some very unfortunate incidents, is that it is usually safer to assume that strategic change will involve a certain measure of human suffering than to assume that it will be a painless, purely rational exercise. With this assumption, it is less likely that one will "under-manage" the human side of a strategic reorganization or the staffing changes that inevitably accompany it.[24]

Conclusion

The major shift in management thinking underlying the selection system described in this article is not in the specifics of the selection methodology, per se, but in the increased attention paid to the link between strategy, organizational design, and selection. As business strategy becomes explicit, and as the organizational structures and managerial behaviors necessary to support this strategy become better clarified, the need to align the staffing process with these parameters becomes almost obvious.

On the other hand, a selection decision, like any other business decision, should primarily be guided by an assessment of the risks and rewards. In the general case we have been discussing, the rewards obviously stem from the ability of selected personnel to successfully implement the chosen strategy. Unfortunately, the risks are somewhat harder to assess: Will the strategy fail without the right person in this particular job? What are the strategic costs of a suboptimal candidate? What are the "disruptions costs" resulting from the removal of an incumbent? If one takes three days instead of one making a staffing decision, invests $50,000 in a new selection system, or removes a questionable candidate instead of leaving him in place, what difference will it make to the company's overall results?

Unfortunately, at this time there is very little basis on which to answer these questions. However, we do know that most executives believe that the business conditions of the '80s demand that their companies be both lean and highly effective. It follows, therefore, that increased attention paid to the link between strategy and selection will be well worthwhile.

Appendix 1: The Dimensions of Senior-Management Effectiveness

Problem Solving

Problem Identification and Analysis (Diagnosis). Recognizing the existence of significant problems—both inside and outside the enterprise—through one's perceptual, analytical, and conceptual abilities; always looking beyond the symptoms to uncover root causes; collecting and analyzing all relevant data to ensure accurate, comprehensive problem diagnoses; developing explicit alternative solutions to problems; examining the implications of each solution.

Solution Implementation. Making, or ensuring the making of, effective and timely decisions to deal with problems; making wise choices even when data are limited; willingness to make decisions on "tough" problems, i.e., problems whose solutions may produce unpleasant personal, interpersonal, or organizational consequences.

Developing practical plans to implement alternatives chosen in the problem-solving process, including the involvement of people and units affected, the delegation of specific assignments, the setting of target dates, the establishment of follow-up mechanisms, and the evaluation of results.

Administration

Execution and Control. Keeping routine activities focused on relevant objectives; directing, monitoring, and redirecting specific work assignments to accomplish objectives.

Communication with Peers, Subordinates, Superiors, and Others. Having the ability to communicate effectively through the use of written material, formal presentations, and verbal interchange, including "listening skills"; possessing a familiarity with all commonly used industrial communications media; choosing the optimum media mix to communicate the desired message within acceptable time and cost constraints; organizing the communication's content to deliver the intended message; keeping relevant persons informed in a timely manner using the appropriate communications vehicles.

Delegation. Allocating sufficient authority and resources to subordinates to enable them to make significant decisions within their areas of responsibility, considering the limits of the subordinates' abilities and the requirements of the work to be done; structuring specific work assignments in a clear, concise manner, while maintaining sufficient room for individual initiative; providing mechanisms to ensure cooperation in delegated assignments of necessary individuals and functions outside one's own; establishing follow-up and control processes that facilitate task accomplishment and the initiation of timely corrective action; having the ability to work with subordinates who are clearly expert in their fields without being either overly deferential or directive.

Crisis Management

Correctly recognizing a crisis situation at the earliest indication of a clear and present danger; identifying the need for specific information/expertise and obtaining these resources within demanding time constraints; making wise decisions under conditions of limited information and significant stress; having the ability to perform competent technical/analytical work under time constraints and emotional pressure; supporting others for extended time periods in a crisis environment.

Negotiation Skills

Demonstrating good judgment in identifying situations requiring negotiation, in contrast to circumstances requiring problem solving; accurately perceiving one's "opponent's" fundamental bargaining demands; persuading the other party to relinquish secondary demands or, in the extreme, to accept much less than they wanted, while maintaining positive relationships; having the ability to satisfy one's own interests while considering the needs of the other negotiating party (i.e., "always leaving something on the table").

Human Resource Management

Integrated Approach.   Recognizing human resource management as an integrated process involving multiple activities (organization design, job specification, manpower planning, recruitment, selection, joining-up, performance feedback, transfer and promotion, management development, and reward/compensation practices); committing one's own time and appropriate resources to the achievement of professional human resource practices within one's own areas of responsibility.

Staffing.   Accurately projecting one's department's requirements for all critical types of manpower over relevant time horizons; articulating the job requirements of subordinates' positions in explicit, concrete terms; possessing a sensitivity to the personality types and management styles that are compatible with the dominant organizational and work group cultures; being able to recruit, select, and integrate subordinates who are technically, managerially, and interpersonally competent; removing nonperforming individuals from positions in a timely and humane manner.

Development of Subordinates.   Ensuring the identification of subordinates' development needs in the context of current and potential future jobs; ensuring the formulation of realistic development plans and timetables; monitoring the implementation of development activities within the department; assessing the impact of development programs on departmental results and relationships; demonstrating the importance of subordinate development by devoting one's own time, departmental personnel, and financial resources to development activities in the face of competing pressures.

Strategy Formulation

Accurately identifying the aspects of the external and internal environments that will exert significant impact on the business unit's future effectiveness and efficiency; establishing mechanisms to monitor the critical indicators within each identified area; formulating strategies and contingency plans to deal effectively with significant opportunities and critical anticipated problems; establishing mechanisms to ensure the timely implementation of formulated strategies and plans; creating a climate that encourages identification between individual managers and the business unit's strategy.

Organizational Leadership

Openness to Innovation and Change. Desire and willingness to learn; willingness to change established strategies, policies, and practices in order to improve the effectiveness and efficiency of the enterprise; willingness to experiment, coupled with creativity in both the technical and managerial aspects of the business.

Interpersonal Empathy and Influence. Recognizing the impact of one's own behavior on others; being sensitive to the moods, feelings, and motivations of others; having the ability to project to subordinates and outsiders an image of company and departmental goals in a way that evokes understanding and commitment; encouraging effective behavior in others through the use of feedback, clarification, logic, and persuasion; possessing a sufficient "behavioral repertoire" to achieve desired results with relevant people in varied situations.

Group Management Skills. Understanding the appropriate circumstances for the use of groups in contrast to individual work assignments; clearly establishing the agenda and objectives to be accomplished in groups; displaying good judgment in the selection of participants, time allocation, and settings; identifying required prework and ensuring its completion; conducting group discussions to maintain both participation and task focus; demonstrating good judgment in dealing with nonagenda items; bringing closure to meetings in a manner that reviews the results achieved and identifies any next steps to be undertaken; ensuring the documentation of outcomes in a managerially useful form.

Large System "Savoir Faire."   Building a robust, informal network to augment formal communication channels; recognizing where to go to get things done outside one's own department; recognizing the need to involve persons, functions, and units outside one's own to achieve departmental objectives; recognizing complex functional and temporal interdependencies; having the ability to deal effectively with political realities; having the ability to see the total organization with an integrated perspective (i.e., to "see the big picture from a helicopter").

Self-motivation.   Working hard to achieve excellence in one's own and departmental work; being comfortable with the use of power in the accomplishment of legitimate organizational purposes; choosing accomplishment-oriented goals over affiliative ones in the face of goal conflict; possessing a strong survival instinct.

Emotional Strength and Maturity.   Resisting short-term and sustained stress; tolerating adversity with a realistic but optimistic outlook for the future; being able to live with the personal consequences of difficult decisions.

Personal Integrity.   Evoking trust in others by being appropriately open about contentious issues and one's own feelings; making decisions that are effective rather than politically expedient; being trustworthy with sensitive information; being consistent in one's behavior toward others in the organization as well as being consistent between what one says and what one does; selectively violating a commitment, if conditions necessitate, to maintain the highest internalized values and standards.

General Management Knowledge

Knowing those areas of content knowledge that a top executive should know, such as economics, financial management, marketing, corporate law, labor relations, information systems, behavioral science and organizational development, governmental dynamics affecting the business, and the technical specifics most salient to one's own business.

Appendix 2: Sample Interview Questions to Assess Senior Management Effectiveness

I. Problem Identification and Analysis

Scenario: Tell me what has been the most perplexing problem for you over the last two years.

1. When did you first become aware of the problem?
2. What were the origins of the situation?
3. What were the most visible manifestations of the problem? What attracted your attention?
4. How did your understanding of the problem evolve as you dug into it?
5. At what point did you feel you really understood the problem and its causes?
6. At what point were you most perplexed about what to do?
7. What was the dilemma?

Scenario: Sometimes things don't work out as we planned, or the information isn't available, or we just plain blew it. Tell me about the most serious error you've made in sizing up a situation in the past two years.

1. What was the reason for the error?
2. When did you realize you had made a mistake?
3. What did you do to cope with that situation?
4. What could you have done differently?

Scenario: Tell me about the best problem solving you have done, taking me step by step through the entire process from the initial "felt need" through the final result.

II. Solution Implementation

Scenario: Some problems are difficult to analyze, but once you know the causes of the problem, it is easy to do something about it; others are vice versa. Give me an example of a problem which you knew the causes and solution for, but for which it was still very difficult to implement the solution.

1. What did you do?
2. How did you plan to implement the solution?
3. How did you try to get support?
4. What obstacles did you encounter, and how did you deal with them?

Scenario: Tell me about the time when your timing in a decision or action was far from optimal.

1. What led to the poor timing? Why?
2. What were the consequences to you?

Scenario: Tell me about the decision you've been most ambivalent about in the past two years.

1. Why were you uncertain? What were the tradeoffs?
2. How did you go about deciding what to do?
3. What did you say to the affected parties?
4. From which party did you get the most anger, resistance, and withdrawal?

Scenario: Tell me about the last high-risk high-judgment decision you have made that had implications for several areas of the business and how you went about implementing it.

1. Did you call a meeting? With whom?
2. Did you issue a memo?
3. How did you specify the involvement of people and units involved?
4. How did you assure follow-up?
5. What was the process you established for evaluating the results of your decision?

8

Managerial Time

Leo B. Moore

Effective time management is a critical factor in managerial success. This article is based on information provided by over 3,000 managers, about 80 percent of whom hold middle-level positions. The survey identified the most common obstacles to effective time management, including interruptions from the telephone, burdensome paperwork, and unannounced visitors. The article groups these and other obstacles into two broad categories and examines steps available to managers who wish to assert more control over their schedules. *SMR.*

One of the most trying problems of every manager is the insidious difficulty of managing his own time. His work has pressures in two time dimensions: accomplishing today's jobs and planning tomorrow's activities. In all he does or attempts, there is an ever-present time problem that cannot be denied or defined. Much evidence suggests that this distinctive personal resource, unique among all the resources of an enterprise, requires more continual constructive attention from the manager than he is inclined to devote. Why then, does this difficulty exist for men who are acknowledged to be capable managers? How effective do they seem to be in dealing with the problem? To what extent can we conclude that the long-run success of every manager is directly related to his effectiveness in time management?

The Study

The investigation of managerial time described here was an adjunct to a more comprehensive comparative study of managerial activities to determine significant differences at various levels of organization. In that study, managers without hesitation reported they found themselves under serious

From *Sloan Management Review,* Spring 1968, Vol. 9, No. 3. Reprinted with permission.

time pressures. Many complained that there were not enough hours in the day and indicated with pride that they worked 60 or 70 hours a week. From reviewing the accumulated data, the conclusions reached immediately were that all managers seem to have many jobs to perform; they select a sequence of tasks using variable priority techniques; they take differing amounts of time and energy to perform similar tasks; and they are prone to work long hours.

The attitudes of the managers are of special interest. How do managers feel about their time problems; why do they devote longer hours to their tasks than others in the organization; and how responsive are they to possible solutions to their time problems? To answer these and other questions, managers were asked to identify and list what they felt interfered with the effective use of their time. They then were asked to suggest and record possible approaches and solutions to these time problems. Individual interviews were first made to collect data; then small groups of six to eight people were organized. Each manager made his two lists prior to the group discussion of the various items. Following the group discussion, a composite listing of interferences and related solutions was prepared.

Over a period of more than six years, almost 3,000 managers (more than 300 groups) have been asked to provide this information. While all the levels and functions of business organization were represented, about 80 percent of the respondents came from middle management. Their companies range in size from ones with small regional businesses to large international corporations. Most of the information was supplied in the course of management-development programs and seminars.

Interferences and Solutions

None of the managers found it a challenging problem to list several interferences in the effective use of time. It was also relatively easy for the managers to define the difficulty involved and to propose solutions to cope with it. The ease and speed with which this material was prepared suggested that managers had given much thought to the matter, perhaps even to the point of complete frustration.

After only a few groups had prepared their lists, a marked consistency of items appeared. As a result, if I ask a management group today to provide this information, I will expect invariably to find the following ten items on their lists: the telephone, meetings, reports, visitors, delegation, procrastination, firefighting, special requests, delays, and reading. They would not necessarily be in this order. In fact, rank ordering by individual managers reveals that each manager has his own list with special adjectives to indicate the exact nature of his personal difficulty with each item. (It might be interesting for the reader to make his or her own list and also to speculate as to what the managers reply when asked what single item and what combination of two items predominate as interferences.)

A brief summary of the difficulties and solutions for each of the interfering items reported by managers might read as follows:

The Telephone.   Problems with the telephone center on the frequency and length of calls that are considered interruptions. Special note is often made of those incoming calls placed by a person who either is not available or is busy on another phone. Having the secretary screen incoming calls and holding all calls during important periods are often suggested solutions. In one company the telephone was considered such a culprit that the entire management group agreed to shut down the telephones for one hour in the morning, with the switchboard operator taking messages during that period rather than putting through any incoming calls.

Meetings.   The complaints about meetings are vehement and numerous, ranging from "too long and too many" to "ineffective and indecisive." The typical solution suggested is to reduce the number of meetings. Some companies have accomplished this by requiring top-executive approval before any meetings can be held.

Reports.   All paperwork, and particularly making out reports, is considered a top time-waster for the manager. The ever-increasing stream of forms, records, memos, mail, and simple informational notes is continually usurping time. Most managers agree that there is apparently no ready answer to this problem; even the computer, with all its promise, seems only to compound an already bad situation. Some companies have instituted forms control and paperwork-simplification programs, but the consensus seems to be that stopping an avalanche is not the same thing as preventing one.

Visitors.   Visitors, particularly those who arrive unannounced, prove difficult for the manager who must decide how to handle the conversation and how and when to finish the interview. This is most trying when they are referred or rerouted by a superior, or when they arrive from the home office. Most managers feel that they simply must live through these endless hours. Some tongue-in-cheek avoidance techniques are: never sitting down, edging the visitor toward the door, and having the secretary openly announce another commitment.

Delegation. Satisfactory delegation is apparently difficult to achieve when measured by the ability of the subordinate to perform without frequent checks with his superior as to what was desired. Many managers agree that subordinates often know what to do, but are eager to let the superior know what progress they are making. Some, however, are more anxious than eager and are willing to let the superior do the job if he succumbs to their pleas for assistance. Too often the manager himself is not exactly certain of the particulars of what he wants or needs, so going over the work instructions carefully and having them repeated are suggested to clarify problem definitions. Specific statements about how time should be allotted and how often progress should be reported should be included in the instructions.

Procrastination. Persistent problems are the order of a manager's day and procrastination is a tempting answer to some of them. Constant interruptions make it difficult to decide the sequence of activity, and certain problems are likely candidates for postponement. Managers are not alike in their selection of priority problems; some are more inclined to start with the complicated, while others are willing first to rid themselves of the easy ones in order to concentrate on the difficult. Most managers agree that they have more problems than they can accommodate, and suggest that the superior establish a priority. The trouble is that he wants them all "yesterday." Delegating some items to subordinates, even when the manager might want to solve them himself, seems the best approach.

Firefighting. The unexpected problem that demands immediate firefighting attention can be expected to occur at a most inconvenient time. Dedicated managers simply respond when the alarm sounds and hope that there will not be too many simultaneously. Crisis prevention is a fond hope of most managers, but too often there is no time to allot to such anticipatory activities. One thought often voiced is that of overcoming the reluctance of subordinates to present bad news sooner; fires only grow worse.

Special Requests. Special requests, particularly those from the head office, are worse than fires. They have a way of enlarging in uncertainty on their path down, so that too often managers put in more time and effort than was originally envisioned. The obvious suggestion to send back a request for further instructions or specifics meets with tremendous resistance and is not often used.

Delays. The military practice of "hurry up and wait" is especially irksome to managers. Delays of all types, particularly of incoming schedules, required information, and planning decisions, upset any manager's best-laid plans and often lead him to a life of quiet desperation.

Reading.   The increasing volume of management literature has made reading a time problem of serious dimensions. Speed-reading courses help a great deal. Digests and abstracts of articles and books prove most beneficial. The company librarian and other readers can help by pointing out material of interest to individual managers.

An Overview

This brief summary represents the initial thinking of management groups about their time problems. On occasion, emphasis has been given to a particular interference, because it reflected a special company condition. However, solutions showed little variation from group to group, because managers tended to provide general answers for what they regarded as specific personal situations. Yet no single answer applied. For that reason a more detailed treatment of these ten recurring difficulties and the suggestions for their elimination or improvement is better left to the individual manager.

My preference is to concentrate on a more interesting aspect of the study. Why did these managers permit the continued existence of these interferences, and which of their own proposed solutions were they prepared to pursue on the job? Their hesitancy and uncertainty in answering these questions prompted broader discussions and led to several conclusions and interesting speculations.

For example, it became apparent that these items fell into two natural groupings. The first five in the sequence presented above are in the communications area, and the second five stem from the professional or operations area. Through an exploration of these major groupings, it was hoped that the true nature of the time-management problem might be developed further.

Communication Problems

Any manager will agree that, to a large extent, he is in the communication business, because he achieves results through others. On the surface, it would seem that of all people, managers would be most adept at communicating effectively with others. So why do they have trouble with communications? I am thoroughly convinced after critical discussion with these groups that communication is the consistent weakness of management. Too many managers acknowledged that they were not trained in even rudimentary techniques for effective communication. They felt they intuitively possessed skills for effective communication, or stated that communication was not a pressing problem.

Meetings provide a good example of the communication problem. Many managers call or attend meetings without a full realization of how necessary meetings are to an organization. There is absolutely no method more effective for sharing information, giving instructions, or solving problems than a meeting of those concerned. The abuse and misuse of meetings is only an indication that there is as much to learn about this important communication method as there is about writing an effective memorandum or making a clear telephone call.

Every effective communication has three requirements; when these are fulfilled, time is saved. Using the example of the meeting, no one should call a meeting without first making a statement in writing of its purpose. From this statement of purpose, he must then plan the details of who should attend, when it should be held, and what facilities he will need. He must determine the presentation he will make, the material he must prepare, and how much time will be required to accomplish his goal. These three essentials for more effective meetings also provide the basis for evoking more constructive contribution from the participants. Proper organization should include informing participants of the meeting early enough to allow for their own preparation. This includes, if necessary, a meeting with their own staff to develop their reasoned and unified recommendations fully. This approach, when used with management groups, has resurrected the meeting as an effective tool for the transfer of information.

Courses in conference leadership methods, involving actual practice, should be considered fundamental to managerial responsibility, and should be followed up with annual refreshers and reviews. Purpose, planning, and technique are equally pertinent to other communication areas. The first two are not serious problems for the manager, once he appreciates the values in this approach, but technique must be learned.

Reports and other formal paperwork should be required to pass the test of suitability of both presentation of data and meaningful use. Too many reports that are prepared with religious fervor end their lives in wastebaskets and files, while their supposed purpose is being fulfilled by special reports prepared by those who need them. This duplication of effort and time is obvious, but corrective action is seldom taken. The technique of an elimination date on every form, report, and the like helps considerably to generate an attitude of questioning the purpose and values of paperwork.

Visitors. I have often recommended to managers that they talk to their purchasing agents about dealing with visitors as a part of their duties. People in purchasing need a technique for speedily handling a full range of visitors with a wide range of purposes without losing cordiality and effectiveness in these contacts.

Delegation. Similar problems exist in delegating responsibility. The subordinate may work for you, but he also feels the time pressure when given an added assignment. The superior shows consideration if requests reflect purpose and planning; this helps to evoke a spirit of cooperation. The principal point is that none of these problems can be avoided; they need correct handling. However, managers seldom are properly trained or urged to learn how best to perform these fundamental communication functions. Too often they have learned the wrong way from their own superior.

Operations Problems

While the superior may mislead some managers in the problems of communication, he is frequently identified as the most important influence in their approach to managing effectively. In the communication area, managers generally admitted and accepted their own personal responsibility for their communication deficiencies. However, discussions among many management groups revealed a strong feeling of a dual responsibility (the manager and his superior) for the five items in the operations area, even though these are essentially concerned with how each manager thinks and solves a wide range of problems that determine his own success.

Procrastination was reported to result most often from indecision on the part of the superior; he should never give a man a job to do without putting a due date on it. When no date of completion is agreed upon, then it follows that a subordinate is placed in a position of deciding on the wrong date. If the superior does not suggest a date, one should be requested by the subordinate. Crises are always generated by the superior, since, as an outside observer, he is easily excited. Fires are not crises to firefighters; they are trained to cope with crises and are best able to assess the critical dimensions. For the manager, a review with the superior of the potential problems arising from any intended action will considerably help to reduce the anxiety caused by an untoward event. The superior frequently views special requests from the top as important interest in his area, and quite naturally he is happy to demonstrate his capabilities. A willingness to place a more sober dimension upon a request by responding to it in a rapid and efficient manner is often suggested as a better approach.

Delays, when viewed objectively, are failures in planning and coordination. Many of them arise because the superior waits to be certain that promises will be kept before he requests commitments from others. Consistently demonstrating the ability to assume responsibility for the full breadth of an assignment does much to convince the superior to make commitments as well as request them.

Planned reading and study is an integral part of the manager's role. A manager who reads with a purpose is not concerned simply about his personal obsolescence, but is eager to learn about new methods and approaches to his problems. Reading is not viewed as a chore but as a necessity. The opportunity to discuss with others, particularly the superior, the implications of new ideas is an important part of learning how to manage more effectively.

While the typical management group is quick to recognize these five operational items as time problems, usually much discussion is required to develop constructive suggestions on means for improvement. Too often the management group is willing to accept the superior as the problem and not see the real problem in themselves and their struggle for managerial competence.

Actual Experiments

The question of the place of the superior in time management suggested the advisability of working with management groups over a period of time to discover how they responded to the use of the improvement ideas they generated for each of the areas. Five management groups, each composed of the superior and the managers who report to him, were willing to explore the problem of managerial time in depth. Particular emphasis was placed upon employing many of the ideas already discussed.

Instruction, demonstrations, group discussions, role playing, and the opportunity to practice were all utilized in an effort to improve skills in the communication area. Feedback concerning performance and improvement was provided through group critiques. An effort was made to motivate the individuals to take a problem-solving approach to their own communication problems. Before such an approach can be attempted, however, a manager first must be made aware of his problems. He then must be convinced that the problem is not completely out of his control and that improvements can be made through systematic effort.

Role playing, through a judicious selection of the plot, provided a particularly good device for making a manager aware of his problems. At later stages, it was helpful in providing the chance to practice more normative techniques. Role playing was used extensively in improving skills in delegation and in handling visitors. As discussed earlier, the focal points of the training in improving the effectiveness of meetings were purpose, planning, and technique. These three principles also were applied to reporting, along with a particular emphasis on brevity and pointedness.

All management groups and all the individual managers reported measurable improvements in the communication area after training. This was particularly noted in the case of meetings when the number was markedly reduced and the length of those held also was reduced. The managers also stated that they felt better about these meetings, because there was adequate discussion, appropriate decisions were reached, and these decisions were in fact implemented. When individual managers reported that they had made improvement, they immediately noted that they had failed to employ what they had learned.

In the operations area, however, no such consistency of results can be reported. In group discussions, the superior readily accepted his impact upon the managers, but also indicated that he was essentially the victim of crises, special requests, and delays from his superior. The necessity to read a constantly increasing volume of material, generated both internally and externally, was an accepted affliction for all managers regardless of rank. Many who were not helped even by speed reading simply stopped reading. Conclusions about the problems that managers faced individually and the methods of improvement that they tried can be only speculative, but a certain amount of generalization is possible. This is particularly true in those instances for which the problem of time management was most serious or for which helpful practices were to some extent employed successfully.

The Challenge of Effective Time Management

By their efforts to solve their own time problems, many managers only compound their organizations' time problems. They fail to realize the extent to which their poor habits affect the people around them. They do not schedule their time effectively and accept the resulting excessive demands on their time as a necessary condition of their employment as managers.

The effect of the inefficient scheduling of time is usually first manifested in missed deadlines. There are always plausible excuses, but nevertheless the performance promised is not delivered on time. Promises easily made are not easily kept. Many management jobs cannot be promptly and fully estimated at first. The manager who has trouble allocating and scheduling his time is prone to make a promise and then struggle valiantly to meet it. He is reluctant even to the last minute to admit the possibility of not finishing on time. This manager is surrounded by activity: His phone is constantly busy, people are in his office, others are waiting to get in, and so on. This manager not only has an effect upon his superior and his associates and subordinates, but his family begins to feel the impact of his time problems with extra hours spent in the office. Obviously, we all exhibit some of these symptoms from time to time. However, it should be recognized that they are most often symptoms of a man who is not managing his time effectively.

No way to solve this time problem is embodied in the same technique employed for managing any other resource. Planning and scheduling the available time is the only answer. A manager would not long be successful if he treated his financial, material, and other resources as he does his time. The concept of control through plans and schedules is fundamental to sound management and to increasing effectiveness. One must decide in advance what he plans to do and what quantity of resource will be needed. To gain his objective as planned, he then schedules, measures, and compares the actual expenditure of the resource with the plan and the schedule. The variance permits him to make decisions about the plan, the schedule, and the performance, and to adjust all three in tune with his objective and the conditions he is facing. This feedback provides a continual review for this integrated sequence of managerial activities. A basic test of excellence in management is the amount of additional resource that is generated in the management process. So it must be with time. The effectiveness of its management can be judged by how much time is made available to be used as desired.

Time Planning.   The planning process consists of listing what to do along with estimates of how long each item will take. The schedule is prepared by dividing the day into fifteen-minute segments and deciding when each item will be accomplished by entering on the schedule allotted time intervals. Note that this is the typical appointment calendar enlarged to include time dimensions and decisions with the intent that they will be kept as entered. All operational activity will be influenced by these entries and the test will be how well the plan and schedule were maintained. To measure this dimension, the schedule sheet should have an additional column that permits the recording of variances both as to time and activity. This sheet then will permit a review of the events of the day and will influence the plans for the coming day. It will also raise questions about ability to maintain promises made, due dates on delegated work, quantity of information and method of handling, and the like. In short, time will be managed and those requirements for its most effective management will be made obvious. They will fall into such groupings as how the work gets done, what work must be eliminated, delegated, or refused, and how future work is planned, committed, and accomplished.

At this point, I have never met a management group that has not immediately raised loud objections and made derisive comments about the impossibility of approaching such a method of operation. The gist of their reaction is that the system would never permit them to schedule their day that completely and that their superior would create the principal interference. The participants insist that time management is a problem of insurmountable dimensions.

Yet plans, schedules, and reviews do provide the basis for knowledge. A manager who tries the process will soon discover that it is not easy, and that the difficulties rest with himself, not with his superior, the system, or the elusive "they." He will find it hard to choose from his first list of things to do and give priority to the items. After all, the list is nothing but an accumulation of many promises made to himself and to others. Many items will have a degree of uncertainty, since no questions have been asked about what is actually desired or needed. The manager will need to review with others to determine the priority and content of many items before he can choose realistically the most important few. Then he will discover that it takes longer to do most things than he had assumed. He will need to review his work methods in order to get the job done better and more easily while still not losing quality and coverage. He will need to develop the ability to think through a job in order to plan its performance. He will need to accept the wisdom of discussing a job thoroughly even to the point of questioning its need without appearing to resist it as an imposition. He will need to establish criteria for deciding what he will do and what he will have others do for him. In essence, he must have time to study himself and how he manages.

It is during the sequence of gaining some knowledge, taking action, and gaining further knowledge for additional action that most managers simply return to their old practices. They will report that it cannot be done; that their day cannot be managed. Is it too much to expect managers to manage their time effectively? Must they simply make the best of a bad bargain? Are the forces acting upon them such that they must yield to the impact rather than discover a means of governing the situation to their advantage and purpose? In the face of so many managers' failures to succeed over the long run with this problem, I have long been in pursuit of the cause, because the condition can only get worse.

The Effective Executive

There is an old proverb which I have found to be largely true—"if you want something done, give it to a busy man to do." Down through the years I have found several such men among the ranks of management and have enjoyed the privilege of interviewing them to discover their understanding of time. Most of them merely reaffirmed the value of planning and scheduling. In their planning they consistently revealed their determination to be constructively selective in the choice of what they would and would not do. They did not take lightly the promise to perform and always included realistic time demands and considered other commitments before accepting an assignment. Talking with such men about their activities regularly revealed the almost offhand ability to discuss at some length and in some detail what they had planned for themselves for many months ahead. Certain significant statements indicate their temper and approach. "I never join an organization simply to attend its monthly meetings and receive the journal. I expect to contribute to that organization and gain something definite from the association. If I do not, then I resign." "I delegate, but I am careful to delegate things I know how to do, reserving to myself those things that I do not know how to do in order to learn myself. Asking a man to do something in vague, uncertain terms, does nothing for him and damages my operations." Their planning and scheduling of time seemed to provide knowledge and conviction about managing time. An atmosphere of quiet effectiveness existed, measured by a range of activities, all deliberately selected and purposively pursued.

Understanding Time Problems

The problem with time as a resource rests in its uniqueness, and it is this uniqueness that makes time a problem for all who would manage. What is the nature of time? Time is a limited resource, but so are other managed resources. We have only so much money, material, manpower, and the like available to the manager. But here the similarity ends: The uniqueness of time exists in its nature. It cannot be accumulated like money, but can only be expended as it becomes available. Herein lies the problem for the manager, because he has never been taught in all his courses on management how to manage a resource that comes at him unceasingly, increment by increment.

A manager must learn how to manage his day. But it is hopelessly impossible for the typical manager to begin this learning process by detailed scheduling. Might I suggest a better learning technique? Make a list of a few things you would like to complete tomorrow. As time goes on, expand the list. Other people will present a continuing problem in meeting these goals. To reduce a part of this problem, secretaries and administrative assistants will have to be transformed from a staff that handles errands to one that assumes delegated responsibilities. The concept of time as a resource to be managed should be communicated to the manager's group. While the process is slow and frustrating, it provides the only answer to more efficient operations and more effective management of your most precious asset, time.

PART III

Organizational Change

9

Strategies for Large System Change

Richard Beckhard

This article explores a topic of growing concern to many managers: the successful implementation of organization change in large systems. Consultant and teacher Richard Beckhard begins by describing a model of change planning applicable to large and complex organizations. He then focuses on five specific intervention strategies that may be required in actual organization settings. The article concludes with an examination of where in the organization to begin a change effort and how to maintain change once successfully initiated. *SMR*.

The focus of this article is on assisting large-organization change through consultative or training interventions. As used below, "client" refers to an organization's leader(s) and "consultant" refers to the intervenor or change facilitator. Note that the consultant can come from within or from outside the organization.

Intervention is defined here as behavior that affects the *ongoing social processes* of a system. These processes include:

1. Interaction between individuals.
2. Interaction between groups.
3. The procedures used for transmitting information, making decisions, planning actions, and setting goals.
4. The strategies and policies guiding the system, the norms, or the unwritten ground rules or values of the system.
5. The attitudes of people toward work, the organization, authority, and social values.
6. The distribution of effort within the system.

Interventions can affect any one or several of these processes.

From *Sloan Management Review,* Winter 1975, Vol. 16, No. 2. Reprinted with permission.

The first part of the article describes a model of diagnosis and strategy planning that has had high utility for the author during the past several years. The second part examines a number of actual strategies in organization and large system change and the issues of where to begin change and how to maintain change.[1]

A Model for Change Planning

The following model is far from perfect. However, its use seems to enable one to ask the "right" questions and to obtain answers that yield a basis for relatively trustworthy judgment on early interventions into the large system. For convenience the model will be discussed under four headings.

Defining the Change Problem

When a change effort is initiated, either the client and/or the consultant, or some other part of the system, has determined that there is some need for change. An initial diagnostic step concerns analyzing what these needs are and whether they are shared in different parts of the system. For example, let us suppose top management in an organization sees as a major need the improvement of the supervisory behavior of middle management and, simultaneously, the personnel staff in the organization sees as a *prior* need a change in the behavior of the top management and a change in the reward system. These are two very different perceptions of the priority of need for initial change, but a common perception that there is a need for change in the organization does exist. As a part of determining the need for change, it is also useful to collect some information from various parts of the system in order to determine the strength of the need.

There are two distinct ways of defining the change problem. The first considers the *organization* change needed or desired. For example, does the need concern changing the state of morale, the way work is done, the communication system, the reporting system, the structure or location of the decision making, the effectiveness of the top team, the relationships between levels, the way goals are set, or something else? The second considers what *type* of change is desired and what the hierarchy or rank-ordering of these types is. One should ask whether the primary initial change requires a change:

1. Of attitudes? Whose?
2. Of behavior? By whom and to what?
3. Of knowledge and understanding? Where?

4. Of organization procedures? Where?
5. Of practices and ways of work?

Rank-ordering the various types of change helps to determine which early interventions are most appropriate.

Having defined the change problem or problems from the viewpoint of both organizational change and change process, one can look at the organization system and subsystems to determine which are primarily related to the particular problem. The appropriate systems may be the organizational hierarchy, may be pieces of it, may be systems both inside and outside of the formal structure, or may be some parts of the formal structure and not other parts. A conscious identification of those parts of the total system that primarily affect or are affected by the particular change helps to reduce the number of subsystems to be considered and also helps to clarify directions for early intervention.

Determining Readiness and Capability for Change

Readiness as stated here means either attitudinal or motivational energy concerning the change. Capability means the physical, financial, or organizational capacity to make the change. These are separate but interdependent variables.

In determining readiness for change, a formula developed by David Gleicher of Arthur D. Little is particularly helpful. The formula can be described mathematically as $C = (abd) > x$, where C = change, a = level of dissatisfaction with the status quo, b = clear or understood desired state, d = practical first steps toward a desired state, and x = "cost" of changing. In other words, for change to be possible and for commitment to occur there has to be enough dissatisfaction with the current state of affairs to mobilize energy toward change. There also has to be some fairly clear conception of what the state of affairs would be if and when the change were successful. Of course, a desired state needs to be consistent with the values and priorities of the client system. There also needs to be some client awareness of practical first steps, or starting points, toward the desired state.

An early diagnosis by the consultant of which of these conditions does not exist, or does not exist in high strength, may provide direct clues concerning where to put early intervention energy. For example, if most of the system is not really dissatisfied with the present state of things, then early interventions may well need to aim toward increasing the level of dissatisfaction. On the other hand, there may be plenty of dissatisfaction with the present state, but no clear picture of what a desired state might be. In this case, early interventions might be aimed at getting strategic parts of the organization to define the ideal or desired state. If both of these conditions exist, but practical first steps are missing, then early intervention strategy may well be to pick some subsystem, e.g., the top unit or a couple of experimental groups, and to begin improvement activities.

The following case illustrates these ideas. A general manager was concerned that the line managers were not making good use of the resources of the staff specialists. He felt that the specialists were not aggressive enough in offering their help. He had a desired state in mind of what good use of staff by line would be. He also had a practical first step in mind: Send the staff out to visit the units on a systematic basis and have them report to him after their visits. The manager sent a memo to all staff and line heads announcing the plan. Staff went to the field and had a variety of experiences, mostly frustrating. The general manager got very busy on other priorities and did not hold his planned follow-up meetings. After one round of visits, the staff stopped its visits, except in rare cases. Things returned to "normal." An analysis showed that the general manager's real level of dissatisfaction with the previous state of affairs was not high enough to cause him to invest personal energy in follow-up reporting, so the change did not last.

Capability as defined here is frequently but not always outside of personal control. For example, a personnel or training manager may be ready to initiate a management-development program but have low capability for doing it because he or she has no funds or support. The president of an organization may have only moderate or low readiness to start a management-development program, but may have very high capability because he or she can allocate the necessary resources. Two subordinates in an organization may be equally ready and motivated toward some change in their own functioning or leadership skills. One may have reached the ceiling of his or her capabilities, and the other may not. Looking at this variable is an important guideline in determining interventions.

Identifying the Consultant's Own Resources and Motivations for the Change

In addition to defining the client and system status, and determining with the client the rank-ordering of change priorities, it is necessary for the consultant to be clear with himself and with the client about what knowledge and skills he brings to the problems and what knowledge and skills he does not have. One of the results of the early dependency on a consultant, particularly if the first interventions are seen as helpful or if his reputation is good, is to transfer the expertise of the consultant in a particular field to others in which his competence to help just is not there.

Concerning motivations, one of the fundamental choices that the consultant must make in intervening in any system is when to be an advocate and when to be a methodologist. The values of the consultant and the values of the system and their congruence or incongruence come together around this point. The choice of whether to work with the client, whether to try to influence the client toward the consultant's value system, or whether to take an active or passive role is a function of the decision that is made concerning advocacy vs. methodology.

This is not an absolute decision that, once made at the beginning of a relationship, holds firm throughout a change effort. Rather, it is a choice that is made daily around the multitude of interventions throughout a change effort. The choice is not always the same. It is helpful to the relationship and to the change effort if the results of the choice are known to the client as well as to the consultant.

Determining the Intermediate Change Strategy and Goals

Once change problems and change goals are defined, it is important to look at intermediate objectives if enough positive tension and energy toward change are to be maintained. For example, let us suppose that a change goal is to have all of the work teams in an organization consciously looking at their own functioning and systematically setting work priorities and improvement priorities on a regular basis. An intermediate goal might be to have developed within the various divisions or sections of the organization at least one team per unit by a certain time. These *intermediate* change goals provide a target and a measuring point en route to a larger change objective.

One other set of diagnostic questions concerns looking at the subsystems again in terms of:

1. Readiness of each system to be influenced by the consultant and/or entry client.
2. Accessibility of each of the subsystems to the consultant or entry client.
3. Linkage of each of the subsystems to the total system or organization.

To return to the earlier illustration concerning a management-development program, let us suppose that the personnel director was highly vulnerable to influence by the consultant and highly accessible to the consultant but had low linkage to the organization, and that the president was much less vulnerable to influence by the consultant and the entry client, here the training manager. The question is, Who should sign the announcement of the program to line management? The correct answer is not necessarily either the president with his or her higher linkage or the personnel manager with his or her accessibility and commitment. The point is that weighing these three variables helps both the consultant and client to make an operational decision based on data. Whether one uses this model or some other, the concept of systematic analysis of a change problem helps develop realistic, practical, and attainable strategy and goals.

Intervention Strategies in Large Systems

The kinds of conditions in organizations that tend to need large system interventions will now be examined.

Change in the Relationship of the Organization to the Environment

The number and complexity of outside demands on organization leaders are increasing at a rapid pace. Environmental organizations, minorities, youth, governments, and consumers exert strong demands on the organization's effort and require organization leaders to focus on creative adaptation to these pressures. The autonomy of organizations is fast becoming a myth. Organization leaders are increasingly recognizing that the institutions they manage are truly *open* systems. Improvement strategies based on looking at the internal structure, decision making, or intergroup relationships exclusively are an incomplete method of organization diagnosis and change strategy. A more relevant method for today's environment is to start by examining how the organization and its key subsystems relate to the different environments with which the organization interfaces. One can then determine what kinds of organization structures, procedures, and practices will allow each of the units in the organization to optimize the interface with its different environment. Having identified these, management can turn its energy toward the problems of integration (of standards, rewards, communications systems, etc.) that are consequences of the multiple interfaces.

The concept of differentiation and integration has been developed by Paul Lawrence and Jay Lorsch.[2] In essence, their theory states that within any organization there are very different types of environments and very different types of interfaces. In an industrial organization, for example, the sales department interfaces with a relatively volatile environment: the market. The production department, on the other hand, interfaces with a relatively stable environment: the technology of production. The kind of organization structure, rewards, work schedules, and skills necessary to perform optimally in these two departments is very different. From a definition of what is appropriate for each of these departments, one can organize an ideal, independent structure. Only then can one look at the problems of interface and communication.

Clark, Krone, and McWhinney[3] have developed a technology called "Open Systems Planning" that, when used as an intervention, helps the management of an organization to sharpen its mission goal systematically; to look objectively at its present response pattern to demands; to project the likely demand system if no proactive actions are taken by the organization leadership; to project an "ideal" demand system; to define what activities and behavior would have to be developed for the desired state to exist; and finally to analyze the cost effectiveness of undertaking these activities. Such a planning method serves several purposes:

1. It forces systematic thinking.
2. It forces people to think from outside-in (environment to organization).
3. It forces empathy with other parts of the environment.
4. It forces the facing of today's realities.
5. It forces a systematic plan for priorities in the medium-term future.

This is one example of large system intervention dealing with the organization and its environment. Another type of intervention is a survey of organization structure, work, attitudes, and environmental requirements. From this an optimum organization design is developed.

There is an increasing demand for assistance in helping organization leaders with these macro-organization issues. Much current change-agent training almost ignores this market need. Major changes in training are called for if OD specialists are to stay organizationally relevant.

Change in Managerial Strategy

Another change program involving behavioral-science-oriented interventions is a change in the *style* of managing the human resources of the organization. This can occur when top management is changing its assumptions and/or values about people and their motivations. It can occur as a result of new inputs from the environment, such as the loss of a number of key executives or difficulty in recruiting top young people. It can occur as women in the organization demand equal treatment, or as the government requires new employment practices. Whatever the causes, once such a change is planned, help is likely to be needed in:

1. Working with the top leaders.
2. Assessing middle-management attitudes.
3. Unfreezing old attitudes.

4. Developing credibility down the line.
5. Dealing with interfacing organizations, unions, regulatory agencies, etc.

Help can be provided in organization diagnosis, job design, goal setting, team building, and planning. Style changes particularly need considerable time and patience, since perspective is essential and is often lost by the client. Both internal and outside consultants can provide significant leadership in providing perspectives to operating management. Some of the questions about key managers that need answers in planning a change in managerial strategy are:

1. To what degree does the top management encourage influence from other parts of the organization?
2. How do they manage conflict?
3. To what degree do they locate decision making based on where information is located rather than on hierarchical roles?
4. How do they handle the rewards that they control?
5. What kind of feedback systems do they have for getting information about the state of things?

Change in the Organization Structures

One key aspect of healthy and effective organizations is that the structures, the formal ways that work is organized, follow and relate to the actual work to be done. In many organizations the structure relates to the authority system: who reports to whom. Most organizations are designed to simplify the structure in order to get clear reporting lines that define the power relationships.

As work becomes more complex, it becomes impossible in any large system to have *one* organization structure that is relevant to all of the kinds of work to be done. The basic organization chart rarely describes the way even the basic work gets done. More and more organization leaders recognize and endorse the reality that organizations actually operate through a variety of structures. In addition to the permanent organization chart, there are project organizations, task forces, and other temporary systems.

To clarify this concept, we examine a case where a firmly fixed organizational structure was a major obstacle to getting the required work done. In this particular consumer-based organization was a marketing organization primarily concerned with competing in the market, and a technical subsystem primarily concerned with getting packages designed with high quality. Market demands required that the organization get some sample packages of new products into supermarkets as sales promotions. The "rules of the game" were that, for a package to be produced, it had to go through a very thorough preparation including design and considerable field testing. These standards had been developed for products that were marketed extensively in markets where the company had a very high share. The problem developed around a market in which the company had a very low share and was competing desperately with a number of other strong companies. Because of the overall company rules about packages, the marketing people were unable to get the promotion packages into the stores on time. The result was the loss of an even greater share of the market. The frustration was tremendous and was felt right up to the president.

Within the marketing organization there was a very bright, technically oriented, skilled, abrasive entrepreneurial person, who kept very heavy pressure on the package technical people. He was convinced that he could produce the packages himself within a matter of weeks, as opposed to the months that the technical people required. Because of his abrasiveness he produced much tension within the technical department, and tensions between the two departments also increased. At one point the heads of the two departments were on a very "cool" basis. The president of the company was quite concerned at the loss of markets. He had attempted to do something earlier about the situation by giving the marketing entrepreneur a little back-room shop in which he could prove his assertions of being able to produce a package in a short time. The man did produce them, but when he took them to the technical people for reproduction, they called up all the traditional ground rules and policies to demonstrate that the package would not work and could not be used.

The client, here the president, had diagnosed the problem as one of noncooperation between departments and particularly between individuals. Based on this diagnosis he asked for some consultative help with the interpersonal problem between the marketing entrepreneur and the people in the technical department. He also thought that an intergroup intervention might be appropriate to increase collaboration between the groups.

The consultant's diagnosis was that, although either of these interventions was possible and might, in fact, produce some temporary change in the sense of lowering the heat in the situation, there was little possibility of either event producing more packages. Rather, the change problem was one of an inappropriate structure for managing work.

The consultant suggested that the leaders of marketing and technical development together develop a flow chart of the steps involved in moving from an idea to a finished promotion package. Then they were to isolate those items that clearly fitted within the organization structure, such as the last few steps in the process, which were handled by the buying and production department. The remaining steps, it was suggested, needed to be managed by a *temporary* organization created for just that purpose. The consultant proposed that for each new promotion a temporary-management organization be set up consisting of one person from packaging, one from marketing, one from purchasing, and one from manufacturing. This organization would have, as its charter, the management of the flow of that product from idea to manufacturing. They would analyze the problem, set a timetable, set the resource requirements, and control the flow of work. The resources that they needed were back in the permanent structures, of which they were also members. This task force would report weekly and jointly to the heads of both the technical and marketing departments. The president would withdraw from the problem.

The intervention produced the targeted result: Promotion packages became available in one-fifth the time previously required. The interpersonal difficulties remained for some time, but they gradually decreased as people were forced to collaborate in getting the job done.

Change in the Ways Work Is Done

This condition is one where there is a special effort to improve the meaningfulness as well as the efficiency of work. Job-enrichment programs, work-analysis programs, and development of criteria for effectiveness can all be included here. To give an example, an intervention might be to work with a management group helping it examine its recent meeting agendas in order to improve the allocation of work tasks. Specifically, one can get the group to make an initial list of those activities and functions that absolutely have to be done by that group functioning as a group. Next, a list can be made of things that are not being done but need to be. A third list can be made of those things that the group is now doing that could be done, even if not so well, by either the same people wearing their functional or other hats, or by other people. Experience has shown that the second two lists tend to balance each other and tend to represent somewhere around 25–30 percent of the total work of such a group. Based on this analysis a replan of work can emerge that can have significant effects on both attitudes and behavior. The output of such an activity by a group at the top means that work gets reallocated to the next level, and thus a domino effect is set in motion that can result in significant change.

Another illustration concerns an organizationwide change effort to improve both the way work is done and the management of the work. The total staff of this very large organization was about 40,000 people. During a six-month period, the total organization met in work teams with the task of developing the criteria against which a team wanted the performance of its work unit to be measured. They then located their current performance against those criteria and projected their performance at a date about six months in the future against the same criteria. These criteria and projections were checked with senior-management committees in each subsystem. If approved they became the work plan and basis for performance appraisal for that group.

With this one intervention, top management distributed the responsibility for managing the work to the people who were doing the work throughout the organization. The results of this program were a significant increase in productivity, significant cost reductions, and a significant change in attitudes and feelings of ownership among large numbers of employees, many of whom were previously quite dissatisfied with the state of things. Given this participative mode, it is most unlikely that any future management could successfully return to overcentralized control. Much latent energy was released and continues to be used by people all over the organization who feel responsible and appreciated for *their* management of *their* work.

Change in the Reward System

One significant organization problem concerns making the reward system consistent with the work. How often we see organizations in which someone in a staff department spends 90 percent of his time in assisting some line department; yet for his annual review his performance is evaluated solely by the head of his staff department, probably on 10 percent of his work. One result of this is that any smart person behaves in ways that please the individual who most influences his career and other rewards rather than those with whom he is working. Inappropriate reward systems do much to sabotage effective work as well as organization health.

An example of an intervention in this area follows. The vice-president of one of the major groups in a very large company was concerned about the lack of motivation by his division general managers toward working with him on planning for the future of the business as a whole. He was equally concerned that the managers were not fully developing their own subordinates. In his opinion, this was blocking the managers' promotions. The vice-president had spoken of these concerns many times. His staff had agreed that it was important to change, but their behavior was heavily directed toward maintaining the old priorities: meeting short-term profit goals. This group existed in an organization where the reward system was very clear. The chief executives in any subenterprise were accountable for their short-term profits. This was their most important assignment. Division managers knew that, if they did not participate actively in future business planning, or if they did not invest energy in the development of subordinates, they would incur the group vice-president's displeasure. They also knew, however, that if they did not meet their short-term profit objectives, they probably would not be around. The company had an executive incentive plan in which considerable amounts of bonus money were available to people in the upper ranks for good performance. In trying to find a method for changing his division managers' priorities, the group vice-president looked, with consultant help, at the reward system. As a result of this he called his colleagues together and told them, "I thought you'd like to know that in determining your bonus at the next review, I will be using the following formula. You are still 100 percent accountable for your short-term profit goals, but that represents 60 percent of the bonus. Another 25 percent will be my evaluation of your performance as members of this top-management planning team. The other 15 percent will be your discernible efforts toward the development of your subordinates." Executive behavior changed dramatically. The reality of the reward system and the desired state were now consistent.

We have examined briefly several types of organization phenomena that need large-system-oriented interventions. We will now look at initial interventions and examine some of the choices facing the intervenor.

Early Interventions

There are a number of choices of where to intervene. Several are listed here with the objective of creating a map of possibilities. The list includes:

1. The top team or the top of a system.
2. A pilot project with a linkage to the larger system.
3. Ready subsystems: those whose leaders and members are known to be ready for a change.
4. Hurting systems. This is one class of ready system where the environment has caused some acute discomfort in a generally unready system.
5. The rewards system.
6. Experiments: a series of experiments on new ways of organizing or new ways of handling communications.
7. Educational interventions: training programs, outside courses, etc.
8. An organizationwide confrontation meeting, bringing together a variety of parts of the organization, to examine the state of affairs and to make first step plans for improvement.[4]
9. The creation of a critical mass.

The last concept requires some elaboration. It is most difficult for a stable organization to change itself—that is, for the regular structures of the organization to be used for change. Temporary systems are frequently created to accomplish this. As an example, in one very large system, a country, there were a number of agencies involved in training and development for organization leaders. The government provided grants to the agencies for training activities. These grants also provided funds to support the agency staffs for other purposes. Because of this condition each agency was developing programs for the same small clientele. Each agency kept innovations secret from its competitors.

In an attempt to move this competitive state toward a more collaborative one, a small group of people developed a "nonorganization" called the Association for Commercial and Industrial Education. It was a luncheon club. Its rules were the opposite of an ordinary organization's. It could make no group decisions, it distributed no minutes, no one was allowed to take anyone else to lunch, there were no dues, and there were no officers or hierarchy.

In this context it was possible for individuals from the various competing agencies to sit down and talk together about matters of mutual interest. After a couple of years it even became possible to develop a national-organization development-training project in the form of a four-week course attended by top line managers and personnel people from all the major economic and social institutions in the country. Only this nonorganization could sponsor such a program. From this program a great many other linkages were developed. Today there is an entire professional association of collaborating change agents with bases in a variety of institutions, but with the capacity to collaborate around larger national problems.

Maintaining Change

To maintain change in a large system it is necessary to have conscious procedures and commitment. Organization change will not be maintained simply because there has been early success. There are a number of interventions that are possible, and many are necessary if a change is to be maintained. Many organizations are living with the effects of successful short-term change results that have not been maintained.

Perhaps the most important single requirement for continued change is a continued feedback and information system that lets people in the organization know the system status in relation to the desired states. Some feedback systems that are used fairly frequently are:

1. Periodic team meetings to review a team's functioning and what its next goal priorities should be.
2. Organization sensing meetings in which the top of an organization meets, on a systematic planned basis, with a sample of employees from a variety of different organizational centers in order to keep apprised of the state of the system.
3. Periodic meetings between interdependent units of an organization.
4. Renewal conferences. For example, one company has an annual five-year planning meeting with its top management. Three weeks prior to that meeting the same management group and their wives go to a retreat for two or three days to take a look at themselves, their personal and company priorities, the new forces in the environment, what they need to keep in mind in their upcoming planning, and what has happened in the way they work and in their relationships that needs review before the planning meeting.
5. Performance review on a systematic, goal-directed basis.
6. Periodic visits from outside consultants to keep the organization leaders thinking about the organization's renewal.

There are other possible techniques, but this list includes the most commonly used methods of maintaining a change effort in a complex organization.

Summary

In order to help organizations improve their operational effectiveness and system health, we have examined:

1. A model for determining early organization interventions.
2. Some choices of change strategies.
3. Some choices of early interventions.
4. Some choices of strategies for maintaining change.

The focus of this article has been on what the third party, facilitator, consultant, etc., can do as either a consultant, expert, trainer, or coach in helping organization leaders diagnose their own system and plan strategies for development toward a better state. This focus includes process intervention but is not exclusively that. It also includes the skills of system diagnosis, of determining change strategies, of understanding the relationship of organizations to external environments, and of understanding such organizational processes as power, reward systems, organizational decision making, information systems, structural designs, and planning.

It is the author's experience that the demand for assistance in organizational interventions and large system organization change is increasing at a very fast rate, certainly faster than the growth of resources to meet the demand. As the world shrinks, as there are more multinational organizations, as the interfaces between government and the private sector and the social sector become more blurred and more overlapping, large system interventions and the technology and skill available to facilitate these will be in increasingly greater demand.

10

Management Transitions for
Newly Appointed CEOs

James N. Kelly

The new CEO is commonly perceived as a powerful individual who rapidly takes charge of a firm through dynamic leadership. The author reports the results of a survey of newly appointed CEOs that sheds new light on how they approach their new positions. Management style, establishment of priorities, and selection of management teams are some of the topics covered in the article. *SMR.*

A new chief executive officer eagerly grabs the reins of his or her new position, and it is done none too soon. His or her predecessor stayed on too long before leaving. The company has become directionless. Divisions have drifted; some have been allowed to continue for too long with unsatisfactory performance, and some have slipped in competitive position without corrective action. Deadwood has accumulated in divisions and on the corporate staff. It is now up to the new CEO to reverse this process through strong leadership and action, particularly during his or her six-month honeymoon period with the board of directors.

Is this dramatic picture of the new CEO accurate? Is the new CEO the bold, assertive leader that we tend to visualize, or does he or she follow a more cautious style? How does the new leader actually lead? To establish some facts about the role and behavior of new chief executive officers, Management Analysis Center surveyed approximately 150 of them.

The Nature of the Survey

Two surveys were conducted: one in 1976 covering 56 executives and a second in 1979 covering 100 new CEOs. New chief executives were identi-

From *Sloan Management Review,* Fall 1980, Vol. 22, No. 1. Reprinted with permission.

fied from the "Who's News" column in the *Wall Street Journal.* In the 1979 survey, written questionnaires were sent to approximately 430 new CEOs; about 23 percent completed and returned the questionnaire. The 1979 respondents averaged forty-eight years in age and fourteen years in the company (when promoted from within), and came primarily from marketing (38 percent), operations (29 percent), finance (22 percent), and general management (20 percent). Approximately two-thirds were promoted from within, two-thirds were in charge of independent companies (not subsidiaries or divisions), and two-thirds were in companies with over $100 million in sales. The CEOs were new to top management jobs in 85 percent of the cases.

The participants of the 1979 survey were divided into two groups: fifty-three who had been CEOs for one to six months and forty-seven who had been CEOs for six months to two years. This was done in order to identify the differences between what new CEOs *thought* they would do at the start of their tenure, and what those on the job slightly longer say they actually *did.* The survey did not cover anyone with more than two years on the job, so that CEOs' perceptions of their initial actions would be fresh in their minds. If differences between planned actions and performed actions were evident, we felt that they would indicate where misconceptions exist in the thinking of new CEOs. Questions were asked about plans and actions during two time periods: the first six months and the subsequent year. This was done in order to establish benchmarks and to keep time horizons manageable from the respondents' viewpoints; six months was not implied to be the time period required to complete a management transition.

Insights into Management Transitions

From this research we have gained four insights into the typical management style, techniques, and priorities of newly appointed chief executive officers:

1. New CEOs move slowly in asserting their authority and establishing their imprint on their organizations.
2. Formulating corporate strategy is not the most important issue for the new chief executive officer.
3. The new CEO establishes a team made up of both incumbent executives and new appointees.
4. New chief executive officers have a short honeymoon period of less than six months before they are held accountable for performance.

These insights, and data from the surveys from which they were derived, are described in the following sections. Unless otherwise indicated, the data presented are from the 100 respondents in the 1979 survey. The 1976 results were similar to and consistent with those for 1979.

Moving Slowly to Assert Authority

New CEOs are often visualized as agents of dramatic change for their organizations. After a great trauma a new CEO is brought in to reverse staggering losses, declining profits, or eroded market shares. In other circumstances a CEO is appointed to replace an aging, retiring executive and to revitalize the organization. The new CEO is perceived as a confident leader striding forward to bring much needed change to the corporation.

Indeed, some of the respondents in the survey subscribe to this concept of an assertive management style for new CEOs. The president and CEO of a $100 million rubber and plastics company said, "Unless you are a true 'driver' and have a particular goal as CEO, why become one?" A similar position, "Establish your platform early—the first thirty days," was advised by the new CEO of a $1 billion interior finishes and industrial chemicals company. This new executive described a formal talk he gave to 500 people in his management group in which he spelled out a new emphasis and new or redirected strategies, all designed in the first thirty days of his assignment. Of the 150 cases studied, such fast-moving behavior and style were exceptional. New executives in most cases move extremely slowly and cautiously. Their style is informal, and their methods are low key. They downplay their own ego and authority, and they go to great lengths to establish personal relationships with their new subordinates.

Table 10.1 indicates this cautious behavior. Opening up the organization is given the highest level of importance. Establishing a personal imprint and moving quickly on personnel and business decisions were given about half the level of importance of opening up the organization. These new CEOs were minimizing turmoil, gaining input, and establishing support; they worked to secure their positions in their companies. Limiting contacts to the top management team is given very low importance; the effort to gain support is not confined to the upper echelons. The new executive attempts to obtain broad input in establishing a base of support.

The basically conservative style of the new CEOs is overwhelmingly demonstrated in the advice of many respondents:

"Move slowly and carefully—a dumb step early in time is hard to recover from." President, $25 million medical-products subsidiary.

Table 10.1 Management Style During Transition

Q:

Which of the following statements describe the philosophy or style you intend (intended) to use during the first six months of your new responsibilities?

	Importance	
A:	Percentage Answering Very High or High	Percentage Answering Moderate, Low, or None
I will try to "open up" the organization to see problems and create new solutions.	87	13
I will attempt to gain input and support from my top management team.	84	16
I will attempt to obtain broad sources of information in order to make good decisions.	71	29
I want to minimize the turmoil or uncertainty caused by my appointment.	56	44
I want to use the opportunity of my appointment to make other changes necessary in the business.	53	47
I want to establish my imprint on the company at an early moment.	48	52
I feel it will be necessary to move quickly on personnel and business decisions to avoid inheriting old problems.	41	59
I feel most short-term decisions will best be made by me with occasional help from other top executives.	29	71
I will limit my contacts to the top management team in order to reinforce their authority.	20	80
	N = 100	

"Move slowly if you have the time. Be careful so that the actions you take are properly understood." President, $290 million metal-products division.

"Take time to think and recognize that 'no' is often a good decision or action." President and CEO, $300 million textile and chemicals company.

"Go slowly and get several opinions. Don't jump to conclusions." President and CEO, $325 million chemical subsidiary.

"Listen to your people; then do what you think is best." President and CEO, $10 million electronics company.

"Stay flexible—don't panic—be patient." Chairman and CEO, $300 million brokerage and banking company.

"Keep learning; sublimate ego." President and CEO, $150 million manufacturing subsidiary.

Defining the CEO's Responsibilities

The new executive's conservative style is also demonstrated in the methods used to define his or her responsibilities. Table 10.2 displays these methods in order of the importance assigned to them by respondents. Discussions with subordinates and private contemplation were overwhelmingly seen as the most important methods used to define responsibilities. Conversely, formal discussions with other CEOs (including predecessors) and the writing out of responsibilities were given relatively little importance:

"Be confident in yourself and the talents that got you to your job; don't 'press.' " President and CEO, $1.7 billion food company subsidiary.

"Continue in previous management style; don't introspect over how a CEO job is 'different.' " President and CEO, $400 million electrical-machinery subsidiary.

"Act like you have been on the job all your life." President and CEO, $50 million health-care company.

Table 10.2 Definition of Responsibilities

Q:

What methods do (did) you intend to use in defining and planning the execution of your new responsibilities?

	Importance	
	Percentage Answering Very Important or Important	Percentage Answering Helpful, Unimportant, or None
A:		
Discussions with subordinates	84	16
Private contemplation	82	18
Discussions with superiors (directors)	60	40
Discussions with predecessor	38	62
Writing out responsibilities	33	67
Discussions with informal advisers	32	68
Study of published material	31	69
Discussions with other CEOs	10	90
	N = 100	

Table 10.3 Management Techniques

Q:

In dealing with new issues and implementing your management style, which of the following techniques do you feel will be (were) most helpful during your first six months?

	Importance	
	Percentage Answering Very High or High	Percentage Answering Moderate, Low, or None
A:		
Personal meetings with key executives	93	7
Special visits to offices, departments, or plants	63	37
Routine management visits	47	53
Changes in formal management systems for organizing, planning, and controlling resources	43	57
Special team-building meetings	42	58
Informal visits to probe into organization	38	62
Outside advice from directors, bankers, others familiar with company	33	67
Task force studies and recommendations	30	70
Formal conferences or seminars	15	85
Informal advice from other CEOs	13	87
Informal social events	10	90
Management consulting assistance	7	93
Management retreats	6	94
	N = 100	

Cautious Management Techniques

As would be expected, the management techniques used by new CEOs are also very cautious. Table 10.3 presents the techniques in order of importance to the respondents. Personal meetings were overwhelmingly emphasized. However, broadening contacts through special visits to offices, departments, and plants was also seen as important. Conversely, outside assistance from management consultants or other CEOs was ranked low, as were nonroutine activities such as management retreats and formal conferences.

During the first six months a new executive works hard to establish personal contacts with a broad spectrum of people in the organization:

"Avoid isolation—take chance of becoming too involved—alternative is worse." President, $140 million steel distributor.

"Know your company." President and CEO, $324 million food-distribution company.

"Get to know the power structure as early as possible." President and CEO, $40 million consumer products company.

"Although remedial action should be expedited, it should not be undertaken until the CEO is fully knowledgeable of the company's operations and of the capabilities of the senior managers." President and CEO, $300 million oil, gas, and minerals exploration company.

"Get to know people first." President and CEO, $65 million medical subsidiary.

"Consolidate people relations first." Chairman and CEO, $150 million electronics distribution company.

"Don't spend too much time on things that are not productive for stockholders, customers, and employees, such as filling out questionnaires." President, banking company.

"Go at a moderate rate; understand other management people and the problems of the company. Act in a fair, firm manner; give associates the opportunity to act." President and CEO, $700 million real-estate company.

"Spend time to get to know the business and your people." President and CEO, $185 million meat-packing company.

"Meet regularly with top and middle managers to evaluate personnel prior to any reorganization changes. Get involved in depth; travel to learn the business firsthand." President and CEO, $200 million soft-drink subsidiary.

"Dig in; be visible; involve yourself in division-level problems at times; and work, work, work." Chairman, President, and CEO, $800 million engineering and construction subsidiary.

"Clearly see where you are before starting out in a new direction." President and CEO, $80 million leisure-products company.

These statistics and statements paint a picture of new CEOs as conservative and cautious. They clearly believe they must go slowly in taking over their new responsibilities. However, there also appears to be a certain amount of uneasiness about this cautious approach. When asked whether they were more concerned about moving too slowly or about moving too fast, the new executives who had been on the job for six months or less were about evenly split between "too fast" and "too slow." The executives in office for six months to two years believed in retrospect that they had moved at about the right speed during their first six months. As Myles Mace observed, new chief executive officers should move quickly slowly.[1] The new CEO is like a contestant in a long-distance walking race, using a necessarily slow and deliberate style to achieve results as quickly as possible.

Corporate Strategy Is Not the Highest Priority

Classic management theory holds that strategic planning and personnel selection must follow the formulation of strategic goals. This theory is presented, for example, in Chandler's work.[2] Executives must determine what they are going to do before dealing with how to do it and who will do it. Change in the top management of an organization should be an excellent time to apply this theory. New leadership can start by establishing new direction. This would be particularly true in companies where executives are appointed from outside the organization, or where the new executives are dealing with poorly performing companies. Some of the new executives agreed with this theory:

"Take time to work out a comprehensive plan before making any other moves." President, $160 million mining company.

"Think through your goals and company objectives first. Then be assertive and don't compromise basic principles to attain those objectives." President and CEO, $200 million food division.

Although these comments were in the minority, the quantitative data also suggest, particularly for the very new chief executives, that strategy is a high-priority item. Table 10.4 compares the relative importance placed upon strategy, organizational structure, and evaluation of top managers by executives in the two groups surveyed. The executives with less than six months in

Table 10.4 Issues or Actions

Q:

During your first six months in your new position, what importance do (did) you place on the following issues or actions?

	Percentage Answering Very Important or Important	
	One to Six Months as CEOs	Six Months to Two Years as CEOs
A:		
Evaluating and changing strategy	76	56
Evaluating and changing organizational structure	62	72
Evaluating and replacing top managers	54	44
	N = 53	N = 47

office establish priorities based upon the classic theory: first, define strategy (76 percent); second, define structure needed to implement strategy (62 percent); and third, obtain the right managers for the intended strategy and structure (54 percent).

This pattern falls apart, however, in the priorities of the more experienced managers. For these executives, structure replaces strategy as the issue they would consider most important during the first few months in the CEO job, as shown in Table 10.4. This switch in priorities from what new executives think will be important and what more experienced managers say was important is revealing. The new executive is perhaps naive in placing such importance on strategy. The executive in office somewhat longer is perhaps more pragmatic in placing the highest priority on structure, while downplaying the more difficult and sensitive areas of strategy and personnel. He or she may also be responding to the immediate practical problems of the business that cause strategic change to be deferred until later than originally anticipated.

The high priority given to structure by the more experienced CEOs raises an interesting possibility about the management process. Perhaps organization is the new manager's most valuable weapon. It can be used to assume control and to implement strategy once control has been established. The more experienced executives recognize that they must eventually deal with strategy. In fact, they rate it the most important activity during the year following their first six months (78 percent very important or important, versus 56 percent during the first six months). For new CEOs, then, we can postulate a new management theory: *Attention to organizational structure should precede formulation of strategy, which will in turn lead to additional changes in structure and in management personnel.* Change in organizational structure is an important and constantly useful management tool.

Establishing a Management Team

Establishing a management team is a concept generally interpreted in one of two ways. It may mean selecting and appointing one's own top managers, or it may mean assuring that top management consists of the best possible people regardless of whether they are appointed or inherited by the new CEO. New executives do not anticipate replacing many of the managers they have inherited. They do not appear to adhere to the first interpretation of establishing their own management team—replacing existing executives with their own team.

For new CEOs with less than six months in office, the anticipated percentage of replacements ran the full range from zero to 100 percent, with a mean of 25 percent and a median of only 10 percent. The more experienced CEOs were very different in this respect. The percentage of top managers that they had appointed or intended to appoint ranged from 20 percent to 100 percent, with a mean of 56 percent and a median of 60 percent. While half of the newer CEOs expected to replace no more than 10 percent of the existing management team, *none* of the other group expected to replace less than 20 percent, and half reported a rate of 60 percent or more.

This increase could be accounted for by any of three factors. First, as new executives gain experience, it may become apparent to them that more executives must be replaced than was originally anticipated. Second, unexpected turnover—subordinates following the old CEO—may add to the replacement statistics. Third, the CEOs may be appointing more executives than they are replacing. They may, in fact, be expanding their management teams beyond the size originally thought necessary when they assumed control, and not replacing many more of the original executives than was anticipated at the outset.

New CEOs appear to follow closely the second interpretation of establishing the management team. They want to ensure that they have the most competent teams possible, whether or not they personally appoint the executives. New CEOs repeatedly referred to the top management team as being essential to their success:

"A competent team is critical." President and CEO, $22 million water utility.

"What is necessary? This isn't a personal need but a corporate one. If good people are functioning well, leave them. If not, replace them." Chairman and CEO, $120 million fabrications subsidiary.

"I am concerned about developing my top management team." President and CEO, $450 million division.

"Know your top management." President and CEO, $1.2 billion life-insurance company.

"As soon as possible, be sure your management team represents the best talent available." President and CEO, $750 million oil and gas subsidiary.

In the process of building a management team, the new CEO uses two aspects of the situation to advantage: time and organizational structure. The passage of time solves some problems as managers reach retirement age. One new CEO who had replaced 20 percent of his top management team dealt with another 20 percent by encouraging early retirement. While one might hypothesize that time works against the new CEO, in fact, our respondents use time as their ally:

"I will do it [replace management] over a period of time so that it should not be a problem." President and CEO, $100 million rubber and plastics company.

"Replacing management is temporarily a problem—but ultimately not at all." President and CEO, $200 million food division.

New CEOs also use structural change to deal with the problem of creating their management teams. In responding to questions about priorities for action, evaluating and changing organizational structure was cited by the new CEOs as having the highest priority. Evaluating and replacing top managers, by comparison, was ascribed half the level of importance. Structural change can mean both adding new people to the organization and realigning the duties of the people already in the organization:

"We'll only realign duties and make additions—[replacing management] is no great problem." President and CEO, $12 million mining subsidiary.

"Reassign—no problem. Made major changes after eleven months; timing was about right." President and CEO, $1 billion interior finishes and industrial chemical company.

"Plan to do some shuffling of responsibilities." President and CEO, $700 million banking company.

Discipline for the CEO's Predecessor

Our data indicate that the new CEO does not appoint a totally new management team, but does work to establish the strongest possible management team for the company. This process requires time and the restructuring of responsibilities. It also can be complicated by the need to discipline the new CEO's predecessor and new subordinates. This issue appeared in a section of the questionnaire dealing with transition of management (see Table 10.5).

The responses in Table 10.5 show surprising differences between the two groups. Those in the job slightly longer seem to recognize that informal techniques of discussing new responsibilities and new reporting relationships with subordinates, and simply working on a day-to-day basis, are less important than initially thought by the newer CEOs. The more experienced executive places a much greater emphasis on such stern actions as "informing subordinates that they should report only to me," "isolating predecessor from continued contact with my new subordinates," and "agreement that my predecessor will pass all communication with my subordinates through me." If the predecessor remains with the firm, as was true for 64 percent of the respondents, developing a strong management team can be more diffi-

Table 10.5   Transition of Management

Q:

If your predecessor remained in the company after you assumed your new responsibility, how do (did) you intend to manage the transition period?

	Percentage Answering Very Important or Important	
A:	One to Six Months as CEOs	Six Months to Two Years as CEOs
By open discussions with subordinates about new working relationships.	90	78
Informally, by day-to-day contact.	74	57
By agreement that my predecessor will pass all communication with my new subordinates through me.	57	77
By giving predecessor a new assignment.	37	46
By isolating predecessor from continued contact with my new subordinates.	15	40
By informing subordinates that they should report only to me.	4	41
	N = 38	N = 26

cult and seems to require more discipline and action than the new CEO initially anticipates.

The team that is finally chosen—although composed of people the new CEO believes are strongest—is thus not generally a team of managers newly appointed by the CEO. This point was clearly made by the president and CEO of a $410 million diversified company when he stated, "I do not believe you must have 'your' team in to do a good job."

The Honeymoon Period for New CEOs

How long do new CEOs have before the problems of the past become their problems? Six months is often cited as a rule of thumb for the honeymoon period. The rule of thumb is inaccurate. The time period varies for different aspects of management and is generally less than six months.

In the 1976 survey we specifically asked executives how much time they

Table 10.6   Timing of Impact

Q:

How long a period of time do (did) you feel will be (was) required for you to have an impact on the following aspects of your business?

| | Timing of Impact | | |
	Immediate	Within Six Months	Beyond Six Months
Aspect:			
Top management personnel	58	35	7
Organizational structure	32	56	12
Business strategy	24	54	22
Marketing programs	18	59	23
Profit performance	16	49	35
Financial position	15	45	40
Resource allocation	14	55	21
Information systems	8	68	24
		N = 100	

had before they were accountable for certain areas of management and performance. In 1979 we asked about the same areas in terms of the time required for the CEO to have an impact. The results were quite similar. Table 10.6 shows how long new CEOs think it will take them to have an impact on some important aspects of their responsibilities. There is a wide range of differences among the various aspects. Top-management personnel, at one end of the spectrum, is an area where the impact is believed to be immediate by about 60 percent of the respondents. At the other extreme, financial position is often described as an area where impact will take place only after six months or more (40 percent of the respondents). For 35 percent of the respondents, profit performance is similar to financial position in requiring more than six months for the CEO to have an impact.

Recognizing that the timing of having an impact is not the same as the timing of accountability, and that it would be interesting to learn whether executives see a difference between the two, our surveys asked about accountability in 1976 and about impact in 1979. If accountability is perceived as coming sooner than the ability to have an impact, this would indicate a transition problem for the new CEO. Table 10.7 shows the results of this distinction in the two surveys.

Table 10.7   Timing of Impact and Accountability

	1979 Study	1976 Study
	Impact within Six Months	Accountability within Six Months
Aspect:		
Top management personnel	93	84
Organizational structure	88	82
Resource allocation	78	NA
Business strategy	78	84
Marketing programs	77	NA
Information systems	76	NA
Profit performance	65	66
Financial position	60	70
	N = 100	**N = 56**

The data indicate that in important areas, such as top-management personnel, almost all new CEOs believe the honeymoon period is less than six months. In many instances, as shown in Table 10.6, they perceive immediate impact and accountability. In other areas, such as financial position and profit performance, a large number (35 to 40 percent) of the executives think that it takes longer than six months before they have an impact and before they become accountable. In general, the honeymoon period appears to be shorter than six months.

Implications of the Research

This survey cannot be used to say whether the priorities and methods reported by new CEOs are correct or incorrect, effective or ineffective. We cannot correlate behavior with results to determine effectiveness. We can, however, report the behavior favored by the respondents. This may be valuable information for other new CEOs to consider as they think about their new responsibilities.

1. New CEOs move cautiously and informally in establishing their authority. Bold action is rarely used. Thought is given to creating ways to delve into the organization to establish lines of contact, information, and support.

2. New CEOs do not attack the large strategic issues as the first priority. They look to the structure of relationships and responsibilities—both formal and informal—in the organization as the first area for thought, concern, and change. They seek to change the infrastructure to gain control of the organization, and then they consider strategy.
3. New CEOs tend to create management teams with equal numbers of new appointees and incumbents. Good people already in the organization can be part of the management team.
4. Most new CEOs feel they are accountable for and can have an impact on many important aspects of their business in less than six months. They plan to be well under way with actions and changes (particularly in the personnel and structure areas) within that time.

The transition period for new CEOs is fraught with problems. They are expected to produce results quickly, yet, as Mace suggests, they "should walk on eggs for a considerable time."[3] A final comment from one of our respondents highlights the paradoxical nature of the new CEO's situation:

"Pray for wisdom, patience, and perseverence, and go like hell." President and CEO, $45 million food-manufacturing and distribution company.

11

How to Implement Radical Strategies in Large Organizations

Yvan Allaire

Mihaela Firsirotu

Carrying out a radical strategy in a large firm is the acid test of corporate leadership. Yet, there are no models available to prepare and guide leaders to take unprecedented actions. The authors in this article address this issue and propose a framework for devising and implementing strategies that are discontinuous with the organization's present course of action. The framework considers four types of radical strategies: reorientation, turnaround, revitalization, and transformation. *SMR.*

The business press has recently chronicled many corporations that are experiencing momentous shifts in strategic orientation. Reference is often made to a corporation's market repositioning, acquisitions and divestitures, structural changes, etc. However, when reporting on such major strategic changes, the press has also begun to emphasize the softer dimensions, such as values, culture, and mind-sets. Thus, it is not entirely accidental that the topic of corporate culture has become a popular issue at a time when many corporations are experiencing major overhauls. Culture, and its resistance to change, provides an explanation for the insuperable difficulties a firm encounters when it attempts to shift its strategic direction. Not only has the "right" corporate culture become the essence and foundation of corporate excellence, but it is also claimed that the success or failure of needed corporate reforms hinges on management's sagacity and ability to change the firm's driving culture in time and in tune with required changes in formal strategies, structures, and management systems.

But while such observations are relevant, even though they are sometimes

From *Sloan Management Review*, Spring 1985, Vol. 26, No. 3. Reprinted with permission.

simplistic or faddish, they fail to inform corporate leaders on two critical issues:

1. What different types of radical strategies are available? And do different strategies call for different implementation procedures? For example, there has to be a difference between a radical strategy to turn around a moribund firm; a strategy to shift a corporation's resources to totally new markets and industries; and a strategy to prepare a healthy organization for major changes in its industry.
2. What lessons have been learned from the experience of corporations that have attempted, succeeded, or failed at radical strategies? Are there emerging frameworks, models, bits of wisdom that can guide corporate leaders facing such a task?

This article addresses these two issues by proposing clear, operational distinctions among four types of radical strategies: reorientation, turnaround, revitalization, and transformation. These four, well-demarcated radical change situations, which all call for very different actions, flow from a simple diagnosis of how the firm *fits* in its present and future environments. We then go on to describe a framework for thinking about, devising, and implementing strategies that are discontinuous with the organization's present course of action.

Four Case Situations

No radical strategy will ever occur if the corporation's leadership is not convinced of the need for dramatic actions. Therefore, a critical first step is for a firm to arrive at an appropriate diagnosis of how it fits in its present environment. A prescription prevalent in the business policy and strategy field has been the need for fit[1] or alignment[2] between the firm's strategy and its environment, present and future. An assessment of a corporation's fit and adjustment to its present and future environments will reveal one of the four possible situations described below.

Case I: Harmony and Continuity

In this first case, the firm's strategy is well adjusted to its present environment, which results in the firm's sound economic performance. The future is an evolutionary, predictable version of the present, for which the firm will prepare in an incremental manner. In other words, the preferred state of affairs, whenever attainable, is for a firm to have a harmonious fit in its

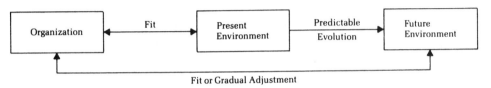

Figure 11.1 Case I: Harmony and Continuity

present environment, while making synchronized, gradual changes to meet anticipated future requirements (see Figure 11.1).

Still, managers and, for that matter, most people, have a strong tendency to cling to this approach even when there are warning signals that a new approach is needed for the firm to cope with the future. (To the extent that the firm's management is not deluding itself into believing that a Case I strategy is the proper diagnosis, the textbook prescriptions and techniques for good management formulated for just such conditions are relevant and useful.)

A company's harmonious fit to present and future environments is most easily achieved in periods of easy economic growth and tranquil technology. However, periods of economic upheaval or economic transformation may disrupt and threaten the status quo of large businesses. If this happens, the business environment becomes "discontinuous," and becomes increasingly characterized by radical changes in the rules of the game. It is as if, in an ongoing game of chess, one of the players or some outside authority were to decree suddenly changes in the rules that govern the moves of chess pieces. Much of the players' past chess experience (and the hundreds of books offering advice on how to play chess) would automatically become obsolete. In the final analysis, if an organization finds that it has to adjust to radically changed circumstances, the Case I scenario is inappropriate, and even dangerous.

Case II: Preemptive Adjustment or Temporary Misfit

Preemptive Adjustment

In this case, the firm is not well adjusted to its present market circumstances, which results in its immediate unsatisfactory performance. However, it is anticipated that the future will be fundamentally different from the present situation. The environment is expected to undergo a sudden breach of conti-

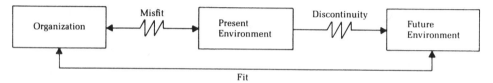

Figure 11.2 Case II: Preemptive Adjustment or Temporary Misfit

nuity or a sharp change from present conditions and trends: The firm is prepared and ready to reap rich rewards when this happens (see Figure 11.2).

A good illustration of this case is provided by Citibank's expenditures on technology and product development, which resulted in poor performances for some years in its retail banking operations. Nonetheless, this orientation has since placed the firm in a favorable strategic position as deregulation of the banking industry has begun to take effect and radically change the competitive and market environments. Another example is MCI Communications, whose quixotic challenge to AT&T in the long-distance telephone market has been made more significant by successive changes in the regulations of the telecommunications industry in the U.S.

Also included in this category are innovating firms that propose radically new products to currently unreceptive or undeveloped markets. Genentech's early foray into the gene-splicing and biotechnology field is a good example. Firms in this situation, if they are persistent and if their resources are sufficient, may eventually be vindicated—unless their ventures were ill-timed and ill-conceived.

Temporary Misfit

Transient, short-lived phenomena may perturb the organization's present environment, thereby creating havoc and misalignment for the firm. Nonetheless, the future could bring a return to normal circumstances to which the organization will be well adjusted. The organization will then resume its past acceptable level of economic performance. Although this scenario may be plausible, it may also be one of wishful thinking, or what Abernathy, Clark, and Kantrow call the "transient economic misfortune" school of thought.[3]

The prevalence of this type of unfounded rationale is particularly evident in industries that are coming to the end of their growth cycle. For example, the leveling off in sales of kerosene heaters, cross-country ski equipment, video games, snowmobiles, and personal computers was characteristically attributed to transient phenomena, such as bad weather or bad economic conditions. It was believed that as soon as the weather and the business climate returned to normal, sales would again surge. Of course, this did not happen. In these cases, sticking to this strategy was damaging, for it led to a postponement of the kind of actions required to adjust these businesses to new realities.

Case III: Transformation or Reorientation

Here, the firm is well adjusted to its present environment and turns in strong, respectable performances. However, its management foresees a future environment that is quite different from the prevailing one as a result of demographic, technological, regulatory, or competitive changes. To cope with, and thrive in, these upcoming circumstances, the organization must undergo a fundamental change (see Figure 11.3).

Transformation

Classic examples of major strategic transformations that have restructured whole industries include Boeing's shift to the production of jet-engine commercial airplanes and IBM's immense wager on the integrated-circuit technology of the 360. More recently, current and anticipated dramatic changes in computer markets and technology have called for major modifications of strategy at IBM and Digital Equipment. In the latter case, K.C. Olsen, Digital's president, "embarked upon a radical transformation of his engineering-oriented company into a tough, market-driven competitor."[4]

At Black and Decker, painful competition from Japanese manufacturers has led the company to bet its future on a "global" market strategy that requires a major transformation of the corporation.[5] The management of Beatrice Foods has also voiced its intention to transform the sprawling food, consumer, and industrial products holding company into a "consolidated marketing giant on the order of Procter & Gamble Co."[6]

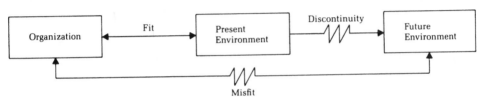

Figure 11.3   Case III: Transformation or Reorientation

In Canada, the Bank of Montreal has undertaken a major transformation of its structures and modes of operation. It is preparing for (and ushering in) an emerging banking environment that is thought to call for radically different operating technologies, management systems, and banking philosophy.[7]

The breakup of AT&T along with the heroic efforts of some of its components (Western Electric, Bell Labs, AT&T Information Systems, etc.) to shift from a monopoly environment to a competitive market context is perhaps the most striking example of a large-scale attempt at strategic transformation.[8]

Transformations may also result from a firm's resolve to change the "center of gravity" of the corporation.[9] For example, Monsanto's move downstream from commodity chemicals to proprietary patented products illustrates a transformation strategy.[10] The displacement of a corporation's center of gravity often means that new skills and radically different modes of operation and styles of management must be brought into the organization in a short period of time. This kind of transformation may result in a company that is temporarily misaligned with its present environment.

Reorientation

A reorientation scenario is one where a company, in anticipation of stagnation and even decline as its present markets mature, may reorient its resources into more attractive markets and industries. The business press is full of accounts of companies that are searching for renewed vitality through reorientation strategies. Below is a list of organizations that either have reoriented or are in the process of reorienting their operations.

- General Electric's shift from traditional electric products to high technology (computer services, factory automation).[11]
- Sears, Roebuck and American Express's invasion of the financial services market.[12]
- Philip Morris's aggressive entry into the beer industry (through Miller) and into the soft-drink industry (through Seven-Up).
- Eaton's shift from reliance on trucks and other vehicle parts to electronics, automation machinery, and fluid-power systems.[13]
- Pillsbury's shift to fast-food and restaurant chains.[14]
- Gould's move from battery operations—the very foundation of the corporation which it recently and symbolically sold—to the production and selling of electronic equipment. Gould Inc. now operates fifty-seven electronic plants in eleven countries.
- Imasco's (a large Canadian cigarette manufacturer) move into the United States' fast-food and retail-drug business.[15]

- Philips' shift to high-tech products.[16]
- Cincinnati Milacron's shift from metal bender to supplier of new robotic technology.[17]
- U.S. Steel's redeployment of assets (Marathon Oil, etc.).[18]
- Singer's expansion into aerospace.[19]
- Johnson & Johnson's recent emphasis on high-tech medical hardware.[20]

Because the environments in which these firms operate do not provide a future with sufficient prospects for growth and profitability, they are seeking to move voluntarily to market environments offering more promise and potential. In such a reorientation of activities, the firm must manage a breach, or discontinuity, between its present and future state.

Case IV: Turnaround and Revitalization

The firm in this case is misaligned with its present environment: Its performance may range from mediocre to dismal. Furthermore, the company is ill-equipped to meet the future (see Figure 11.4). The business press reverberates with stories of dramatic efforts of companies salvaging and turning around large organizations, such as Chrysler, Massey-Ferguson, International Harvester, American Motors, Montgomery Ward, AM International, Geico, Clark Equipment, A&P, Braniff, Pan-Am, Boise Cascade, Allis-Chalmers, Dome Petroleum, Eastern Airlines, and Western Union.

But whether the situation calls for revitalization or turnaround actions hinges on the severity of the problems. There is, for example, a difference between a Burroughs' or a Westinghouse's lackadaisical profit performance, sagging market share, and groping adjustment to changing markets on the one hand and, on the other hand, a Chrysler, Massey-Ferguson, or International Harvester on the brink of bankruptcy.

A company is in a turnaround situation if it has experienced such grave losses that its very survival is at stake if improvements are not achieved

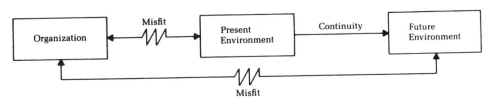

Figure 11.4 Case IV: Turnaround and Revitalization

swiftly. However, a corporation may not be in any immediate danger, but may show mediocre or below-average results, calling for a revitalization of its performance in the marketplace. Recent examples of businesses undergoing a revitalization are Prudential-Bache Securities,[21] Continental Corp.,[22] Corning Glass,[23] Burroughs,[24] Goodyear,[25] Sears' retailing division,[26] J.C. Penney,[27] Westinghouse,[28] and Sherwin-Williams.[29]

A Framework to Devise and Implement Radical Strategies

Leaders faced with the challenge of transforming, reorienting, revitalizing, or turning around a large corporation will find few relevant models or useful prescriptions to guide their actions. Instead, they will most likely fret about culture and about how to create and sustain the kind of values they should want for their organizations. They may even be bullied by popular infatuation into a "search for excellence" that promotes specific and contingent observations as universal and compelling management principles.[30]

Based on the experiences of many leaders who assumed the role of corporate revolutionaries, we have devised a framework for implementing radical strategies. The framework is broken down into six basic steps: (1) making a proper diagnosis; (2) formulating a metastrategy for radical change; (3) assessing the company's culture and structure; (4) defining the goals of the company's culture and structure; (5) proposing a broad agenda for radical change; and (6) stabilizing the organization.

Step 1: Making a Proper Diagnosis

Perhaps the most pernicious aspect of a corporation's present culture and structure is the way it can shape corporate mind-set that makes its leaders and managers immune or oblivious to signals of danger.

For example, a corporate leadership persuaded that it is in a Case I situation of harmony, continuity, and incremental adjustments may be right. However, the leaders may be deluding themselves or they may be impervious to indications of dramatic industry changes. They may even deny the reality of their present difficulties and shortcomings, and they may cling to a Case II diagnosis of a transient, self-correcting phenomenon, thereby attributing the company's poor performance to factors beyond their control. They may, therefore, feel that no radical actions are called for on their part.

Obviously, the first step in implementing any radical strategy is to make sure that the diagnosis of the firm's state of adjustment to its present environment and its preparedness for future circumstances is based on a tough, lucid, and unbiased assessment. Radical strategies must be considered if the leadership concludes, on the basis of that assessment, that it must either transform, reorient, revitalize, or turn around the corporation. Each of these strategies has its own particular dynamics and set of considerations. Although the contents and rate of change will reflect each company's particularities, these four radical strategies (in particular, turnaround, revitalization, and transformation) should unfold in a pattern of steps and actions, sometimes sequential but often overlapping and concurrent.

The Four Radical Strategies

Reorientation

Of the four radical strategies, reorientation is the easiest to implement. If a reorientation calls for the gradual divestment of present businesses and the acquisition of businesses in new fields—as General Electric and Gould are doing—corporate management would acquire the cultures and structures of the newly acquired firms. On the other hand, if a reorientation calls for the addition of new businesses to a mature, but profitable business—as Philip Morris, Pillsbury, and Imasco have done—the culture and structure of these businesses should not be disturbed if they are functioning well. Nevertheless, there are a few pitfalls that a company should be aware of when implementing a reorientation strategy. These are described below:

Corporate Management's Mind-set.   The fundamental requirement of a successful reorientation is corporate leaders' awareness that they are entering new territories and that their past experiences and specific skills might therefore be of limited relevance, if not totally inadequate. It is tempting, but dangerous, to assume that what has made a company successful in its present businesses will also make it successful in other industries. Such an attitude is sometimes reinforced by leaders emphasizing the similarities between the new and old businesses. For example, General Foods bungled in the fast-food business (with Burger Chef) precisely because it first attempted to have this totally new business managed by people from its old business.

This trap is particularly dangerous when a corporation moves into new fields incrementally. For example, the chief executive of Johnson & Johnson challenged *Business Week's* cover story that stated that J&J would have to change its corporate culture as it moved more and more into high-tech medical hardware.[31] In his letter to *BW,* Mr. Burke retorted, "It is well known that Johnson & Johnson has been a high-technology company for decades. . . ."[32] Obviously, J&J's leadership diagnosed the situation as a Case I scenario (continuity), whereas *Business Week* concluded that it was a Case III situation (reorientation).

The Lure of Efficiency through Integration

Even though corporate management may consciously acknowledge that a newly acquired or a newly formed business is different from the existing mature business, it may be tempted to integrate some of the new business's functions with the old one in order to take advantage of the cost savings. This temptation must be resisted, however, for the old business's culture may permeate the new business, thereby making it increasingly difficult for the new business to adjust to its own competitive environment. Woolworth is a case in point. When Woolworth, a successful, but mature variety-store business, formed the discount store Woolco, it decided to integrate some of Woolco's functions (in particular, purchasing) with Woolworth's operations. This led to Woolco's ultimate failure—in part because its operations were permeated by Woolworth's "five-and-dime" thinking. In contrast, Kresge managed its successful K mart division as a completely autonomous business.[33]

A successful reorientation calls for a corporate leadership that knows it does not know how to run the new businesses it is either acquiring or forming. Every attempt should be made to keep the cultures and structures of both the new and old businesses separate and distinct.

Turnaround

When a corporation's very survival is threatened, its leaders must carry out emergency actions that will stave off bankruptcy and buy them the time required to implement a radical strategy. The leadership must quickly find a new, more suitable market strategy that offers a compelling long-term solution to the firm's present plight. Often what is required to get the firm out of its rut is a new top-management team that will challenge taken-for-granted "facts" and assumptions. Such a crisis provides top management with a formidable tool to carry out changes that would otherwise be impossible. However, the level of stress among managers and employees must be monitored and managed. Too much stress may well lead to counterproductive actions (e.g., rash decisions).

Revitalization

Before a revitalization strategy can be implemented, an organization must first come to terms with two pervasive issues: (1) that there is no immediate evidence of crisis or threat to the firm's survival; and (2) that mediocre performances are often justified by putting the blame on external factors thought to be beyond the control of management. Given this backdrop, it is up to corporate leaders to make a looming crisis tangible and to make known the dangers the corporation faces. The leaders must make the case vivid and persuasive. Corporate management must also develop a sense of control and responsibility for the firm's performance.

Transformation

Of all the radical strategies, transformation requires the most demanding and skillful leadership. What is needed is a genuine revolution initiated by a leader with a vision of the corporation's future and the will to achieve it. However, the typical scenario is one where the corporation's present performance is satisfactory—maybe even excellent—and thus there is no impetus and no obvious justification for change.

Transformation strategy also involves other risks. Top management frequently makes the mistake of focusing exclusively on the structural aspects of change and of assuming implicitly that an appropriate culture will emerge quickly and inevitably from the new structural arrangements. In addition, in the course of transforming the organization to meet impending changes, top management may bring about a misalignment that is similar to a Case II misfit situation. Corporate management must be aware that some degree of confusion and disarray among employees and clients may be unavoidable during the process of transformation and may result in a lower level of economic performance for a period of time.

Step 2: Formulating a Metastrategy for Radical Change

To achieve radical change, the organization should be instilled with the new strategies, structures and systems, and supporting values deemed necessary to make such a change successful. Obviously, the leader, who is usually the CEO, must be able to distance himself or herself from the ongoing operations in order to set in motion the processes of change. This means that when present or anticipated events indicate that change in an organization's culture and structure is necessary, the leader must be able to formulate a strategy to implement a radically different strategy in the organization. This strategy is known as a metastrategy.

The leader's metastrategy is unwritten and communicated to very few people, at least in its early stages of implementation. At the beginning, the metastrategy may consist of a leader's tentative search for broad goals and directions. He or she will then set up or activate multiple (internal and external) channels to consult and discuss the goals and orientations.

When a leader becomes convinced—the sooner the better—that particular goals and directions are appropriate, he or she will then take the necessary steps to broaden support for the chosen direction through a well-thought-out sequence of symbolic actions and structural changes. The leader's metastrategy will reflect some hard thinking and firm conclusions about the kind of values that should be built into the organization. However, this does not mean that the leader should hold corporatewide seminars on the "culture we should have." (Culture is in the realm of feelings and sentiments and does not develop well under clinical observation.) Rather, the metastrategy process is formal and well-mapped-out and leads to a new, explicit strategy for the organization. In this way, the organization's future is dependent upon the quality of this present leadership's metastrategy.

Currently, the business press is full of sagas of leaders going about the task of major corporate overhauls. The accounts of these struggles and our own research of specific cases lead to a firm conclusion: Radical strategies have been successfully implemented only where corporate leaders were equipped with an effective metastrategy.

Step 3: Assessing the Corporation's Present Culture and Structure

The objective here is to understand the organization as a sociocultural system, to chart the socialization that the corporation actually provides, and to get at the organization's mind-set. If the leaders emerge from the ranks of the corporation, this step requires that they examine the values, beliefs, and mind-sets (including their own) imparted by the organization. On the other hand, if the leaders are newcomers, this step calls for their fast and sensitive learning of the organization's tangible and occult properties. In either case, the process may be helped by finding answers to the following questions:

- What are the tacit background assumptions and expectations in the corporation? Where do they come from?
- What are the values and frames of mind that flow from the particular nature of the industry? How did the industry's peculiar technology, regulations, labor-management relations, nature of competition, and econom-

ics form the beliefs and behavior of the organization? These factors almost always play a critical role in shaping the mind-set of a corporation. Yet, this factor is generally overlooked in the recent crop of books and articles on corporate culture, which tends to view culture merely as the product of past or present charismatic leaders.

- What stories, legends, myths circulate concerning the corporation's history, its past and present leaders? How are its successes and misfortunes explained?
- What are valued behavior, promotion paths, and critical skills for success in the corporation?
- What reinforcement of present culture is afforded by recruitment, training, promotion, organization structures, management systems?
- What is the implicit or explicit process of socialization in the corporation? Who are the role models? What cues and messages are conveyed to new employees? What values are communicated in training sessions?
- What is the degree of employee involvement in the corporation? Is there widespread commitment or calculative, limited participation on the part of management and employees? Are there groups (divisions, departments, etc.) with a subculture substantially at odds with the rest of the corporation?

The end product of this inquiry should be a statement of the basic values, assumptions, or expectations that have emerged from the organization's particular history, leadership, and contingency factors and that are supported by present-day management policies and practices. Below are brief examples of the set of assumptions that deeply permeated the operations of two large corporations, AT&T and Canadian National.

W. Brooke Tunstall, assistant vice-president of AT&T, found that AT&T's operations were deeply influenced by the following:[34]

- AT&T's role is to provide the best universal service at the lowest possible cost in a regulated environment.
- AT&T must have "one system," "one policy" throughout the organization to fulfill its role.
- AT&T is a three-legged stool: It must achieve a fair balance in the treatment of its employees, customers, and shareholders.
- Operational efficiency, technical skills, and a high level of effort to create a favorable regulatory climate are the keys for success.
- AT&T is a big family that cares for its employees.

In her study of Canadian National (CN), a state-owned railway company (now diversified to a large extent), Firsirotu discovered the assumptions underlying this corporation:[35]

- CN has a public-service responsibility to Canadian communities.
- Independence from government interference is a necessary condition of successful operation.
- CN has a degree of control over its market environment.
- Revenues for commercial viability are to a large extent dependent upon regulatory and political decisions and orders.
- Costing expertise and technical skills are critical to success in the corporation.
- Long-range financial planning is essential to successful management of the corporation.
- Additional volume of business is always good and will be sought through pricing actions rather than through better service offerings.
- CN is a big, patriarchal family with a top-down flow of authority and wisdom.

These two studies are instructive in that:

- They identify two sets of assumptions that have their roots in their respective industry's character, not in charismatic leadership. These assumptions are quite functional for the industry and context in which these organizations are operating; however, they would (and did) become very burdensome in different markets and contexts (e.g., AT&T in communications/information systems, or CN in the trucking business).
- Some assumptions may be conflicting, even mutually exclusive (e.g., independence from government and viability that depends upon political decisions), thereby creating tensions, variations in emphasis, and different means of reconciliation at various turns in the organization's history.
- These values and assumptions are shared and supported with different intensity in different parts of the organization. For instance, the union's leadership at CN is suspicious of the "big family" concept, but it stresses at every opportunity the "public service" role of CN as a functional rampart against the cutbacks and rationalizations that a strictly commercial role would impose on it.

Step 4: Defining the Goals of a Company's Culture and Structure

A leader aiming to radically change the corporation must set up processes that lead to some definition of the company's goals in terms of its culture and structure. What would the transformed, revitalized, or turned-around corporation look like? What values, expectations, and assumptions are consistent with, and indeed necessary to, the effective implementation of the firm's changed strategic posture and new operating requirements? This determination must be respectful of the factors that have shaped the corporation and that continue to influence its development. Thus, in attempting to change an organization's culture and structure, the leadership should heed the following observations.

Coherence with Contingency Factors

The values, strategies, and management systems that are proposed for the corporation should have an increasingly functional role in ensuring the survival and success of the firm, as well as providing rewards to its employees. If contingency factors (e.g., regulations, competition, technology) are not changing, the proposed culture must build on the assumptions and expectations that flow from these factors. For example, despite repeated attempts, it has proven very difficult to instill a "marketing orientation" in banking firms operating in a regulated environment where the critical tasks, and, therefore, skills, consist of credit rationing, that is, of deciding which loan supplicants will be favored.

It will also be futile to, say, exhort the employees of a regulated monopoly offering a public service and requiring large capital investments to become "close to the customer," to show a "bias for action," to manage with "simple form and lean staff," and to preach "autonomy and entrepreneurship." The requirements for success, imposed by the economics and regulations of these industries, are pushing very hard in another direction, and attempts by management to instill a culture that works against these forces will, therefore, be counterproductive.

However, when changes in contingency factors do occur, it is management's responsibility to ensure that these factors are quickly made visible to the organization's members and that these mutations are used as levers in working out changes in the organization's values and mind-set.

Multiple Linkages with the Present Culture

In the process of reviving or transforming a corporation, the leader must strive to preserve, emphasize, and build upon aspects of the present culture that are positive and compatible. The leader may even propose a culture that is a modernized version of old values and traditions that once made the corporation successful.

For example, Pistner, the CEO of Montgomery Ward, until very recently, declared his intentions of "replacing Ward's post-office mentality" and of returning to the "homely, honest virtues that made Montgomery Ward a powerful retailing force fifty or seventy years ago."[36] Similarly, Warren, the

CEO of the newly formed Canada Post Corporation, proposed to postal employees a return to the proud values of reliable service that once upon a time made their work honorable and respected in the community.[37]

A present culture may exhibit inherent contradictions in values and assumptions. The proposed culture should then build on these, either emphasizing some assumptions or values and downgrading others, or proposing a novel reconciliation of them. Finally, aspects of a present culture and structure that are antagonistic to the proposed culture and structure should be identified and opposed directly. For example, in the overhaul of a Canadian bank, it was found that any reduction in the number of branches was resisted, because the size of the network had become a measure of the institution's success and importance. Having recognized this, the leadership marshaled arguments in direct attack of that belief.

Step 5: Proposing a Broad Agenda for Radical Change

Figure 11.5 offers a useful schema for this step. The aim of radical strategies is to bring about required major changes in the structure—new goals and market strategies and new organizational designs and systems. But the challenge of radical strategies is to bring about the changes in culture and individual mind-sets deemed necessary to support and reinforce the changes in structure. If this is not achieved, structural changes will be ineffective, or even, counterproductive. However, it should be emphasized that the three dimensions of any organization (culture, structure, individuals) are not to be changed through the same mechanisms.

Table 11.1 summarizes the issues raised by radical, discontinuous, strategic change. It underlines the fact that management has a high degree of control on structural variables (formal goals, strategy, design, management systems). These may be changed at moderate to high speed, through the application of good technical, analytical management and competent political management of internal coalitions. In addition, if structural changes are legitimated by the present culture, management can implement such changes swiftly and easily.

However, when it comes to changes in cultural properties of the firm, management has, at best, only a moderate degree of control. Changes at that level tend to be slow and must be effected in part through symbolic management, accompanied by suitable structural reinforcements.[38] In order for this to happen, management must understand and make a conscious attempt to channel the complex social processes through which symbols, meanings, and values are created.

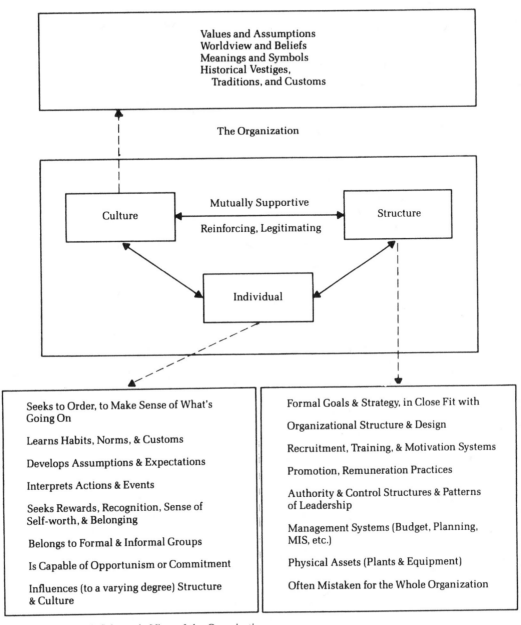

Figure 11.5 A Schematic View of the Organization

Table 11.1   Dynamics of Strategic Change

The Organization	Degree of Control by Management	Rate of Change	Mode of Change
Structure	High	Moderate to high	Political and technical management plus cultural legitimacy
Culture	Low to moderate	Low to moderate	Symbolic management supported by structural changes
Individual	Low to moderate	Low to moderate	Conversion through replacement, training, reeducation, and restructuring of assumptions and worldviews

Effective changes in culture and structure must be carried out in a well-coordinated sequence of actions, which mutually reinforce, legitimate, and aim to reorient and restructure the mind-sets of management and employees. In the process, some tension between culture and structure is inevitable as changes at one level are not rooted in the other. However, this tension must be calibrated, so that it does not reach a point where the linkage is severed and the present culture becomes antagonistic to the new structure. The resulting confusion, disarray, and disorientation among the members of the organization would be most disruptive.

To guard against a cultural clash, individual members should be provided with powerful symbolic materials and tangible structural evidence of a new corporate order. These should contain a compelling explanation of the corporation's present problems and future actions, as well as clear messages about the modes and norms of behavior that will be successful and rewarded henceforth. This agenda for radical change would typically include political and symbolic actions as well as recruiting change agents.

Political Actions

1. Broaden the political support for radical actions.
2. Raise the level of dissatisfaction and discomfort with the present situation.
3. Sensitize key actors to the need for change.

If necessary, use outside consultants or research results to underline the risk of the present course and to offer a compelling case for change. For example, when Pistner took over as CEO of Montgomery Ward, he prepared a dramatic document that he called, "A Charter for Survival." Pistner wrote, "Survival is the right word. It implies that the company is in trouble and that its future is in doubt unless drastic measures are taken. The trouble is real, and an immediate change must be made."[39]

Symbolic Actions

1. Communicate forcefully a new image that captures the external strategy and proposed culture to be implemented.
2. Use all available media channels to disseminate them (in-house journals, orientation sessions, training).

Here the leader should become the articulate embodiment of the new goals, directions, and values. For example, Smith of GM is synthesizing the new spirit he wants in the corporation by embodying "the 3 Rs—risk, responsibility, and rewards."[40] Similarly, Sullivan of Borden is trying to capture in an acronym, ROSE (return on shareholder's equity), his target for a revitalized company: "He sent ties with a ROSE logo to the top 200 managers. . . . He instituted incentive programs to reward executives for meeting financial goals, including bonuses tied in part to ROSE. . . ."[41]

Change Agents

1. Identify or recruit, train, and disseminate throughout the organization change agents who are favorable to the new orientation and who explain and propagandize it.
2. Maintain a liaison relationship.

Step 6: Stabilizing the Organization

During periods of transition, more than any other time, the members of the organization will be looking out for signals—watching for clues, inferring intents and motives—to see which way the organization is going. Any discrepancy between the leadership's words and deeds will be spotted. Furthermore, any contradictory or ambiguous signal can sidetrack or slow down the process of change. For example, at AT&T, the former IBM executive Archie McGill had become the symbolic embodiment of the utility company's resolve to become an effective marketer and competitor in the information systems field. The ups and downs of his career at AT&T were interpreted as evidence of the leadership's real intentions concerning this new orientation. For this reason, his recent departure from AT&T created confusion and uncertainty, a feeling that the new style and spirit of management that had sprung up in parts of the corporation might be quickly uprooted.[42]

Therefore, when stabilizing the organization, the following steps should be taken:

1. Ratify and reinforce the emerging worldview in the organization with public decisions and announcements by promoting persons identified with the new vision.
2. Establish tight consistency and coherence between words and actions.
3. Use tactical decisions to support fundamental changes in orientation.
4. Control and channel socialization processes.
5. Ensure that recruitment, selection, and training of employees are consistent with the new orientation.

Conclusion

Implementing a radical strategy in a large organization has proved to be an immensely difficult task, the acid test of a leader's skills. The difficulty of the task is compounded by a great deal of confusion about the very meaning of radical change and the paucity of models to guide management in such endeavors. However, we feel that the concepts and guidelines offered in this article provide a useful framework to think about and devise radical strategies and to manage strategic discontinuities.

Of course, in these matters, nothing can replace a leader's intuitions, his or her experience, and natural skills. Nevertheless, these necessary attributes will work better when they are supported by a clear understanding of how one should go about transforming a social system and of how a corporation can be radically changed.

PART IV

Organizational Culture

12

Does Japanese Management Style Have a Message for American Managers?

Edgar H. Schein

Many managers and observers, concerned about U.S. market share and productivity and impressed with Japanese success in these areas, have developed a sudden preoccupation with Japanese management methods. In this article, the author addresses the fundamental issue of what American managers can really learn from the Japanese through an analysis of two current best-sellers on Japanese management. He finds that the books fail to answer the critical question: Can management methods embedded in one culture be effectively transferred to another? As he explains, so little is understood about culture and its relationship to management methods that it is risky to assume that a method that works well in Japan will also work well here. *SMR*.

One of the greatest strengths of U.S. society is our flexibility, our ability to learn. When we see a problem, we tinker with it until we have it solved, and we seem to be willing to try anything and everything. One of our greatest weaknesses, on the other hand, is our impatience and short-run orientation. This leads to fads, a preoccupation with instant solutions, a blind faith that if we put in enough effort and money anything is possible, and an inability or unwillingness to see the long-range consequences of some of the quick fixes we try. Complicated solutions that require long-range planning, resolute implementation, and patience in the face of short-run difficulties are harder for us to implement.[1]

The tension between flexibility and fadism can be seen clearly in the current preoccupation with Japanese management. Two recent books, Ouchi's *Theory Z* and Pascale and Athos's *The Art of Japanese Management,* are currently on the *New York Times* best-seller list.[1a] Why this sudden

From *Sloan Management Review,* Fall 1981, Vol. 23, No. 1. Reprinted with permission.

interest, and what are the implications of it for management theory? I would like to examine some of the theses of these two books and put these theses into a historical perspective. From this perspective I will draw some tentative conclusions about cultural themes in the U.S. and the implications for U.S. management.

Some Historical Perspective: Indoctrination

In 1961 I published an article called "Management Development as a Process of Influence" attempting to show that many of the socialization methods used by some of our largest corporations (such as IBM and General Electric) were essentially similar to processes of indoctrination that one could observe in many other settings.[2] Such socialization methods were under strong attack by W.H. Whyte (in *The Organization Man*) and others who saw in them a tendency to create "men in grey flannel suits" who would cease to think for themselves and just parrot the corporate line, thus reducing the innovative and creative capacity of the organization and the individuality of the employee.[3] Ironically, the companies that had built such indoctrination centers (such as IBM at Sands Point, N.Y., and General Electric at Crotonville, N.Y.) were very proud of the spirit and common way of thinking that they could induce in their employees and managers. Such spirit was viewed as one of the key sources of strength of these enterprises.

But the pendulum swung hard during the 1960s, and it became the fashion to move away from producing conformity toward stimulating self-actualization.[4] "Indoctrination" either moved underground, was relabeled, or was replaced by "development" programs that emphasized opportunities for the integration of individual goals with organizational goals. Models of development shifted from the engineering model of "molding or shaping people to fit the organization" to more agricultural models of permitting people to flourish according to their innate potential; the obligation of the organization was to provide sunshine, nutrients, water, and other environmental supports. (Little was said in this model about pruning, transplanting, and uprooting, by the way.) The IBM songbook was put away, and managers who used to be proud of their ability to motivate people by inspiring them through common rituals and activities were made to feel ashamed of using "manipulative" tactics.

In the 1970s we discovered the concept of "organizational culture" and have begun to rethink the issue once again.[5] Even if a company does not deliberately and consciously indoctrinate its new employees, its important beliefs, values, and ways of doing things will, in any case, powerfully socialize anyone who remains in the organization and wishes to move upward and inward in it.[6] Such socialization processes and their effects in producing either conformity or innovation have been described and analyzed, and the tactics which stimulate innovation have received special attention.[7]

Now, with the "discovery" that some Japanese companies are effective because of their ability to involve and motivate people, and the assertion that such involvement results from socialization tactics that induce a high degree of loyalty and conformity, we may be headed back toward the ideology of indoctrination so forcefully put aside a mere twenty years ago.

Human Relations and Participation

A similar pendulum swing can be identified with respect to two other human relations values: whether or not one should treat people holistically, and whether or not one should make decisions from the bottom up by participation and consensus mechanisms. Many Americans have grown up with a tradition of bureaucracy, of strong bosses, of hiring people as "hands" to provide certain activities in return for certain pay and benefits. But most students of industrial-relations systems note that there has been a historical trend in such systems from a period of autocracy through a period of paternalism toward the present more consultative and participative models.[8] In the paternalistic phase American companies have treated employees very holistically: building company towns; funding company sports activities; providing country clubs, counseling services, day-care centers, medical facilities, uniforms, and so on. Indeed, one of Ralph Nader's most powerful films deals with the town of Kannapolis, N.C., where the Cannon Mills Co. not only provides lifetime employment but owns all of the housing, uses its own security force as the town police force, and provides all the services needed by the town. What alarmed Nader was the possibility that the citizens of this town were not developing any skills in self-government, which would leave them very vulnerable if the company should move or cease to be so totally paternalistic.

We may also recall that one of the major results of the now historic studies of the Hawthorne plant of the Western Electric Company was the recognition that employees were whole people who brought their personal problems with them to their place of work. In the 1930s the company launched a counseling program that involved company-employed counselors to help employees deal with any personal problems on a totally confidential basis.[9] Though it has been a tradition in our military services that officers not fraternize with the men (presumably because it might be difficult to be objective when individuals must be sent into dangerous situations), there is no such tradition in industry generally. Office parties, company picnics, and other forms of fraternization have been considered legitimate and desirable in many organizations and by many managers, though they are clearly not so institutionalized in the U.S. as they are in Latin America and Japan.

The human relations training programs for foremen that were rampant in the 1940s were clearly aimed at teaching managers to treat their employees as whole people, to consider their needs, to fight for them when necessary, and to build strong loyalty and team spirit. The leadership and sensitivity training which flourished in the 1960s was similarly aimed at truly understanding the needs and talents of subordinates, peers, and bosses, so that appropriate levels of participation could be used in solving increasingly complex problems in organizations.[10] The writings of McGregor on Theory Y showed the importance of trust and faith in people; the writings of Argyris showed the necessity of permitting people in organizations to function as adults instead of reducing them to dependent children.[11] Likert argued cogently for System 4, a more participative form of organization in which consensus management plays a big role; and Maslow first introduced the idea of Theory Z, a self-actualizing organization.[12]

Many managers saw the point immediately, and either felt reinforcement for what they were already doing or began to retrain themselves and their organization toward some of the new values and technologies of participative decision making. But as a total ideology this approach clearly has not taken hold. Many organizations discovered:

- That high morale did not necessarily correlate with high productivity.
- That autocratic systems could outproduce democratic systems (at least in the short run).
- That high productivity even when achieved by autocratic methods could build high morale.
- That the costs in terms of time and effort which participation entailed were often not affordable in certain kinds of environments.

Human Relations Japanese Style

Now the pendulum appears to be swinging once again on the issue of paternalism, managing the whole worker, and creating worker involvement through participation. We are told that the Japanese are extremely paternalistic and holistic in their approach to employees, that they tend to employ people for life, and that supervisors take care of the personal as well as the work needs of subordinates (sometimes even helping an employee find a wife). The Japanese use bottom-up consensual decision making and encourage high levels of trust across hierarchical and functional boundaries.

Theory Z

Ouchi has for some time been arguing that the essential differences between American (Theory A) and Japanese (Theory J) management systems lie in some key *structural* issues and *cultural* values that make it possible for certain kinds of management styles to flourish. Specifically, he points out that major Japanese companies:

- Employ their key people for "life" (i.e., until forced retirement at the age of fifty-five to sixty).
- Rotate them through various functions.
- Promote them very slowly and according to more of a seniority than a merit system.
- Place responsibility on groups rather than on individuals (a value of the Japanese culture).

These determinants make it possible for Japanese companies:

- To treat their employees as total people.
- To build the kind of trust that facilitates bottom-up consensual decision making.
- To control employees in a subtle, indirect manner.

In contrast, Ouchi points out, the bureaucratic model often associated with pure American management methods emphasizes:

- Employment contracts that last only as long as the individual is contributing.
- Specialization of function with rotation reserved only for people on a general managerial track.
- Little concern for the total person.
- Rapid feedback and promotion.
- Explicit formal control systems.
- Individual responsibility (a strong cultural value in the U.S.).
- Individual top-down decision making.

The crucial insight Ouchi provides is to identify another model, which he calls Theory Z, that is found in many American companies, that fits into our culture, and that combines certain features of the A and J models. Such companies have:

- Lifetime employment.
- Slower rates of promotion.
- Somewhat more implicit, less formal control systems.

- More concern for the total person.
- More cross-functional rotation and emphasis on becoming a generalist.
- Some level of participation and consensual decision making.
- A continued emphasis on individual responsibility as a core value.

Though he does not give much evidence in his book, Ouchi has shown in other papers that a U.S. company that approximates the Theory Z criteria generated higher morale, higher loyalty, and generally more healthy, positive feelings at all levels of the hierarchy than did a comparable Theory A company. What is missing, however, is convincing evidence that those companies fitting the Theory Z model are more *effective* than comparable companies operating more on the Theory A bureaucratic model. Furthermore, Ouchi acknowledges that the Theory Z companies he has studied generate less professionalism, have a harder time integrating mavericks into their ranks because they generate strong conformity pressures (leading them to be sexist and racist), and may only be adaptive for certain kinds of technological or economic environments. In fact, the only way a Theory Z company can manage the instabilities inherent in running a successful business in a turbulent environment is to limit lifetime employment to a small cadre of key people and to keep a large percentage of the labor force in a temporary role, policies that resemble more closely the bureaucratic A model. In order to survive, it may be necessary for Theory Z companies to subcontract much of their work or to rely on a set of satellite companies to absorb the instabilities. (The latter is the typical Japanese pattern.)

Implications of Theory Z

After describing how this notion of an industrial "clan" can facilitate certain kinds of long-range involvement on the part of employees, Ouchi argues strongly that U.S. companies should think seriously about becoming more like clans, and lays out a program of how they might do it. Neither the argument that a company should be more like Z, nor the proposed steps for how to get there, are at all convincing, however. The theoretical sophistication displayed in the analysis of types of organizational control is followed by naive and superficial prescriptions about how one might think about a change program designed to help a company to become more like a clan (if, indeed, this is even possible). In effect, the manager is invited to be more open and trusting and to involve his or her people more. Little attention is given to the issue of why a given organization would be less trusting and participative in the first place, or to the problem of transferring managerial values from a culture in which they fit very well to one in which the fit is not at all clear.

But Ouchi makes a strong sales pitch, and it is here that our tendency to embrace the quick fix may get us into trouble. If someone tells us that Theory Z is closer to the Japanese model, and that the Japanese are getting a lot of mileage out of their model, do we all get on the bandwagon and give our employees tenure, push decision making down the hierarchy, and slow down promotions? Do we turn everyone into a generalist, throw out formal control systems, and treat each person as a total human being? If we do, will our productivity shoot right back up, so that we can regain our once dominant economic position? Sounds too simplistic, does it not? Unfortunately, that is just what it is, because it takes into account neither the uniqueness of Japanese culture, the uniqueness of U.S. culture, the technological and environmental conditions that ultimately will dictate whether an A, a Z, or some other form will be the most effective in a given situation. What the Ouchi book leaves out, unfortunately, are criteria to help a manager decide whether or not a Z, an A, or some other form is appropriate.

On the positive side, the analysis focuses on the importance of the human factor, and Ouchi's seven criterion categories are certainly important in assessing the options for managing people. The identification of the clan mechanism as a way of organizing and controlling people brings us back to what many companies know intuitively—"we are one big family in this organization"—and legitimizes the kind of indoctrination that used to be more common. We can see more clearly that between autocracy and democracy there lies a full range of choices, and that a high degree of paternalism is not necessarily incompatible with bottom-up, consensual, participative decision making. The manager can also see that the way people feel about an organization can be explicitly managed even if the relationship to long-range effectiveness is not completely clear. As Etzioni noted long ago, a person can be involved in an organization in a variety of ways, ranging from the "alienated prisoner" or calculative employee to the participating member who is fully and morally involved.[13] Two serious questions to consider are whether U.S. economic organizations can claim moral involvement (as some Japanese firms apparently do) and whether such levels of involvement are even desirable in our culture.

The Ouchi analysis closes with a useful reminder that what ties the Japanese company together is a *company philosophy,* some dominant values that serve as criteria for decisions. What permits bottom-up consensual decision making to occur is the wide sharing of a common philosophy that guarantees a similarity of outlook with respect to the basic goals of the organization.

Ouchi provides some case examples and displays a method by which a company can determine its own philosophy.

Integrating the Seven S's

Pascale and Athos make their argument at a different level of analysis, though they also stress the importance of managing *people* as key resources and the importance of superordinate goals, sense of spirit, or company philosophy. Ouchi is more the social scientist, presenting a theoretically grounded sociological argument for a structural approach to human resource management. Pascale and Athos are less theoretical and more didactic. They are the teachers/consultants, distilling some of the wisdom from the analysis of the Japanese experience, and they try to transmit that wisdom through a more down-to-earth writing style. The managerial reader will learn more from this book, while the social scientist will learn more from the Ouchi book.

As already indicated, Ouchi has seven basic criteria for distinguishing A from J. Pascale and Athos (with due apologies for the gimmicky quality of the scheme) draw on a formulation developed by the McKinsey Co. that includes the following seven basic variables:

1. Superordinate goals.
2. Strategy.
3. Structure.
4. Systems.
5. Staff (the concern for having the right sort of people to do the work).
6. Skills (training and developing people to do what is needed).
7. Style (the manner in which management handles subordinates, peers, and superiors).

Within this structure, Pascale and Athos identify what they term the "soft S's" and the "hard S's," and explain that the superordinate goals are critical in tying everything together. They argue that Japanese companies are effective because of their attention to such integration and their concern for those variables which have to do with the human factor, the soft S's. These are the factors American managers allegedly pay too little attention to: staff, skills, and, most important, style. The hard S's are strategy, structure, and systems.

Through a detailed comparison of the Matsushita Corp. and ITT under Geneen, the authors bring out the essential contrast between Japanese attention to the soft S's and Geneen's more "American" preoccupation with very tight controls, autocratic decision making, and concern for the bottom line. Yet the Geneen story also illustrates that a system that is as internally consistent as ITT's was can be very effective. Its weakness lay in its inability to survive without the personal genius of a Geneen to run it.

The Japanese Style

Following this dramatic contrast, Pascale and Athos analyze the Japanese management style and explain how a culture that values "face" and is collective in its orientation can breed managerial behavior that makes the most of ambiguity, indirection, subtle cues, trust, interdependence, uncertainty, implicit messages, and management of process (instead of attempting to develop complete openness, explicitness, and directness in order to minimize ambiguity and uncertainty). "Explicit communication is a cultural assumption; it is not a linguistic imperative," they remind us.[14]

The lesson for American managers is diametrically opposite in the two books. Ouchi's proposal for how to get to Theory Z is to be more open; Pascale and Athos imply (from their positive case examples of U.S. managers who use indirection, implicit messages, and nondecision as strategies) that we might do well to learn more of the arts of how to be less open. Though we in the U.S. often imply that to worry about "face" is a weakness and that it is better to "put all the cards on the table," in fact, there is ample evidence that Americans no less than Japanese respond better to helpful face-saving hints than to sledgehammers. "When feedback is really clear and bad, it's usually too late."[15] "The inherent preferences of organizations are clarity, certainty, and perfection. The inherent nature of human relationships involves ambiguity, uncertainty, and imperfection. How one honors, balances, and integrates the needs of both is the real trick of management."[16]

The analysis of face-to-face communication, drawn from an article by Pascale called "Zen and the Art of Management," is full of valuable insights on the subtleties of how and why indirection, tact, and concern for face are not merely niceties but necessities in human relations. It is crucial to recognize, of course, the distinction between *task* relevant information (about which one should be as open as possible in a problem-solving situation) and *interpersonal* evaluative information (about which it may be impossible to be completely open without running the risk of permanently damaging relationships).[17] Sensitivity training in which people attempted to tell each other what they thought of each other only worked in so-called stranger groups, where people did not know each other before and knew that they would not have to work or live with each other after the program.[18]

Interdependence

Pascale and Athos supplement their analysis of face-to-face relations with an excellent analysis of groups and the dilemmas of interdependence. Noting that the American tradition is one of independence and that the Japanese tradition (based on their limited space and the technology of rice farming) is one of interdependence, they show how groups and meetings can work in this context by members being more restrained, self-effacing, and trusting. As Ouchi points out, getting credit in the long-run, instead of worrying (as Americans often do) about being recognized immediately for any and all accomplishments, is made possible by the knowledge of lifetime employment, i.e., if people have to work with each other for a long time, true contribution will ultimately be recognized. Both books indicate that such group relationships combined with lack of specialization of careers give the Japanese company the ability to integrate better across key functional interfaces, because everyone has more empathy and understanding for other functions.

Superior-Subordinate Relationships

Long-term relationships and a culture in which everyone knows his or her place in the status hierarchy lead to a different concept of superior-subordinate relationships in Japan. The boss is automatically more of a mentor, teaching through subtle cues rather than blunt feedback, exercising great patience while the subordinate learns how to interpret cues and to develop his or her own skills, and reinforcing the basic company philosophy as a conceptual source that helps subordinates to decide what to do in any given situation. This point is critical, because it highlights one of the most important functions of superordinate goals or organizational philosophy. If everyone understands what the organization is trying to do and what its values are for how to do things, then every employee who truly understands the philosophy can figure out what his or her course of action should be in an ambiguous situation. No directives or explicit control systems are needed because the controls are internalized.

Individualism and Authority

Pascale and Athos take the issues of power and authority into the cultural realm in a more subtle fashion than does Ouchi, who merely labels J companies as having collective responsibility and A and Z companies as having individual responsibility. But we must ask what individual or collective responsibility means in each culture. Can we assume that the American model of individual rights, independence, equal opportunity under the law, and related values and norms is in any sense the opposite of or even on the same dimension with the Japanese notion of group responsibility? Is the issue simply that the group would be sacrificed for the individual in the U.S., whereas the individual would be sacrificed for the group in Japan?

A more appropriate formulation is to assume that in every culture and in every individual there is a core conflict about how self-seeking or self-effacing to be for the sake of one's group or organization. At the extremes where either nationalism or anarchy is involved, the conflict is easier to reduce, but in a pluralistic society it is a genuine dilemma. (This is exemplified in U.S. sports organizations, which try to create a team while maximizing the individual talents of the players.) In a recent analysis of individualism, Waterman has indicated that in political and social science writings there have always been two versions of individualism: one focuses on selfishness and takes advantage of the group, and one focuses on self-actualization in the interest of maximizing for both the individual and the group the talents latent in the members.[19] Those writers who argue for a humanistic solution to organizational problems are espousing the second definition, which assumes that integration is possible.

In my experience the effective organization is neither individualistic nor collective; rather it attempts to create norms and procedures that extol stardom and teamwork equally. The manager's job (just like the good coach's) is to find a way to weld the two forces together. The Japanese solution to this dilemma appears to be aided immensely by the fact that basic traditions and cultural values strongly favor hierarchy and the subordination of the individual to those above. However, this solution has potentially negative consequences, because it reduces the creative talent available to the organization. One might suspect, however, that the effective organization in Japan finds ways of dealing with this dilemma, and that the highly talented individual is not as pressured to conform as the less talented individual.[20]

The Japanese company in the Ouchi model could be expected to be more innovative on those tasks requiring group solutions, while the American company could be expected to be more innovative on those tasks that require a high level of individual expertise and creativity. Company effectiveness would then depend on the nature of the tasks facing it, its ability to diagnose accurately what those tasks are, and its flexibility in transforming itself—what I have termed an "adaptive coping cycle."[21] Whatever its human virtues and in spite of its ability to integrate better, a Theory Z organization might have more trouble both in seeing changes in its environment and in making the necessary transformations to adapt to those changes. Because of its strong commitment to a given philosophy and the pressure for everyone to conform, it is more likely to produce rigid paradigms for dealing with problems.

Implications for U.S. Management

Both books call for a reexamination of U.S. paradigms of how to organize and how to manage. While one can only applaud this challenge and use the models which the books present to gain perspective for such reexamination, one must be concerned about the glibness of the lessons, recommendations, and advice, given the meager data base on which they are based. Neither book makes much of an effort to decipher what may be happening in our own culture and society that would explain our tendency toward Theory A (if, indeed, it can be shown that such a tendency exists). Why do we have difficulty with some of the solutions the Japanese apparently find natural and easy? And, most important, what are the strengths in the U.S. system that should be preserved and built upon?

For example, Ouchi is quick to point out the negative consequences of the American tendency to try to quantify everything. Most of us would agree that for managing the human system of the organization, quantification may be more of a trap than a help, but one might also argue that our desire to quantify reflects some of the best tradtions of Western science and rationalism. The trick is to learn what to quantify and to know why quantification is helpful. In designing quality-control programs or in setting sales targets, it may be crucial to state a goal in quantifiable form in order to measure progress toward the goal. On the other hand, attempting to quantify managerial traits as part of a performance-appraisal system may distort communication and reduce the effectiveness of the whole system, because people would begin to feel like "mere numbers." The effective manager in any cultural system would be the one who knows what to quantify.

Many of the formal control systems that have become associated with the concept of bureaucracy (and that are seen by Ouchi, Pascale, and Athos as dysfunctional relative to the more indirect controls associated with the Japanese style) imply that all organizations face similar control problems. One suspects, however, that controlling the design and building of a large aerospace system might require more formal control mechanisms than the control of an R&D organization in a high-technology industry. Ouchi's comparison of formal bureaucratic with informal clan mechanisms misses the point that Galbraith made so effectively: As any organization evolves, it develops organizational structures that are needed *at that stage* to deal with its information-processing and control problems. A geographically dispersed organization dealing with local variants of a given market has different problems from a high-technology company that has standard products that work more or less in any market. Galbraith's analysis reveals at least six or seven variants of control systems from simple rules to complex matrix structures.[22]

But the most important issue to examine before we race into new organizational paradigms is whether or not we even have the right explanation for Japanese success. Neither Ouchi nor Pascale and Athos presents much evidence to justify the premise that the Japanese organizations cited are successful because of the management system described. In addition, no evidence is shown that such organizations are, indeed, the most successful ones in Japan. For example, it may well be that both Japanese productivity and management style are the reflection of some other common historical, economic, and/or sociocultural factor(s) in Japan.[23] Neither book tells us enough about the following important issues:

- The role of postwar reconstruction.
- The opportunity to modernize the industrial base.
- The close collaboration between industry and government.
- The strong sense of nationalism which produces high levels of motivation in all workers.
- That lifetime employment is possible for roughly one-third of the employees in some Japanese organizations, because of the system of temporary employment for the rest of the employees and the existence of satellite companies that absorb some of the economic fluctuations.
- That all employees retire fairly early by U.S. standards (in their mid- to late fifties).
- That many of the best companies are family dominated and their strong company philosophies may be a reflection of founder values that might be hard to maintain as these companies age.
- That the cultural traditions of duty, obedience, and discipline strongly favor a paternalistic clan form of organization.

Neither book refers to the growing literature that compares managerial style and beliefs in different countries and that contradicts directly some of the books' assertions about U.S. and Japanese management approaches.[24] For example, although both books extol the virtues of Japanese indirection, subtlety, and ability to live with uncertainty and ambiguity, Hofstede found in a sample of forty countries that U.S. managers reported the highest levels of tolerance of ambiguity, while Japanese managers reported some of the lowest levels. On many dimensions U.S. and Japanese managers are surprisingly similar in their orientation, which suggests that the real answer to organizational effectiveness may be to find those combinations of strategy, structure, and style that are either "culture free" or adaptable within a wide variety of cultures.

Knowing What Is Cultural

If we are to have a theory of organizations or management that is culture free or adaptable within any given culture, we must first know what culture is. This is surprisingly difficult, because we are all embedded in our own culture. What can we learn from Japanese managers if we cannot decipher how their behavior is embedded in their culture? Can we attempt to adapt managerial methods developed in other cultures without understanding how they would fit into our own?

The first and perhaps the most important point is that we probably *cannot really understand another culture* at the level of its basic world view. The only one we can really understand is our own. Even understanding our own culture at this level requires intensive analysis and thought. One cannot suddenly become aware of something and understand it if one has always taken it completely for granted. The true value of looking at other cultures is, therefore, to gain perspective for studying one's own culture. By seeing how others think about and do things, we become more aware of how we think about and do things, and that awareness is the first step in analyzing our own cultural assumptions and values. We can use analyses of Japanese management methods and their underlying cultural presumptions to learn about the hidden premises of U.S. managerial methods and our own cultural presumptions.

If we can grasp and become aware of our own premises and values, we can then examine analytically and empirically what the strengths and weaknesses of our own paradigm may be. This process of self-analysis is subtle and difficult. Not enough research has been done on managerial practices in our own culture; thus, the methods of analysis and tentative conclusions presented below should be treated as a rough first cut at analyzing our own cultural terrain.[25]

Levels of Culture

In thinking about culture, one should distinguish surface manifestations from the essential underlying premises that bind the elements of any given culture. As shown in Figure 12.1, there are at least three interconnected levels:

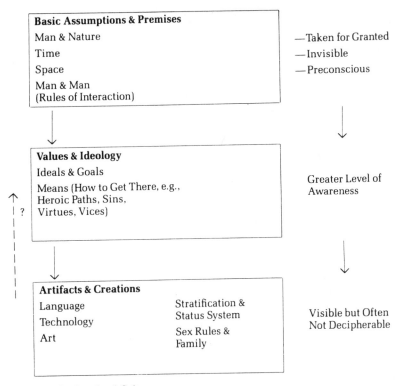

Basic Assumptions & Premises

Man & Nature — Taken for Granted

Time — Invisible

Space — Preconscious

Man & Man
(Rules of Interaction)

Values & Ideology

Ideals & Goals

Means (How to Get There, e.g.,   Greater Level of
Heroic Paths, Sins,   Awareness
Virtues, Vices)

Artifacts & Creations

Language   Stratification &
                  Status System   Visible but Often
Technology   Not Decipherable
                  Sex Rules &
Art   Family

Figure 12.1 The Levels of Culture

1. *Artifacts and creations* are the visible manifestations of a culture (which include its language, art, architecture, technology, and other material outputs) and its visible system of organizing interpersonal relationships, status levels, sex roles, age roles, etc. Though this level is visible, it is often not decipherable in the sense that the newcomer to the culture cannot figure out "what is really going on," what values or assumptions tie together the various visible manifestations.
2. *Values and ideology* are the rules, principles, norms, values, morals, and ethics that guide both the ends of a given society (group) and the means by which to accomplish them. Values and ideological statements usually define what national goals, intergroup relationships, and interpersonal relationships are appropriate to strive for. They are taught to children and reinforced in adults. Generally the level of culture we first encounter is how to achieve the goals (i.e., we encounter the appropriate rules of conduct that govern relationships between nations, groups, and individuals within the society). This is also where differences are felt most

strongly, because of the penalties associated with behaving inappropriately. This level of culture, although partly conscious and partly unconscious, can be revealed if people reflect analytically about their own behavior.

3. *Basic assumptions and premises* are the underlying and typically unconscious assumptions about the nature of truth and reality, the nature of human nature, "man's" relationship to nature, "man's" relationship to "man," the nature of time, and the nature of space.[26] These assumptions create the cultural core or essence, provide the key to deciphering the values and artifacts, and create the patterning that characterizes cultural phenomena. This level is hardest to examine, because it is taken for granted and, hence, outside of awareness.

If we analyze U.S. culture and managerial assumptions in terms of some of the categories around which basic assumptions are built, what perspective does this provide, and how does this help us to learn from Japanese managerial practices?

Some Key Assumptions of U.S. Culture

"Man's" Relationship to Nature: Proactive Optimism

It is a premise of most Western societies (particularly of the U.S.) that nature can and should be conquered, that "man" is ultimately perfectible, and that anything is ultimately possible if we put enough effort into it. The philosophy "Where there's a will there's a way," buttressed by "Every day we do difficult things; the impossible just takes a little longer," sets the tone for how we approach tasks. We feel constrained by the environment only if we do not have the knowledge or technology to control or alter it, and then we proactively seek whatever knowledge or technology is necessary to overcome the obstacle.

Such proactive optimism underlies the values surrounding equality of opportunity in that we take it for granted that anyone might be able to accomplish anything, if given the opportunity. In other words, man is ultimately perfectible, as the thousands of self-help books in book stores proclaim. The notion of accepting one's "fate" (limiting one's aspirations according to one's social position or some other nontechnological constraint) is simply not part of the underlying ideology, however much empirical data might argue to the contrary.[27]

Given this core assumption, what kinds of organizational forms are possible in the U.S.? Can an industrial clan (a Theory Z organization) with its intrinsic conservative orientation survive in a cultural environment that emphasizes change, progress, innovation, and novelty? Or would this cultural orientation begin to erode the very core of such an organization—the stability that produces the comfort?

Similarly, can a culture that encourages people to find better ways to do things independently, to resist arbitrary authority if it interferes with pragmatic problem solving, and to value individual accomplishment produce an integrated system like the Pascale/Athos Seven S model? Perhaps the most notable characteristic of U.S. managerial practice is that we are never satisfied and are forever tinkering to find a better way. This will always undermine efforts toward integration. For many U.S. managers, integration equals stagnation. I have observed repeatedly that as soon as a system becomes routine, managers begin to think about "reorganization." Perhaps we deeply mistrust stability and are culturally "pot stirrers."

"Man's" Relationship to "Man": Individualistic Egalitarianism

Every society or group must resolve the issue between individualism and collectivism. The underlying U.S. assumption appears to be that the individual always does and should do what is best for himself or herself, and is constrained only by respect for the law and the rights of others. The rule of law implies that there are no philosophical and moral principles that can ultimately determine when another's rights have been violated, and, therefore, the legislative and judicial process must decide this on a case-by-case basis through a confronting, problem-solving process judged by a jury of peers. Buried in these assumptions is a further assumption that the world can be known only through successive confrontations with natural phenomena and other people; that the nature of truth resides in empirical experience, not in some philosophical, moral, or religious system; and that the ultimate "philosophy," therefore, might as well be one of pragmatism. Ambition, maximizing one's opportunities, and fully utilizing one's capacities become the moral imperatives.

These assumptions, in turn, are related to the Western rational scientific tradition, which emphasizes experimentation; learning from experience; open debate of facts; and a commitment to truth, accuracy, measurement, and other aids to establish what is "real." The openness and pluralism that so many commentators on America emphasize are closely related to the assumption that truth can be discovered only through open confrontation and can come from anyone. The lowliest employee has as good a chance to solve a key problem as the president of the company, and one of the worst sins is *arbitrary* authority ("Do it because I am the boss, even if you think it is wrong" or "If I'm the boss, that makes me right").

Yet teamwork is an important value in U.S. sports and organizational life. It is not clear to me how to reconcile the need for teamwork with the assumptions of individualism, and neither Ouchi nor Pascale and Athos offers much guidance on how consensual methods can be fitted to the notions of individual responsibility that U.S. managers take for granted. One of the greatest fears U.S. managers have of groups is that responsibility and accountability will become diffused. We need to be able to identify who is accountable for what, even when the realities of the task make shared responsibility more appropriate. According to Ouchi and Pascale and Athos, the Japanese deliberately blur individual responsibility and adapt their decision making to such blurring. If that is so, their version of the consensus method may have little to teach us.

Participatory methods can work in the U.S., but they must be based on a different premise: the premise that teamwork and participation are better ways to solve problems, because knowledge, information, and skills are distributed among a number of people. We must, therefore, involve those people who have relevant information and skills. But the goal in terms of U.S. assumptions is better problem solving and more efficient performance, not teamwork, consensus, or involvement per se. Unless Japanese consensus methods are built on the same premise of effective problem solving, they are in many senses culturally irrelevant.

Similarly, the Japanese concern for the whole person may be based on premises and assumptions that simply do not fit our core assumptions of individualism and self-help. U.S. managers are scared of paternalism and excessive involvement with subordinates, because they see them as "invasions of privacy." If an individual is taken care of by an organization, he or she may lose the ability to fight for himself or herself. Our whole system is based on the assumptions that one must "be one's own best friend" and that the law is there to protect each and every one of us. Dependency, security orientation, and allowing others to solve our problems are viewed as signs of failure and lack of ambition and are considered to be undeserving of sympathy. On the other hand, if it is necessary to take care of the whole family in an overseas transfer in order to enable the primary employee to function effectively, then we do it. Pragmatism, necessity, and efficiency override issues of what would be more humane, because of the underlying belief that we cannot philosophically agree on basic standards of what is "best" for everyone. What is best for people must be decided on the basis of negotiation and experience (ultimately expressed in laws, safety codes, and quality of work-life standards).

A culture based on such premises sounds harsh and cold, and the things we are told we should do to "humanize" organizations sound friendly and warm. But cultures are neither cold nor warm, because within any given culture both warmth and coldness have their own meaning. We may not like certain facets of our culture once we discover their underlying premises, and we may even set out to change our culture. However, we cannot produce such change simply by pointing to another culture and saying that some of the things they do *there* would be neat *here*. We have not yet begun to understand our own culture and the managerial paradigms it has created. This article is a beginning attempt to stimulate such self-understanding, which is a prerequisite for any "remedial" action.

13

Cultural Assumptions and Productivity: The United States and China

Edwin C. Nevis

Based on the premise that the study of another culture is a useful tool for learning about one's own environment, the author compares and contrasts major cultural characteristics of the U.S. and China. Although he guards against the idea of blindly adopting major Chinese cultural assumptions, the author feels that the U.S. may benefit economically by looking toward China to find new insights and fresh approaches to help the U.S. better cope with prevalent economic ills—low productivity and lack of innovation in the work force. *SMR.*

In recent years there has been a profusion of books and articles about the Japanese economic success and about how the U.S. might improve its own economic performance by learning from and adopting some of the Japanese practices and norms. This enthusiasm has brought new popularity to the study of comparative management. Inevitably, questions have been raised as to whether it is feasible to transplant specific practices and policies from one culture to another. For example, is the lifetime employment of large Japanese firms workable in the U.S.? Drucker, Hofstede, Schein, Pascale and Athos, and Ouchi are among those who have addressed such issues, particularly with regard to the Japan-United States exchange.[1] Consequently, new questions have emerged: What is culture? Can a person of one culture truly understand another culture?[2]

Drawing upon my recent work in the People's Republic of China (PRC) and my years of working with U.S. managers in the areas of motivation, creativity, and innovation, this article attempts to contribute to the growing body of literature in this area. During my stay in China (from May to September of 1981), I heard repeated comments and read numerous articles

From *Sloan Management Review,* Spring 1983, Vol. 24, No. 3. Reprinted with permission.

concerning two major problems plaguing that country: low productivity and difficulty in applying innovations that would improve the Chinese worker's motivation and performance in all areas of work.[3] I was immediately struck by the similarity of these concerns and the concerns of U.S. managers regarding low productivity and lack of innovation in the United States. Though the industrial base and the standard of living in the two countries are considerably different, these issues are critical to the economic well-being of both nations.

While I do not think that one culture can borrow from another, the study of another culture can be a very useful tool for learning about one's own environment. In particular, the contrasts that arise from such cultural comparisons heighten our awareness of cultural characteristics that distinguish one culture from another. Cultures are not fixed, closed systems that can be understood in static, mechanistic terms. By using an analysis of basic cultural assumptions in the People's Republic of China and in the U.S., and by looking at recent developments in the two societies, this article attempts to isolate the kinds of Chinese practices and norms that might illuminate ways for the U.S. to bring about positive changes in America's productivity and innovation.

Background on the People's Republic of China

Immediately following China's liberation in 1949, the Chinese poured forth enormous energy to support the development of a new society. Though there was much suffering and deprivation during this period, most Chinese speak well of the times. The development of the country—particularly in agriculture and health—proceeded until the Cultural Revolution began in 1966. The Cultural Revolution, which lasted until 1976, brought much unrest. Policies and structures were dismantled, and intellectuals or those showing a strong individualism were suppressed. This led to fear, poor morale, and apathy. Survival came to mean an unquestioning loyalty to Chairman Mao.

The Cultural Revolution nonetheless brought about two major cultural attitudes. First, great caution about standing out in any way became the norm. It was too risky to assert a great deal of initiative unless one was certain of how it might be received. Since such clarity was generally lacking, few people dared to take this risk. Second, in order to reward loyalty to the work unit and the nation as a whole, the concept of sharing equally became prevalent. Everyone was to make equal sacrifices; the idea being to make sure that all shared in the relatively meager rewards or outcomes. Since the standard of living was low and incomes were marginal anyway, it was considered better to have everyone share equally what little there was than to give extra rewards to those who had earned more by being more productive. Thus, poor performance was rewarded equally with good performance.

Maoism

Mao was adamant that national unity and loyalty were not to be compromised, and much of the suffering and deaths that occurred during this period stemmed from an absolute application of this policy. He was also quite firm about developing agriculture as a main priority, putting it ahead of industrial development. Thus, he saw the need to feed the country adequately and to establish a higher standard of living for the enormous number of peasants and rural dwellers. Farms were to be only communal; no individual farming was allowed. Industry was to be controlled and operated by the state, leading to the development of a large bureaucracy that included, for example, eight ministries of machine building. Each of these ministries was to own and operate thousands of factories, as well as support organizations, including colleges and training schools. In addition, Mao stressed the concept of "perpetual revolution." As classes began to form in the new China, it became necessary to take strong actions to suppress them so that a classless society would prevail. The most dramatic example of this was the unleashing of the Red Guards to attack the growing managerial and intellectual classes in the Chinese society. Another major aspect of the new China was "de-sensualization." Mao believed that a bland, austere society was essential in building the desired classless society. The lack of color in clothing reflected the desensitized environment Mao so highly encouraged.

But probably the most fundamental aspect of the Chinese culture under the Mao regime was the extensive use made of work groups to promote the development of an agricultural society. Most factories and agricultural organizations were broken down into small units. In the factories, work was carried out in units called workshops, which ranged from cost centers to small groups of people working around two or three machines. Likewise, smaller units such as brigades and teams were employed on the communal farms. From the beginning work was organized and controlled in small groups. While changes have been made over the years regarding the correct size and structure of these groups, the basic concept has remained intact. Since so much of one's life was oriented toward the work unit—with housing, education, and medical care often being part of the fringe benefits—the life pattern of the typical Chinese person was strongly group oriented. Thus, it followed from this structure that people would help each other not only with work problems but also with personal problems. Chairman Mao also encouraged and rewarded the propriety of intervening in the lives of friends, neighbors, and coworkers for the purpose of "correcting" deviant behavior.

Cultural Assumptions Underlying Chinese Management Concepts

The following is a list of the most apparent cultural assumptions gleaned from this study of Chinese management structures and practices. These traits reflect the cultural changes since 1949 and represent the basic aspects of the new society.

- Loyalty to the country is of the utmost importance: the nation has priority over everything.
- Emphasis is placed on central planning and the creation of a powerful state.
- Consideration for the family is very important.
- Personnel selection (i.e., leadership) is based upon exploits or ideological contribution.
- Great respect is shown for age and traditional ways.
- Equity is more important than wealth.
- Saving and conserving (money, resources, etc.) are highly valued.
- Personal credit for accomplishments is denied; conformity is enforced.
- Every decision must take ideology into account.
- Communal property is considered more important than private possessions. Collectivism is the best economic mechanism.
- Emphasis is placed on group forces for motivational purposes.

The fundamental premise that governs these cultural assumptions is that a contributing and valuable member of society is one who puts group goals before individual needs. A sense of "belonging"—a moral imperative—acts as the driving force or core value. From this premise, other cultural traits follow: equity, avoidance of personal credit for accomplishments, the importance of communal property, and an emphasis on group forces for motivation.

A group-oriented system of equal pay and equal reward reached its height during the Cultural Revolution. Today this practice extends so far as to honor "model workers." Every factory displays in a prominent place the pictures and names of those workers whose attitudes and behavior best exemplify the revolutionary ideals. Obviously, other workers are exhorted and are expected to follow suit. In addition, a member of a work unit is entitled to free or very inexpensive housing, schooling for his or her children, medical care, and recreational activities. The power of this combination of incentives and rewards has been great. If you thank a Chinese worker or recognize his or her accomplishment, the reply is something like: "I'm only doing my job"; or "It's my duty." Though there have been some changes in the size and composition of work units over the past six years, these assumptions and practices still prevail to a large extent.

Although today there is a great need to restructure and improve Chinese businesses, the underlying principle that governs Chinese management is "respect for age." It is rare to find a high-potential young manager supervising an older manager. The older managers—or "leaders" as the Chinese prefer to call them—are also trusted contributors of the Revolution and the Party. In an important speech given in 1981, Chairman Hu Yaobang stressed the need to promote younger people into higher positions of leadership.[4] However, it is recognized that this will be a very slow process: Older people will not be passed over to accommodate aspiring young managers.

Cultural Assumptions Underlying U.S. Management Concepts

In contrast to the cultural assumptions of the PRC, the culture of the U.S. has developed out of assumptions that stress the individual and a decentralized government. The following list describes the most critical cultural concepts. (The list is expanded from an extensive analysis by W.H. Newman and reflects what Lodge and others have referred to as the Lockean or Jeffersonian perspective of human nature.)[5]

- The ideology of self-determination is espoused. In other words, there is the belief that individuals can substantially influence the future.
- Freedom of expression and opinion is highly valued. Individualism is encouraged.
- "To get ahead" is taken for granted: there should be equal opportunity for all.
- Independent enterprises are the most effective economic instruments; competition is the most effective mechanism.
- Private property is highly valued; limited state involvement is sought.
- Personnel selection is based on merit.
- Decisions must be based on objective analysis.
- Continual quest for improvement and change is encouraged. A pragmatic orientation toward change is upheld.
- High value is placed on specialization in all fields.
- There is a dominant view of the country as virtually having unlimited resources—the "streets paved with gold" hypothesis is espoused.
- "Fairness" is the guiding principle for the integration of the individual and group needs.

While U.S. management practices and structures are not always true to these assumptions, they are, nonetheless, the guiding values of our culture. The contrast between the assumptions and practices of the U.S. and those of the PRC is striking. Even where there may be some cultural overlap with regard to fringe benefits and welfare, the ideology or strategy is quite different: The Chinese uphold loyalty to the state and national unity; Americans uphold the integrity of the individual. A Chinese work unit, such as a factory, has many features of the "company town" that today are anathema to most Americans. In short, the Chinese assumptions are organized around the actualization of the group, organization, and state. U.S. assumptions, on the other hand, encourage the actualization of the individual. As Veroff et al. point out in their large-scale survey of Americans, we now seek to use "interpersonal intimacy" rather than social organizations as a means of integrating our lives.[6] Finally, it should be noted that U.S. assumptions reflect equality of opportunity, while Chinese assumptions focus on equality in the sharing of output.

Difference between U.S. and China Hierarchy of Needs

Figure 13.1 illustrates Maslow's classic formulation of Western culture's hierarchy of needs.[7] According to his thesis, the foundation of the American society is based on an individual's personal development. (This is manifested through our preoccupations with continuing education, health care, and ca-

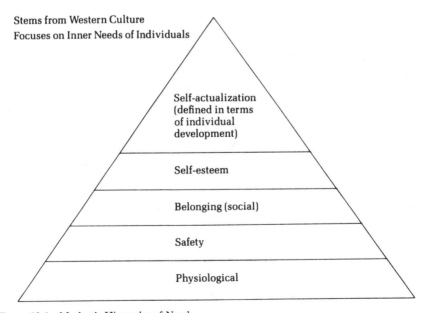

Figure 13.1 Maslow's Hierarchy of Needs

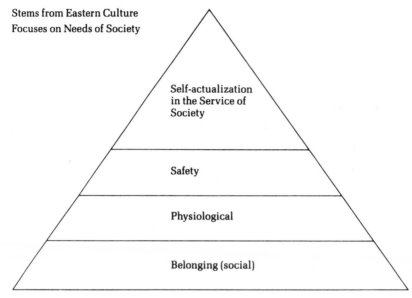

Stems from Eastern Culture
Focuses on Needs of Society

Self-actualization
in the Service of
Society

Safety

Physiological

Belonging (social)

Figure 13.2   Chinese Hierarchy of Needs

reer planning.) From this viewpoint, the individual is expected to develop the "self" in terms of achieving personal goals. In other words, the definition of self-actualization in the U.S. is seen in terms of the individual recognizing his or her own full potential as an independent, self-sufficient human being. Through Maslow's interpretation of the hierarchy of needs, it is clear that the belongingness aspect of our society plays a diminished role in the development of the individual.

In juxtaposition to Maslow's hierarchy, I have constructed a Chinese hierarchy of needs based on Eastern culture. As Figure 13.2 shows, the belonging aspect of the Chinese hierarchy is the focal point or bedrock of its society. This hypothesis is one way to explain how the basic life needs of the Chinese people are met only after the belonging needs of the individual are satisfied. It also helps us to understand the underlying cultural assumption of group loyalty and national unity. In other words, the Chinese concept of self-actualization is defined in terms of one's service to the community.

Recent Developments in the Two Societies

If either country is to enhance its industrial productivity and quality of life, core assumptions and values must be supported even while new trends and ideas are considered. However, if we remain too respectful of accepted assumptions, we may be merely ensuring the status quo, leaving no room for the possibility of true innovation through experiment. Perhaps changes in basic assumptions can be achieved only through revolutionary means—by looking for and supporting radical experiments—even if they violate core values. But here too, it would seem that in order for new values and concepts to become acceptable through revolutionary tactics they must build upon or relate in some way to traditional values. For example, the Chinese sense of loyalty to the nation was surely founded on centuries of feudalistic subservience that existed right up to the time of the Revolution.

Current Developments and Experiments in the People's Republic of China

Table 13.1 lists current major developments and experiments in the PRC. The list suggests that, in a broad sense, the Chinese today are moving more

Table 13.1 Summary of Current Developments and Experiments in China

Although centralized control is well-established and a powerful state is fully in charge, there are signs of public self-criticism by leaders.

There is a large, cumbersome bureaucracy with overlapping, often conflicting subsystems and goals.

There is a general acceptance of national, superordinate goals, but there is growing concern about how well the Party is doing in achieving these goals.

Successful achievements in agriculture are being made; a large population is fed reasonably well.

Success of state and work units in providing necessities for people has produced a welfare mentality. People believe that they will be cared for in one way or another.

Growth of free market system as abundance makes surpluses possible in some areas. Planning and market economies are allowed to coexist.

There is a growing consumerism and individualism in taste. A need for greater privacy is becoming evident.

Select organizations are allowed to retain profits, pay taxes, borrow money at interest, and make own investment decisions.

Experiments are being conducted to find more flexible organizational formats and a way to decentralize authority.

Both individual and group bonuses now exist. Many variations in incentive plans are being tried.

Individual ownership of enterprises is now allowed and encouraged (mostly in small service organizations).

Product quality is now highly stressed. Quality incentives have emerged.

Contract system in industry and job responsibility system in agriculture are upheld. MBO variations with accountability and reward mechanisms to support the objectives are established.

There is a revival of worker's congresses, which function as advisers to leaders. They also watch over welfare needs of workers and select supervisors and managers at all levels.

toward accepting some American cultural assumptions. An important theme emerging in China is the allowance for more individual accountability and reward. Another theme that is being considered is the adoption of a pragmatic ideology, which will serve as a counterforce to pure ideology. The recent appointment of a new chairman and the demotion of the old one in June 1981 symbolizes this trend.

On the other hand, one wonders whether past adherence to a centralized leadership, group work forces, and state welfare will allow the concepts of entrepreneurship and innovation to flourish. Recent data, although meager, show that belongingness and survival needs are still major preoccupations of the Chinese worker (see Tables 13.2 and 13.3). How representative these data are remains a question. What is important to note, in any event, is that new developments have not weakened the resolve of the Chinese leaders to ensure that loyalty to the nation is still the highest priority.

Current Developments and Experiments in the U.S.

Despite the prevalence of troublesome issues such as economic and job uncertainty and poverty, self-fulfillment still remains a strong goal for the American society at large. However, what is beginning to change is the definition of self-fulfillment. Today Americans are becoming more concerned about the quality of their lives, not simply in terms of materialistic

Table 13.2   What Is Important to a Chinese Worker[a]

To realize the four modernizations[b]
To raise bonuses and wages
To believe in Communism
To have ambition
To have a happy family
To bear an honorable title
To be a famous expert
To be promoted
To have no strong beliefs

[a]Items are listed in order of importance.
[b]National goals articulated in 1978 for the socialist modernization of agriculture, industry, national defense, and science and technology.
Source: Based on the 1980 study of 343 Chinese workers by Dr. Xu Lian-Cang of the Chinese Academy of Science.

Table 13.3 What "Chills" a
Chinese Worker's Motivation[a]

Unhealthy tendency[b]
Low wages
Housing problems
Privileges of cadres
Dull life
Dissatisfaction with job
Factional strife
Problems with children's education

[a]Items are listed in order of importance.
[b]Any thought or action by leaders (managers) deviating from or not supporting the current ruling ideology.
Source: Based on the 1980 study of 343 workers by Dr. Xu Lian-Cang of the Chinese Academy of Science.

gains (i.e., how much they *own*), but in terms of consciously choosing a lifestyle that is both psychologically and aesthetically pleasing.

Table 13.4 presents some of the major recent developments in the U.S. society. Similar to the Chinese society, some of these developments represent broad trends; others are more specific experiments or unusual solutions to difficult problems. However, one theme that emerges despite this period of great change is that the concepts of individualism and self-actualization, which are basic U.S. cultural assumptions, have been carried to a very high evolutionary level. In this respect, we are well into the higher level of the hierarchy of needs.

However, many of the economic ills that are afflicting the U.S. seem to be aggravating the means and methods of satisfying needs at the safety and belonging level of the hierarchy. Some of the items described in Table 13.4 are an attempt to address and come to terms with these economic problems. As a result, two major attitudes seem to be emerging: a desire for close, more affiliative relationships at work as well as in other spheres of life; and an appearance of intergroup cooperation to achieve superordinate goals in situations that typically would be left to competitive, adversary mechanisms.

While both of these trends seem to conflict with the basic cultural assumptions of individualism and competition, they relate to social requirements associated with the belonging level of the hierarchy of needs: Many experiments are taking place at this level, including the use of groups in quality of work-life programs. There are also signs that the American people are join-

Table 13.4 Summary of Current Developments and Experiments in U.S.

Self-fulfillment is at a high point and there are high expectations in terms of satisfying many needs and actualizing "self."

Institutions and methods for the development of the "authentic self" have been established.

There is an increase in the number of people living alone as a result of relative failure of the communal experiments of the 1960s. Yet sharing of housing seems to be increasing, particularly among young adults and the elderly.

There is a strong focus on interpersonal intimacy. Friends, family, personal "little" worlds have become important. Individuals are less willing to move or make job changes that have negative impact on these relationships.

Quality of relationships in large institutions has become a concern among workers. In other words, workers are striving for less manipulative, warmer, generous relationships than were formerly associated with the business world.[a]

There is a decreasing desire for dominance in leadership roles among young managers, and for being an entrepreneur or working for oneself.[b]

Increased acceptance of deviation from traditional roles is evident.

There is a deterioration of faith in government and ability of leaders to govern. As a result interest groups have emerged. Lobbying as a means of gaining objectives has also become popular.

There is a deterioration in industrial growth rates and productivity decline and a noticeable decline in the quality of products and services.

Equal-employment opportunity and affirmative-action programs supported by federal laws have been established. Nonetheless, these programs are threatened by economic problems and unemployment increase.

The size of organizations has grown in all spheres. Conglomerates and huge enterprises are beginning to dominate industry.

Advocates of laissez-faire seem to be prevailing over state intervention in significant areas.

Electronic devices and automation have been implemented in the work place.

Many organizations are experimenting with work innovations, such as quality of work-life programs, quality circles, flextime, Scanlon-type incentive plans, and autonomous work groups.

Workers are making changes that better support their social and group needs (e.g., the "Lordstown Case").

Community intervention to help the independent enterprise (such as Lockheed or Chrysler bailouts) is on the rise. The Municipal Assistance Corporation of New York City (MAC) is an example of group cooperation to meet a superordinate goal.

Possible beginnings of new union-management relationships are seen in the reopening of contracts (e.g., the Ford-UAW agreement).

There have been cases of agreements among workers and managers at different levels to share jobs and take pay cuts instead of having some coworkers laid off.

---

[a]See: D. W. Bray and A. Howard, "Today's Young Managers: They Can Do It. But Will They?" *Wharton Magazine,* Summer 1981, pp. 23–28; and J. Veroff, E. Douvan, and R. A. Kulka, *The Inner American* (New York: Basic Books, 1981).

[b]See Bray and Howard (Summer 1981); and A. Shapero, "Why Don't Your Kids Want To Be Entrepreneurs?" *Inc.,* September 1981.

ing groups—although largely for the purpose of political action. Thus, if the Chinese seem to be moving in the direction of individualism by permitting more flexibility in group forces and lessening centralized controls, is it possible that we are moving toward supporting and furthering group units and a communitarian way of thinking? Numerous people have addressed this recent phenomenon. For example, Yankelovich calls for a "new social ethic"; Lodge espouses a "communitarianism" philosophy; Driscoll proposes a cooperative theory of management.[8]

Although many may question the appropriateness of adopting such an orientation, perhaps if we thought of these new developments in terms of expanding our concept of individualism, we would be more receptive and accepting of such attitudinal changes. In fact, a study of our history of the past fifty to sixty years does show periods of group cooperation and consensus at critical times. Some noteworthy examples of these are:

- Camaraderie and group spirit of large segments of the working class in the early days of unionism.
- Sharing and a sense of community by victims of the Great Depression.
- Patriotic attitudes—sacrifices and mobilization of people—manifested during World War II.
- Broad-range support for the space program during the period after the Russians launched the Sputnik.
- Advances in intergroup relations after World War II and the heightened appreciation for group forces brought about by the group dynamics/sensitivity training movement.[9]

Superordinate Goals.   As the above list shows, in hard times, Americans have been able to put aside the idea of individualism temporarily, and rally around superordinate goals. It may now be that we are in a critical period where attention to the belonging level of the social order may help us to deal more effectively with current problems. President Carter appeared to have some insight into our need for this kind of superordinate thinking, but his personal style and the mood of the American people combined to minimize his impact at the time. However, this may have been only a temporary setback to a growing awareness that communal thinking is in order in our society.

Another emerging awareness is that human development specialists in America have been stressing unduly a definition of self-identity as the outcome of a private consciousness and the satisfaction of inner needs, thus ignoring or playing down identity as an outcome of shared meanings and of the individual relating to human units greater than one. But most importantly, what these specialists seem to have overlooked is that self-fulfillment is as likely to be obtained from participating in important social processes as it is from inner exploration and development. Both approaches are legitimate endeavors, but complete concentration on the latter has led to a confusing preoccupation with self-fulfillment.[10] Perhaps unwittingly, the human-potential movement often sounds as though the criterion of the fully actualized person is that of the fully developed, independent individual living in full splendor and alone on some lofty mountain peak. While this state may be attainable if everything around us were working well and lower-order needs were being met, the complexity and necessary interdependence of modern living make it highly unlikely to achieve.

The work of Felix Rohatyn and the MAC to save New York City from bankruptcy, and the bailouts of Lockheed and Chrysler by the federal government are examples of superordinate thinking at a high level. Each of these situations poses a more complicated issue regarding assumptions of free markets, competition, and a limited state. From the standpoint of such assumptions, these actions were inappropriate and possibly harmful. However, such actions may also indicate that we no longer are a society of unlimited resources and that our assumptions do not hold up as well as they did earlier in our history. What stands out beyond adherence to any assumptions is that many people and a significant number of social systems would have been severely damaged if these rescue attempts had not been made.

Implications for U.S. Management Practices

Given the current picture of the U.S. and of our fundamental cultural assumptions, actions to solve our complex modern problems that involve centralized planning or a tightening of organizational controls are likely to be ineffective. A more fruitful approach would be to make greater use of relatively autonomous groups or small social units for producing needed changes. It is my belief that both self-fulfillment through individual expression and identification with meaningful social experiences can be satisfied this way, as well as the desire for deeper or more generous relationships with other people.

Sharing Information. American managers have traditionally mistrusted group decision making. However, this mistrust has been in reaction to pressures for consensus that emphasize the sharing of power and authority. If we can shift our focus somewhat—that is, away from the pressure for shared responsibility to a more pragmatic approach to a sharing of information in the service of better problem solving—we may be able to support newer models for group action in the U.S. Schein has suggested that for groups to be more palatable in the U.S., the focus must be on the need to share information held by many people, instead of attempting to spread responsibility as the Japanese model of group decision making does.[11]

For example, it may not be entirely unrealistic to propose in a group that, unless all the individuals give up something in the service of a larger good (a superordinate goal), all will suffer. This would require the higher levels of authority involved to give up something too, but they would give up something other than individual authority or responsibility and accountability for results. While it may require great skill and inventiveness to implement this approach, it is critical that all parties learn to yield on some aspect or degree of personal goal satisfaction and follow a principle of equity. (This suggests an approach in which all share each other's fate—a central theme in John Rawls's treatise, *A Theory of Justice.*)[12] Certainly this is in keeping with the American cultural assumption of "fairness."

Encouraging "Entrepreneurs."   Another way of making use of small groups in the U.S. is to structure them along entrepreneurial lines. Beckhard and others have suggested this approach as a way of inspiring workers to be creative and productive.[13] Such groups would need the authority and access to the resources necessary to operate as though they were in business for themselves. This approach is similar to the Yugoslavian use of the smallest basic unit of associated labor (BOAL) as a profit center. But more significantly, it is in keeping with the American cultural assumptions of individualism, independent enterprises, and competition to the extent that is possible in these times of large, centrally dominated corporations. It is only a few steps away from the use of Scanlon plans and other cost-saving incentive plans that implement group cooperation.

Small Groups.   In order for this kind of social unit to be effective, however, it must remain small. If we examine the Chinese group units, which are very large, it becomes evident that the major problems standing in the path of their success are the size of the units and their restrictive centralized controls. The breaking down of a large, cumbersome, low-productivity bureaucracy is essential if the Chinese want to achieve economic growth.

In the U.S. also, there are now much data to show that the largest of our industrial organizations perform less well than do moderate-sized ones. For example, one study showed that per dollar of research and development money, smaller companies produced twenty-four times more major innovations than did large ones.[14] Likewise, between 1969 and 1979, firms with fewer than twenty employees accounted for 66 percent of all new jobs.[15]

As automation, teleconferencing, and other communications technology become the order of the day, employees will be driven even further to achieve a greater sense of identity and self-fulfillment. Although such structural changes may produce more challenging jobs for some people—mostly for skilled professionals—this kind of technology will lead to more impersonal relationships. Thus, to manage such an impersonal and technical work environment, relationships with others may become even more critical than job enrichment—which may be quite limited for most people no matter what kind of work they do. In their recent survey of American attitudes and well-being, Veroff et al. reach this very conclusion from their data.[16] Thus, I believe that only through a more innovative use of the small group will a workable solution be found that integrates the belonging needs of individuals and the needs of society as a whole. Loyalty and commitment are much easier to attain in small social units than in large ones, particularly in a culture where individualism is a central value. If anything, our large organizations lean toward collectivism and may actually be more supportive of Chinese cultural assumptions than those of the U.S.

Conclusion

In the final analysis, I propose that the small social unit be examined at a basic strategic and tactical level. This will mean that management considerations will have to include the effect of varying structure, use, and composition of groups. It may also entail decisions to move people less frequently than has been customary in the past in order for a group to work together long enough to become effective. Data such as Katz's findings that research and development groups are most effective between the second and fifth years of their existence need to be utilized and expanded upon for such planning to be effective.[17]

Group Incentives.   Likewise, greater use of group incentives will be necessary. As the Chinese are finding out, it is possible to have both group and individual incentives within the same work group: a group award for achievement of objectives or quotas may be subdivided by the group to allow for individual awards reflecting differential contributions. It is time for American managers to become aware of the possibilities inherent in group goal setting and group incentives.

It is interesting to note here that recently in several instances U.S. workers have agreed as a group to accept pay cuts or to delay pay raises, so that no members of the group need be laid off. While this seems to violate the notion of seniority or expectations of salary progression, it certainly shows respect for group or community needs. It also shows an acknowledgment at a superordinate level of the importance of the well-being of others. The recently completed negotiations between Ford Motor Company and the UAW may be a sign that more of this kind of thinking is beginning to take place. In a recent article in the *New York Times,* Raskin presents several cases in which such cooperation is now taking place between labor and management.[18]

Career Planning.   Still another area to examine from a small group perspective is that of career planning. Currently, we use small groups to educate managers, but essentially, career planning is still centralized at the top of the organization. It would be very interesting to see some experiments in which small groups or organic work units are given responsibility for ongoing career planning on the job. This need not detract from the importance of the individual, and it might even produce a more supportive environment. Here, too, I would anticipate a workable way of integrating organizational needs and individual goals. Some years ago I participated in a highly successful program in which supervisors were selected by subordinates who were adhering to criteria developed by the organization. The Chinese now do this as a matter of routine for first-line supervisors and, more and more frequently, at higher levels of management. Assuming that most American organizations will not allow delegation of this kind of final decision-making authority, I believe that intermediate or *developmental* steps of career planning are possible at the small-group level, with members of given groups acting as "career consultants" to each other.

The proposal to involve a work group in career planning will undoubtedly raise fears in the minds of many that I am advocating a form of invasion of privacy, or that I am unduly influenced by the Chinese use of group forces and their tendency to intervene in the lives of their neighbors and fellow workers.

Despite such reservations, American managers today are beginning to adopt a consultative style of management. The model they use is the consulting/helping process and its special variation, third-party intervention. It is from the model of third-party intervention that I see the most fruitful source of new approaches at the group and intergroup levels. Typically, this model provides a basis for dealing with a crisis or breakdown in relationships. It requires great skill and sensitivity to use it effectively, considering that a major problem is to gain entry and acceptance in two or more tightly bounded systems. We think of Kissinger or Carter in the Middle East, Rohatyn in New York City, or the great labor negotiators as special cases where people functioned well when all else failed. But there are now signs that such people, and even less skilled experts, are playing *voluntary,* experimental roles as bridging agents or coordinators. Some time ago an article appeared in the *New York Times* describing a coalition of organizations that usually do not agree with each other: The American Hospital Association, The American Medical Association, The Blue Cross and Blue Shield Associations, The Business Roundtable, The Health Insurance Association of America, and The American Federation of Labor and Congress of Industrial Organizations.[19] This coalition, nonetheless, has agreed to take on the task of establishing local coalitions around the country to scrutinize the medical costs and the use of hospital services. The effort was organized by John Dunlop, the noted economist and labor expert, but it is an example of what may be done by all kinds of people. At the community level it is just the sort of intervention needed as an adjunct to the social-action groups that unilaterally line up on one side of an issue. The approach respects the independence of the groups involved but recognizes the need for negotiating and integrating models where intergroup consensus is not a viable solution.

Creating a "Helping" Role.   It occurs to me that the "American Way" to promote more group-oriented consultation or third-party intervention is to have small groups initiate requests for assistance. Ideally, this would be done in the early stage of a problem before a crisis develops. Our norm is to have help ordered into action, such as when corporate staff managers are sent to divisions to "fix things." But if the use of requested help becomes popular everywhere in an organization, we could institutionalize a new kind of helping role. This approach would do less violation to the individual responsibility of a manager than it would if other "actors" were forced into his or her arena as a last resort. While I am aware of the strength of the norm this works against, I cannot think of a better way to release cooperative group energy at work and to balance the isolation of self-fulfillment with commitment to superordinate goals. Under this charter I would include seeking help from another part of the organization where problems may be only peripheral to one's own responsibilities. To ensure that this approach would be implemented successfully, training in negotiating and consulting skills is necessary.

If we are to take seriously the need to repair and improve the ways in which we deal with the social and belonging aspects of our society, we must begin to engage in some kind of innovative thinking. Although we cannot simply adopt Chinese practices, which will seem burdensome and obtrusive to most Americans, we should be looking toward community-oriented approaches and alternatives to help us create a cooperative and productive society.

14

Cultural Transition at AT&T

W. Brooke Tunstall

Corporate culture is increasingly recognized as a sine qua non for the long-term success of a corporation. In this article, the author provides a framework for managing cultural change within the context of his involvement in AT&T's divestiture process. His clear view of the cultural impact of disassembling the world's largest corporation illustrates the challenges of adapting culture to changes in a large organization. *SMR.*

At AT&T Operational Headquarters in Basking Ridge, New Jersey, a remote 20 × 32 foot room serves as the status control center for the staggering job of disaggregating the Bell System. The magnitude and complexity of this job are only suggested by the component divestiture of $125 billion in operating telephone company assets from the parent AT&T Company. The walls of this "Corporate Divestiture Management Center" are adorned with timeline charts, schedules, and graphic representations of critical issues. A computer terminal in one corner instantly displays any one of the 300 corporate assumptions, 2,000 work activities, and/or 150 major events underlying divestiture planning. Yet nowhere in this room or in the computer's memory can be found the one single element that may ultimately be most critical to AT&T's success, through divestiture and beyond. That element is AT&T's corporate culture.

Clearly, the culture must be reshaped, adapted, and reoriented to bring the value systems and expectations of AT&T people into congruence with the corporation's new mission and to prepare them for the competitive telecommunications battles looming ahead. Yet no AT&T manager is charged specifically with the management of the corporate culture. No task force is studying its dimensions. No committee is planning approaches to altering its underlying aspects.

From *Sloan Management Review,* Fall 1983, Vol. 25, No. 1. Reprinted with permission.

245

The reason is that the culture is as broad as the enterprise itself, as pervasive as a value system that evolved over a century of service, and as amorphous as the attitudes and expectations of one million employees. Managing the required changes in culture is not an event underlying divestiture; rather, divestiture is one of the causal factors underlying change in the culture. No one manager is assigned responsibility for managing the change because all managers must be responsible for it.

The road to such responsibility is neither broad nor well marked. The idea of managing corporate culture has only recently surfaced and is still considered an unknown art. No disciplined analytic method exists for objectively assessing cultural attributes and their proportionate influence on corporate performance. No accepted conceptual model of corporate culture exists for diagnosis and orderly change of corporate culture requirements.[1] In fact, there is not, as yet, even a clear consensus on how to define culture, although a number of different approaches have been suggested in the research and business literature. For example, Pettigrew emphasized such elements as rituals, symbols, ideologies, and myths in reporting his longitudinal study of organizational culture.[2] Baker referred to an "interrelated set of beliefs, shared by most of their (corporations') members, about how people should behave at work and what tasks and goals are important."[3] Kilmann described corporations' cultures as "the collective will of their members," manifested through the development of work-group norms, rites, rituals, and myths.[4]

More broadly, corporate culture may be described as a general constellation of beliefs, mores, customs, value systems, behavioral norms, and ways of doing business that are unique to each corporation, that set a pattern for corporate activities and actions, and that describe the implicit and emergent patterns of behavior and emotions characterizing life in the organization. Taken together, the elements in the culture encompass the very meaning of the organization, and increasingly, they are recognized as a virtual sine qua non for its ultimate success. In fact, it has been observed that the culture can play as significant a role as either strategy or structure in the long-term performance of the company, especially for the large corporate organization experiencing significant changes in its markets and/or business environment. This may be AT&T's greatest challenge. The concept of corporate culture holds the fascinated attention of many at AT&T who are charged with helping to steer the corporate ship through the stormy seas of divestiture. In fact, as we near the end of this figurative voyage, some see it as a virtual observatory of cultural change in "real time," not only because of the challenge of adjusting a clear-cut, well-established cultural heritage to a new business environment, but also because of the critically compressed time frame in which the change must occur.

The Context of Change

The root causes for AT&T's impending transition lie in a decade of extended debate on whether the nation's telecommunications industry should be opened to competition and, if so, how. Throughout the 1970s, scores of FCC dockets, dozens of private antitrust suits, several proposed legislative bills, and a Justice Department antitrust suit combined in an avalanche of change on the corporate consciousness of Bell management. Decision after decision by governmental bodies moved the industry incrementally toward greater competition. Finally, in late 1981 and early 1982, two cataclysmic federal government mandates opened the floodgates of change. The first was the FCC Computer Inquiry II Order; the second was the divestiture agreement with the Department of Justice.

The magnitude of the structural changes flowing from these mandates can hardly be overstated.

- The FCC ordered AT&T to form a separate subsidiary to provide, on a detariffed basis, all new customer-premises equipment (telephones, push-button systems, PBXs) and "enhanced services" (e.g., digital network) by January 1, 1983. The dimension of the change was such as to require a complete overhaul of the way AT&T markets, sells, and distributes its products and systems. This subsidiary is AT&T Information Systems.
- The divestiture agreement required that a major part of each of the twenty-two Bell Operating Companies be spun off from AT&T early in 1984, without specifying the precise form of their restructuring. Subsequently it was decided to regroup the twenty-two companies into seven regions with a centralized service staff. The charter of each region would provide local exchange service and access to local customer lines for long-distance companies (e.g., AT&T, MCI, and Southern Pacific). An eighth entity, a mutually owned and operated service corporation, would provide central staff services for the seven regions. The surviving AT&T, the ninth entity, would be reorganized to provide interstate and intrastate long-distance services, and to supply and maintain telephone equipment on the customer's premises through its subsidiary, AT&T Information Systems.

The seven Regional Bell Operating Companies (RBOCs) were to be, of course, completely severed from the parent AT&T, joining the vast clan of 1,700 independent U.S. companies whose only relationship to AT&T is to interconnect lines in order to complete customer calls. The RBOCs, large corporations with assets ranging from $12 to $20 billion, are now [1983] in the throes of major reorganization. Each newly appointed RBOC chief executive officer must build a new corporation, a new identity, a new management team, and a new array of product and service offerings.

The surviving AT&T must also accomplish a vast restructuring, because of losing its local lines. As the end of 1983 approaches, this task is almost complete. The restructuring involves the following essential elements:

- The large AT&T headquarters staff is currently being drastically reduced. When the divestiture agreement was signed, the headquarters staff numbered 15,000 people. The utlimate level of the new headquarters staff will be approximately 2,000 people. Former staff members will be redeployed to the RBOCs and its central staff and to the newly formed subordinate units of AT&T.
- Two large sectors are being formed. AT&T Communications will provide *inter*exchange service nationwide, and it will still be under the watchful eye of the FCC. AT&T Technologies will consist of Western Electric Manufacturing, Bell Laboratories Research and Development, AT&T Information Systems (to provide customer equipment), and AT&T International (to serve overseas markets).

Essentially, AT&T is moving from its former geographical profit centers (Bell Operating Companies) to nationwide lines of business serving discrete markets. As with the regional companies, this involves a radical change in many aspects of the way the company operates, including its culture. Its "interconnectedness" with its former operating subsidiaries will be through tie lines and contracts, as opposed to structure and culture.

While the critical research, manufacturing, and long-distance operating capabilities of AT&T remain intact, it must be recognized that the two government mandates will mean the *disintegration* of the Bell System as the nation has known it. This, of course, strikes at the heart of Bell's historical legacy—*its sense of unification* over the course of a century.

The culture shock created by these changes is difficult to exaggerate. In fact, when Bell System people began to verbalize their feelings on January 8, 1982 (the day divestiture was announced), they spoke in metaphors of personal grief, almost as if they had been deserted or there had been a death in the family. Gradually, the initial shock began to abate, helped along by occasional flashes of grim humor. "My initial reaction," one company president said, "was that my best horse had just been shot out from under me."[5]

Every one of its million employees knew that the company would be changed forever, that the postdivested entities would constitute a new ball game, and that they would be working for new companies requiring new skills and new ways of doing things.

Interest in Culture

All of this is happening at the precise moment when the American business community is experiencing a virtual explosion of interest in corporate culture. "Corporate culture," the *New York Times* recently reported, "is the magic phrase that management consultants are breathing into the ears of American executives."[6]

Corporate culture appears to be an idea whose time has come. Yet, it is vaguely reminiscent of Mark Twain's observation on the weather—no one seems to be doing much about it. In fact, the authors of *Corporate Cultures,* a book devoted entirely to the subject, figuratively throw up their hands at the prospect of trying to manage cultural change. "Let's be candid about this," write Allan A. Kennedy, a former principal at McKinsey, and Terrence E. Deal, a professor at Harvard's Graduate School of Education. "We don't know this area any better than anyone else. Cultural change is still a black art as far as we are concerned."[7]

Unquestionably, culture within the corporation is difficult to pin down, nearly impossible to quantify or measure, and remarkably resistant to change. However, the culture can be positively influenced by consistent, thoughtful managerial action. Clearly, no cookbook recipes for change are possible, since each corporation's culture, like each individual's personality, is made up of elements unique to itself. But certain concepts will not change from corporation to corporation. The most basic concept is that managing cultural change is a three-step process:

- First, management must understand the meaning and impact of corporate culture and must ascertain, largely through empirical methods, the elements of its own culture.
- Second, the "cultural wheat must be separated from the chaff." Decisions must be made about which elements support future goals and strategies and must be retained, and which elements are no longer appropriate and must be changed.
- Third, appropriate actions must be taken to effect the required changes in a way that leaves the desirable elements unaffected.

This article will explore each of these elements as they are currently going forward at AT&T.

I. Ascertaining AT&T's Corporate Culture

It has been said that the Bell System contained all the necessary attributes of a nation: territory, idiomatic language, history, culture, and government.

The assertion may have been slightly exaggerated, but its cultural component was unarguably accurate. That culture, in fact, generated the energy to drive the enterprise to become the world's largest—in terms of both assets and employees.

To understand Bell's culture, one must understand that it evolved in a precise way to directly support the corporate mission: achieving universal service in a regulated environment. Everything related to culture was affected: the kind of people Bell companies hired, their shared value system, and the infrastructure of processes to run the business. For most of this century, Bell System people believed that the surest way to achieve universal service was to manage the entire telecommunications system "end-to-end" as a single entity, with both vertical and horizontal integration. (Within this context, universal service meant the design and implementation of a pricing structure that would enable everyone to afford a telephone.)

These two driving forces—the goal of universal service and the concept of end-to-end responsibility—shaped the network, guided Bell Laboratories' technology, permeated Western Electric manufacturing, forged operational methods and practices, and even influenced the depreciation schedules. Equally important, these forces fashioned a corporate culture that was entirely congruent with the corporate mission.[8]

It is significant that neither the mission nor the culture evolved accidentally. They were molded successively by two historic Bell System leaders: Theodore Vail and Walter Gifford. It has been said that if Alexander Graham Bell invented the telephone, then Vail invented the Bell System. Interestingly, Vail patterned the structure of the Bell System after the U.S. government's local/federal division of responsibilities. He then coined a six-word mission statement that would provide direction for the enterprise for more than seventy years: "One System, One Policy, Universal Service." This doctrine became the driving force behind the integrated telephone network, the pricing of products and services, and the unified administrative systems, from Vail's day to the present.

Just as Vail provided the structural blueprint and mission, AT&T President Walter Gifford in 1927 provided the value system to realize them. Gifford stated that the Bell System's goal was to strike a fair balance in the treatment of employees, customers, and shareholders. His philosophy was to "furnish the best possible service at the lowest possible cost, consistent with fair treatment of employees and shareowners."[9] This guideline permeated the Bell System's decision-making process and soon became symbolized as the "three-legged stool" (Gifford's vision of balanced responsibilities to customers, shareowners, and employees). Thus, Vail provided Bell System employees with a clarity of mission and a sense of unification, and Gifford provided a sense of fairness, establishing patterns of managerial actions and employee relations that would continue to the present day.

Bell System Cultural Attributes

Vail's "oneness" and Gifford's "fairness" doctrines had an enormous impact on the attitudes of Bell's employees over the years. Vail's ideal of universal service provided the common purpose that would unite and motivate generations of management and craft people. Gifford's concept of balancing the interests of employees, customers, and shareholders further defined that purpose. A mutually reinforcing set of elements evolved into the intrinsic descriptors of Bell's culture. The first element involves treatment of employees, a prominent part of the psychological contract between company and employee.

Employees. Lifetime careers is an essential aspect of Bell's culture. A high proportion of Bell employees spend their entire working lives within the corporate boundaries of the Bell System; many managers may have as many as fifteen different assignments in a variety of departments and territories. (Layoffs have been almost unknown except at Western Electric, which has closed factories in some episodes of economic decline.)

Career longevity is accompanied by intense loyalty to the company (a second attribute). Almost nationalistic in its fervor, corporate loyalty extends even beyond retirement when former Bell System employees are united in an immense and extremely active fraternity called Telephone Pioneers of America.

A quid pro quo for Bell employees' dedication and loyalty is their perception of fair treatment by the company. Employment security, good salary and benefits, and enormous emphasis on employee safety are facts of life under the protection of "Ma Bell." Over time, employee perception of fair treatment gradually crystallized into a general sense that senior management cared about each employee's welfare.

Bell's policy of up-from-the-ranks management succession is another deeply ingrained aspect of the culture. One veteran manager wryly observed that if faced with the need for a troop of ballerinas, the company would reassign and retrain a group of telephone operators.

Despite its strengths, such a self-contained human resources development system gives rise to mores that may, over time, become less than entirely productive. For example, throughout the Bell System there is a powerful level consciousness—an extreme deference to the status inherent in each level of the managerial hierarchy. There is also a powerful bias toward consensus management, which was exacerbated in past years by a functional organization structure that required a high degree of coordination between the functional departments. (It is interesting to note that the attributes cited are prominent cultural characteristics of Japanese management. It is too early to know whether these attributes are appropriate to the U.S. business environment in general and to AT&T's environment after divestiture.)

Customers. Another cluster of cultural attributes relates to the second leg of the three-legged stool—customers. Dedication to the service ethos is an especially powerful value shared by Bell System people. The importance of quality service is instilled early in every employee's career and is constantly reinforced by senior management. A highly sophisticated and quantified "quality of service" measurement system has long provided the basis for evaluating managerial performance and is a critical part of the organizational infrastructure. Employees anxiously wait to receive the "Green Book," the monthly accounting of finite service indexes in every Bell company in the nation. Prints of Angus McDonald, the nineteenth-century Bell System lineman fighting a blizzard to keep the lines open, have long been part of Bell office decor and are another reminder of the spirit of service.

Shareholders. Finally, shareholder accountability, the third leg of the stool, is safeguarded by those elements of corporate culture that foster productivity and sound financial management.

Through the years, the emphasis on productivity measurements and customer service has been perhaps the most powerful shaper of the Bell value system. There has been intense competition among Bell Telephone Companies to achieve ever greater operational efficiencies. One of AT&T's major managerial challenges in the 1980s will be to redirect this internal competition toward the external environment. However, the shift of this internally directed competitive spirit toward the external marketplace can already be seen in the attitudes of many of the managers in AT&T's regional companies. In a *Fortune* article, one of AT&T's consultants observed, "I've never seen managers so willing to change."[10]

Another dominant aspect of Bell's culture has been its predisposition toward operational and technical skills. Since management of the network has been the central core of the Bell System's historic mission, managers with technical and operational skills have tended to predominate; this can be seen in Bell's senior management profile.

From a strategic standpoint, senior officers in the telephone companies and at AT&T have by necessity maintained a strong focus on regulatory matters. Former Chairman John deButts said that a colleague once asked,

"Wouldn't it be nice if on coming to work some morning we found ourselves thinking not about the FCC or the Justice Department or the state commissions or even the Congress, but thinking first about the customer?"[11] In the absence of external competition, Bell management necessarily focused high-level attention on the industry's regulators, working assiduously to create a favorable "regulatory climate" in Bell territories.

When taken together, these important Bell System cultural attributes explain a great deal about the patterns of behavior and the expectations of generations of Bell System people. Their effect was extended and extraordinary success in protecting the well-being of employees, the investments of shareholders, and the quality of service to customers. Corporate mission and corporate culture have rarely been so well matched. Detractors ("outsiders") might have viewed the environment as a stifling cocoon. However, for most Bell people, the culture provided a "good place to work" and security against the economic vicissitudes of the competitive marketplace.

The match between mission and culture was sustained for decades, primarily because the environment remained largely unchanged. Then suddenly, as 1981 faded into 1982, it became clear that the principle of universal service had essentially been achieved, and that the principle of end-to-end responsibility would have to be abandoned. As the regulated environment gave way to a competitive one, many of the bedrock philosophical doctrines of the Bell System would have to be overhauled to fit the new realities of the marketplace.

II. Separating Cultural Wheat from Chaff

Sensing impending change, a conferee at an AT&T management seminar asked a senior manager if "in its ardor to become a successful competitive enterprise, the Bell System would become a 'shlock' outfit?"[12] The question strikes at the very heart of what many employees fear in the loss of cherished and still valuable aspects of an idealistic cultural heritage.

Clearly, both the FCC Computer Inquiry II Order and the divestiture agreement will bring about monumental changes. Any tampering with the corporate value system during the transition must be executed with great care. As noted previously, it is extremely important to make the distinction between those cultural attributes that are to be preserved and nurtured through periods of change and those that are to be discarded or, at least, reshaped and redirected.

For example, AT&T management recognizes that if employees begin to question whether the corporation has their best interests at heart, this would represent a severe setback that could not be easily repaired. Thus, as this "family" of one million is broken apart and hundreds of thousands of people are reassigned, management must consistently demonstrate that it continues to care about each employee as an individual. Although AT&T can no longer follow Vail's historic vision of "oneness," it is imperative that it not lose sight of Gifford's vision of "fairness."

AT&T also recognizes that in a competitive arena where service quality may provide the competitive edge, it must continue to foster the service doctrine as a strong corporate value. The importance of efficiency of operations must be preserved. Productivity rates of Bell companies have exceeded those of other industries because efficiency has been a "way of life" permeating every job and a primary element used in evaluating managerial performance. It must remain so.

Other cultural characteristics need to be changed. These begin with the way Bell people think about conducting daily business and extend to broadening the paths of managerial succession.

Adapting Managerial "Mind-set"

As AT&T moves toward a fully competitive environment, the mind-set of its management will shift toward a market orientation, a welcome change for senior managers long embroiled in a quagmire of regulatory, legal, and legislative matters. Such a shift will impact not only the ways Bell people think about doing daily business, but also the ways in which business is done. For instance, strategic planning will employ competitive analysis techniques for the first time; a functional organizational structure will move further toward market-segmented lines-of-business structures; costing and pricing methodologies will move from a basis of cross subsidies and national price averaging to product-by-product and service-by-service computation schemes; capital recovery formulas will be overhauled to recognize the shorter product life inherent in competitive products. Such changes reverberate intensely throughout the corporation.

Conforming to a More Risk-Oriented Management

As AT&T moves toward a more competitive environment, its management style must adapt accordingly. In the process its managers must recognize that marketplace uncertainty will replace regulatory uncertainty, and that the cultural mores will change to value more entrepreneurial types of managers than in the past. Attitudes toward risk taking vary considerably among corporations and are an essential ingredient in the total makeup of the corporate culture. Regulated firms like AT&T, with their more predictable forecasts of sales volumes, are not prone to promote risk taking as a valued managerial attribute. This is not a pejorative statement; indeed, it would be foolish to take risks where the rewards are not compensatory. However, in competitive industries that experience sharp shifts in market share and in which greater sensitivity to economic conditions prevails, conservatism is tantamount to default in the marketplace. Unquestionably, AT&T's managers of the future will be more inclined to risk taking than care taking.

Accepting Organizational Change as a Continuing Phenomenon

The "steady state" organizational structure, once part and parcel of the corporate culture in the Bell System, must continue to adapt and readapt to meet changing needs in the future. Certainly nothing in the realm of corporate culture is so ingrained as the corporate organization chart, perhaps because the hierarchical structure is the predominant way decision-making power is distributed among managers of the enterprise. By the same token, it is an entirely human trait to seek stability of structure in an uncertain world. For half a century the Bell System enjoyed a stable structure that was ideally suited to its regulated world. But in the past ten years, two major reorganizations have been implemented, and now [1983] Bell is poised for the third and most far-reaching restructuring of all. As strategies change to meet changing market conditions, so must organizations adapt to implement these strategies. Such adaptation will be a continuing phenomenon that must become a part of every employee's system of expectations.

Broadening the Routes to Power

Under regulation, operational and technical skills were paramount. Line operating jobs were the developmental assignments for managers with high potential to progress first to the coveted operating vice-president spot in the operating companies and then to levels of even greater responsibility at AT&T. In the future new patterns of executive succession may be more appropriate, because a substantial portion of the operating units will be divested, and because the success of competitive strategies will be highly dependent on technological development, marketing prowess, manufacturing know-how, and financial acumen. This is not to say that operating line experience in the surviving regulated sector will no longer be a path to the top; however, it may not be the only path. Conference Board studies show that the routes to top management in Fortune 500 companies are consistently through three channels: production and engineering, marketing and sales, and finance.[13] Future generations of top AT&T executives will undoubtedly include people from these areas, in contrast to the traditional, almost exclusive selection from telephone company operations.

Change at the Grass Roots

Not surprisingly, it is considerably easier to project generalized objectives for cultural change than to predict accurately how change will manifest itself at the grass-roots level of the organization. Intensive effort is required to discern, as fully as possible, the changes that employees are experiencing individually, in terms of their attitudes toward the company and toward their work.

In the various Bell System Companies, studies and surveys have monitored changes in employees' moods and attitudes virtually from the day divestiture was announced—often with dramatic results. As one recent study report noted, "The mere mention of the word 'divestiture' to employees can summon up visions of a legacy eliminated . . . of job opportunities foregone . . . of promises broken."

It is incumbent upon management to demonstrate, in both word and deed, that Bell's promises were made to be kept; that the future of its dedicated employees is secure; and that management's concern for their well-being, like its concern for the quality of service, will continue undiminished.

III. Management Actions to Effect Change in Corporate Culture

A recent article in *Fortune* addressed "just how tractable elements like shared values really are." It posed the following question: "Can a company deliberately change its culture, as it can its strategy or structure?"[14] Although there are no cookbook recipes, once a corporation's culture is defined and its cultural attributes are analyzed to determine which should be preserved and which need modification, actions can be taken to effect the changes. Such actions are now under way at AT&T. (It should be noted that in some instances, influencing the corporate culture is not the exclusive objective—i.e., the actions themselves constitute well-established management practice.)

1. Set the Example

Cultural changes cannot be delegated to the employee information staff. They must begin at the top of the organization with the chief executive officer and have the support of his or her inner circle of top officers. There are numerous examples of how enlightened leadership can transform organizations in military as well as corporate histories. The chief executive officer whose behavior is consistent with the norms and values he or she has articulated for the company has an enormous head start.

Several years before the process of divestiture began at AT&T, Chairman Charles L. Brown began to set the stage for cultural change in a speech before the Commercial Club in Chicago. In that speech, Mr. Brown asserted that "there is a new telephone company in town . . . a high technology business applying advanced marketing strategies to the satisfaction of highly sophisticated customer requirements." He questioned whether the label "Ma Bell" was appropriate to describe such a business. He then asked his audience to pass the word that "Mother doesn't live here anymore."[15] For Bell employees, the statement carried powerful messages about their culture, including the need to set aside symbols of the past (even so venerable a symbol as "Ma Bell").

It seems evident that AT&T has a clear vision of its new mission. The process of strategic change, which has already begun, includes the formation of an overseas subsidiary (AT&T International) and a subsequent joint venture with Philips of Holland, the reorganization of Western Electric and Bell Laboratories into new lines of business, the introduction of a host of newly developed telephones and telephone systems, and the restructuring of long-distance pricing schemes to reflect the realities of competition.

These are just a few of the changes already achieved. However, the process of change is having a striking effect on Bell's employees. AT&T managers and craft people are begining to think of themselves as competitors. As the corporate managerial focus shifts from regulators to the marketplace, the culture will also reflect the shift in outlook.

2. Revamp the System of Management

Even the influence of leadership, of course, has its limits, particularly in large corporations where the principal management is far removed from day-to-day middle and lower management functions. Cultural norms, then, must be reoriented by changing the system of management—the many management processes, the organizational structure, and the management style that drive the corporation. AT&T is clearly communicating the patterns of values and behaviors it wants to achieve by changing reward systems, reorienting resource-allocation processes, and restructuring the organization and establishing its new identity.

For example, the basic job of restructuring postdivestiture AT&T involves a move from its former geographical profit-center orientation to a national line-of-business profit-center orientation. As mentioned earlier, 13,000 employees in AT&T's corporate staff are being redeployed to the prospective postdivestiture division or subsidiary staffs. The relatively small number of employees who remain with AT&T's postdivestiture corporate staff will be organized around a policy/strategy/financial management framework appropriate for the new market-based businesses. The new AT&T organization will, of course, reflect the separation of the detariffed portion of the business from the remaining portions (as required by Computer Inquiry II). It will also influence virtually every assumption, expectation, and belief system of AT&T's employees concerning the company and their positions within it.

3. Articulate the Value System Explicitly

It is critically important to communicate to all employees in specific terms precisely what the corporate value system is, especially in periods of change. At AT&T a carefully recast document, "A Statement of Policy," sets forth the corporation's evolving goals. From the day divestiture was announced, the principal officers have voiced clear messages of corporate positions and expectations. When asked how he wanted the business to be viewed in five years, Chairman Brown replied, "I really want the business to be regarded as one that adapted itself to what the public expected of it, was not a prisoner of embedded thinking, was alert to opportunities, and was able to take its place in a different setting with the same high regard for ethical conduct in a well-managed business that it has always had."[16]

These goals—to adapt appropriately, to think and act creatively, to maximize opportunities, to continue as a highly ethical, well-managed, powerful business—will shape the behavioral norms and ways of doing business at AT&T in the future. The articulation of these goals by the chairman is an important first step toward their achievement, and it will have a powerful influence on the corporation's culture.

4. Gear Training to Support Cultural Values

Another mechanism for effecting change in the corporate culture is management training that is explicitly geared to modify behavior in support of new corporate values. The Bell Advanced Management Program, a developmental experience for high performance fourth- and fifth-level managers of the business, exemplifies such training. Its components include business strategy formulation and implementation, financial challenges, strategic marketing, and the management of change. It seeks to prepare participants to create and implement strategies that will keep the company at the leading edge of change, and to anticipate and respond to strategic issues of the future in a rapidly changing business environment. It emphasizes entrepreneurship. Another example is AT&T's Corporate Policy Seminars, in which the top 2,000 subsidiary managers are brought in for policy presentations and discussions.

5. Revise Recruiting Aims and Methods

Professor Wickham Skinner of the Harvard Business School wrote that "acquiring and developing the right talents for the business as it changes strategy, technology and products requires more shrewd, wise, long-range planning than any other corporate endeavor."[17] He might have added that recruitment of such talent is a powerful, if indirect, means of influencing the corporate culture. In addition, potential problems of "culture clash" can be avoided by making certain that the individual value systems, personalities, and educational backgrounds of younger managers coming aboard are in harmony with the corporation's aims.

AT&T has a long history of recruiting and developing managers for a regulated milieu. This process tended to produce what Michael Maccoby, author of *The Gamesman,* described as "company men"—i.e., employees who are dedicated to the business, who equate their personal success with the corporation's long-term development, and who have exceptional managerial skills.[18] Although much of this should be preserved, an added dimension is required for the competitive marketplace: the propensity to play a higher risk, higher reward game. Indeed, a share of Maccoby's prototype "Gamesman" may be in order for future years—perhaps to be found among the numerous managers recruited from outside the Bell System to staff sales and marketing jobs.

6. Modify the Symbols

Sociologist Emile Durkheim proclaimed that shared symbols are necessary for cultural cohesion.[19] By the same token, modification of symbols is a necessary component of change.

At AT&T, for example, the loss of the Bell name and logo is a serious one. However, this does afford an opportunity to reinforce Mr. Brown's message, both internally and externally, that "Ma Bell doesn't live here anymore." By continuing to use AT&T as a trade name, the corporation capitalizes on its long-standing reputation throughout the world. By replacing the familiar logo (Bell within a circle) with a globe symbolically girdled by electronic communications, AT&T has a new symbol that "suggests new dimensions—of our business and our future."

Of course, not all symbols change. For example, another long-standing symbol, a 1917-vintage, 16-foot bronze statue personifying the Spirit of Communications, has been taken from the top of the old headquarters building, refurbished, and placed in the lobby of the new headquarters building. This statue, affectionately known to generations of AT&T people as "Golden Boy," will continue to stand for excellence in providing service (now around the world) in the years that follow divestiture. As Angus McDonald and other time-honored symbols begin to slip into corporate folklore, "Golden Boy" will continue to be a shared symbol, serving as a bridge between the past and the future.

Transition

With divestiture, AT&T will experience a metamorphosis that would challenge the most boastful caterpillar. The organizational, technological, and operational complexities to be faced are literally without parallel. Yet, more than one informed observer maintains that changing the corporate culture is still the most difficult task facing management.

The fact that corporate culture cannot be quantified makes it no less real and no less important as an ingredient in a corporation's fortunes than return on investment, market share percentage, hurdle rates, or debt ratios. AT&T Chairman Brown summed up both the objective and the importance of changing the corporate culture: "If we are able to adapt our marvelous culture to a different environment—and if we remember that the business in the '80s cannot be run by memory—we can set the course for the next century."[20]

15

C̶ ... New Awareness of
(... Culture

I... nt to decipher an organization's culture, this author claims that we
must dig ... w the organization's surface—beyond the "visible artifacts"—and uncover the basic underlying assumptions at the core of the organization's culture. To
do this, he provides a tool—a formal definition of organizational culture that emphasizes how culture works. With this definition in hand, the author feels that one
can come to understand the dynamic evolutionary forces that govern a culture, and
also explain how the culture is learned, passed on, and changed. *SMR.*

The purpose of this article is to define the concept of organizational culture
in terms of a dynamic model of how culture is learned, passed on, and
changed. As many recent efforts argue that organizational culture is the key
to organizational excellence, it is critical to define this complex concept in a
manner that will provide a common frame of reference for practitioners and
researchers. Many definitions simply settle for the notion that culture is a set
of shared meanings that make it possible for members of a group to interpret and act upon their environment. I believe we must go beyond this
definition: Even if we knew an organization well enough to live in it, we
would not necessarily know how its culture arose, how it came to be what it
is, or how it could be changed if organizational survival were at stake.

The thrust of my argument is that we must understand the dynamic evolutionary forces that govern how culture evolves and changes. My approach to
this task will be to lay out a formal definition of what I believe organizational culture is, and to elaborate each element of the definition to make it
clear how it works.

From *Sloan Management Review,* Winter 1984, Vol. 25, No. 2. Reprinted with permission.

Organizational Culture: A Formal Definition

Organizational culture is the pattern of basic assumptions that a given group has invented, discovered, or developed in learning to cope with its problems of external adaptation and internal integration, and that have worked well enough to be considered valid, and, therefore, to be taught to new members as the correct way to perceive, think, and feel in relation to those problems.

1. Pattern of Basic Assumptions

Organizational culture can be analyzed at several different levels, starting with the visible artifacts—the constructed environment of the organization, its architecture, technology, office layout, manner of dress, visible or audible behavior patterns, and public documents such as charters, employee orientation materials, and stories (see Figure 15.1). This level of analysis is tricky, because the data are easy to obtain but hard to interpret. We can describe "how" a group constructs its environment and "what" behavior patterns are discernible among the members, but we often cannot understand the underlying logic: "why" a group behaves the way it does.

To analyze *why* members behave the way they do, we often look for the *values* that govern behavior, which is the second level in Figure 15.1. But as values are hard to observe directly, it is often necessary to infer them by interviewing key members of the organization or to analyze the context of such artifacts as documents and charters.[1] However, in identifying such values, we usually note that they represent accurately only the manifest or espoused values of a culture. That is, they focus on what people say is the reason for their behavior, what they ideally would like those reasons to be, and what are often their rationalizations for their behavior. Yet, the underlying reasons for their behavior remain concealed or unconscious.[2]

To really understand a culture and to ascertain more completely the group's values and overt behavior, it is imperative to delve into the underlying assumptions, which are typically unconscious but which actually determine how group members perceive, think, and feel.[3] Such assumptions are themselves learned responses that originated as espoused values. But, as a value leads to a behavior, and as that behavior begins to solve the problem that prompted it in the first place, the value gradually is transformed into an underlying assumption about how things really are. As the assumption is increasingly taken for granted, it drops out of awareness.

Taken-for-granted assumptions are so powerful because they are less debatable and confrontable than espoused values. We know we are dealing

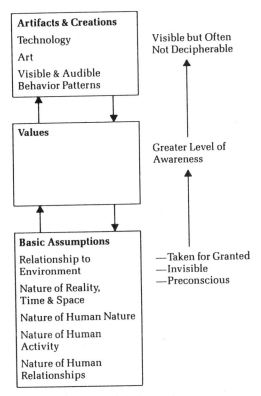

Figure 15.1   The Levels of Culture and Their Interaction

with an assumption when we encounter in our informants a refusal to discuss something, or when they consider us "insane" or "ignorant" for bringing something up. For example, the notion that businesses should be profitable, that schools should educate, or that medicine should prolong life are assumptions, even though they are often considered "merely" values.

To put it another way, the domain of values can be divided into (1) ultimate, nondebatable, taken-for-granted values, for which the term *assumptions* is more appropriate; and (2) debatable, overt, espoused values, for which the term *values* is more applicable. In stating that basic assumptions are unconscious, I am not arguing that this is a result of repression. On the contrary, I am arguing that as certain motivational and cognitive processes are repeated and continue to work, they become unconscious. They can be brought back to awareness only through a kind of focused inquiry, similar to that used by anthropologists. What is needed are the efforts of both an insider

who makes the unconscious assumptions and an outsider who helps to uncover the assumptions by asking the right kinds of questions.[4]

Cultural Paradigms: A Need for Order and Consistency

Because of the human need for order and consistency, assumptions become
patterned into what may be termed cultural "paradigms," which tie together
the basic assumptions about humankind, nature, and activities. A cultural
paradigm is a set of interrelated assumptions that form a coherent pattern.
Not all assumptions are mutually compatible or consistent, however. For
example, if a group holds the assumption that all good ideas and products
ultimately come from individual effort, it cannot easily assume simultaneously that groups can be held responsible for the results achieved, or that
individuals will put a high priority on group loyalty. Or, if a group assumes
that the way to survive is to conquer nature and to manipulate its environment aggressively, it cannot at the same time assume that the best kind of
relationship among group members is one that emphasizes passivity and
harmony. If human beings do indeed have a cognitive need for order and
consistency, one can then assume that all groups will eventually evolve sets
of assumptions that are compatible and consistent.

To analyze cultural paradigms, one needs a set of logical categories for
studying assumptions. Table 15.1 shows such a set based on the original
comparative study of Kluckhohn and Strodtbeck.[5] In applying these categories broadly to cultures, Kluckhohn and Strodtbeck note that Western culture tends to be oriented toward an active mastery of nature, and is based
on individualistic competitive relationships. It uses a future-oriented, linear,
monochronic concept of time,[6] views space and resources as infinite, assumes that human nature is neutral and ultimately perfectible, and bases
reality or ultimate truth on science and pragmatism.

In contrast, some Eastern cultures are passively oriented toward nature.
They seek to harmonize with nature and with each other. They view the
group as more important than the individual, are present or past oriented,
see time as polychronic and cyclical, view space and resources as very limited, assume that human nature is bad but improvable, and see reality as
based more on revealed truth than on empirical experimentation.

In this light, organizational culture paradigms are adapted versions of
broader cultural paradigms. For example, Dyer notes that the GEM Corporation operates on the interlocking assumptions that: (1) ideas come ultimately from individuals; (2) people are responsible, motivated, and capable
of governing themselves; however, truth can be pragmatically determined
only by "fighting" things out and testing in groups; (3) such fighting is

Table 15.1 Basic Underlying Assumptions around Which Cultural Paradigms Form

1. **The Organization's Relationship to Its Environment.** Reflecting even more basic assumptions about the relationship of humanity to nature, one can assess whether the key members of the organization view the relationship as one of dominance, submission, harmonizing, finding an appropriate niche, and so on.

2. **The Nature of Reality and Truth.** Here are the linguistic and behavioral rules that define what is real and what is not, what is a "fact," how truth is ultimately to be determined, and whether truth is "revealed" or "discovered"; basic concepts of time as linear or cyclical, monochronic or polychronic; basic concepts such as space as limited or infinite and property as communal or individual; and so forth.

3. **The Nature of Human Nature.** What does it mean to be "human" and what attributes are considered intrinsic or ultimate? Is human nature good, evil, or neutral? Are human beings perfectible or not? Which is better, Theory X or Theory Y?

4. **The Nature of Human Activity.** What is the "right" thing for human beings to do, on the basis of the above assumptions about reality, the environment, and human nature: to be active, passive, self-developmental, fatalistic, or what? What is work and what is play?

5. **The Nature of Human Relationships.** What is considered to be the "right" way for people to relate to each other, to distribute power and love? Is life cooperative or competitive; individualistic, group collaborative, or communal; based on traditional lineal authority, law, or charisma; or what?

Source: Reprinted, by permission of the publisher, from Edgar H. Schein, "The Role of the Founder in Creating Organizational Culture," in *Organizational Dynamics*, Summer 1983 © 1983 Periodicals Division, American Management Associations. All rights reserved.

possible because the members of the organization view themselves as a family who will take care of each other. Ultimately, this makes it safe to fight and be competitive.[7]

I have observed another organization that operates on the paradigm that (1) truth comes ultimately from older, wiser, better educated, higher status members; (2) people are capable of loyalty and discipline in carrying out directives; (3) relationships are basically lineal and vertical; (4) each person has a niche that is his or her territory that cannot be invaded; and (5) the organization is a "solidary unit" that will take care of its members.

Needless to say, the manifest behaviors in these two organizations are totally different. In the first organization, one observes mostly open office landscapes, few offices with closed doors, a high rate of milling about, intense conversations and arguments, and a general air of informality. In the second organization, there is a hush in the air: Everyone is in an office and with closed doors. Nothing is done except by appointment and with a prearranged agenda. When people of different ranks are present, one sees real deference rituals and obedience, and a general air of formality permeates everything.

Nonetheless, these behavioral differences make no sense until one has discovered and deciphered the underlying cultural paradigm. To stay at the level of artifacts or values is to deal with the manifestations of culture, but not with the cultural essence.

2. A Given Group

There cannot be a culture unless there is a group that "owns" it. Culture is embedded in groups, hence the creating group must always be clearly identified. If we want to define a cultural unit, therefore, we must be able to locate a group that is independently defined as the creator, host, or owner of that culture. We must be careful not to define the group in terms of the existence of a culture however tempting that may be, because we then would be creating a completely circular definition.

A given group is a set of people (1) who have been together long enough to have shared significant problems, (2) who have had opportunities to solve those problems and to observe the effects of their solutions, and (3) who have taken in new members. A group's culture cannot be determined unless there is such a definable set of people with a shared history.

The passing on of solutions to new members is required in the definition of culture because the decision to pass something on is itself a very important test of whether a given solution is shared and perceived as valid. If a group passes on with conviction elements of a way of perceiving, thinking, and feeling, we can assume that that group has had enough stability and has shared enough common experiences to have developed a culture. If, on the other hand, a group has not faced the issue of what to pass on in the process of socialization, it has not had a chance to test its own consensus and commitment to a given belief, value, or assumption.

The Strength of a Culture

The "strength" or "amount" of culture can be defined in terms of (1) the homogeneity and stability of group membership, and (2) the length and intensity of shared experiences of the group. If a stable group has had a long, varied, intense history (i.e., if it has had to cope with many difficult survival problems and has succeeded), it will have a strong and highly differentiated culture. By the same token, if a group has had a constantly shifting membership or has been together only for a short time and has not faced any difficult issues, it will, by definition, have a weak culture. Although individuals within that group may have very strong individual assumptions, there will not be enough shared experiences for the group as a whole to have a defined culture.

By this definition, one would probably assess IBM and the Bell System as having strong cultures, whereas, very young companies or ones that have had a high turnover of key executives would be judged as having weak ones. One should also note that once an organization has a strong culture, if the dominant coalition or leadership remains stable, the culture can survive high turnover at lower ranks, because new members can be strongly socialized into the organization as, for example, in elite military units.

It is very important to recognize that cultural strength may or may not be correlated with effectiveness. Though some current writers have argued that strength is desirable,[8] it seems clear to me that the relationship is far more complex. The actual content of the culture and the degree to which its solutions fit the problems posed by the environment seem like the critical variables here, not strength. One can hypothesize that young groups strive for culture strength as a way of creating an identity for themselves, but older groups may be more effective with a weak total culture and diverse subcultures to enable them to be responsive to rapid environmental change.

This way of defining culture makes it specific to a given group. If a total corporation consists of stable functional, divisional, geographic, or rank-based subgroups, then that corporation will have multiple cultures within it. It is perfectly possible for those multiple cultures to be in conflict with each other, such that one could not speak of a single corporate culture. On the other hand, if there has been common corporate experience as well, then one could have a strong corporate culture on top of various subcultures that are based in subunits. The deciphering of a given company's culture then becomes an empirical matter of locating where the stable social units are, what cultures each of those stable units have developed, and how those separate cultures blend into a single whole. The total culture could then be very homogeneous or heterogeneous, according to the degree to which subgroup cultures are similar or different.

It has also been pointed out that some of the cultural assumptions in an organization can come from the occupational background of the members of the organization. This makes it possible to have a managerial culture, an engineering culture, a science culture, a labor-union culture, etc., all of which coexist in a given organization.[9]

3. Invented, Discovered, or Developed

Cultural elements are defined as learned solutions to problems. In this section, I will concentrate on the nature of the learning mechanisms that are involved.

Structurally, there are two types of learning situations: (1) positive problem-solving situations that produce positive or negative reinforcement in terms of whether the attempted solution works or not; and (2) anxiety-avoidance situations that produce positive or negative reinforcement in terms of whether the attempted solution does or does not avoid anxiety. In practice, these two types of situations are intertwined, but they are structurally different and, therefore, they must be distinguished.

In the positive problem-solving situation, the group tries out various responses until something works. The group will then continue to use this response until it ceases to work. The information that it no longer works is visible and clear. By contrast, in the anxiety-avoidance situation, once a response is learned because it successfully avoids anxiety, it is likely to be repeated indefinitely. The reason is that the learner will not willingly test the situation to determine whether the cause of the anxiety is still operating. Thus all rituals, patterns of thinking or feeling, and behaviors that may originally have been motivated by a need to avoid a painful, anxiety-provoking situation are going to be repeated, even if the causes of the original pain are no longer acting, because the avoidance of anxiety is, itself, positively reinforcing.[10]

To fully grasp the importance of anxiety reduction in culture formation, we have to consider, first of all, the human need for cognitive order and consistency, which serves as the ultimate motivator for a common language and shared categories of perception and thought.[11] In the absence of such shared "cognitive maps," the human organism experiences a basic existential anxiety that is intolerable—an anxiety observed only in extreme situations of isolation or captivity.[12]

Second, humans experience the anxiety associated with being exposed to hostile environmental conditions and to the dangers inherent in unstable social relationships, forcing groups to learn ways of coping with such external and internal problems.

A third source of anxiety is associated with occupational roles such as coal mining and nursing. For example, the Tavistock sociotechnical studies have shown clearly that the social structure and ways of operation of such groups can be conceptualized best as a "defense" against the anxiety that would be unleashed if work were done in another manner.[13]

If an organizational culture is composed of both types of elements—those designed to solve problems and those designed to avoid anxiety—it becomes necessary to analyze which is which if one is concerned about changing any of the elements. In the positive-learning situation, one needs innovative sources to find a better solution to the problem; in the anxiety-avoidance situation, one must first find the source of the anxiety and either show the learner that it no longer exists, or provide an alternative source of avoidance. Either of these is difficult to do.

In other words, cultural elements that are based on anxiety reduction will be more stable than those based on positive problem solving because of the nature of the anxiety-reduction mechanism and the fact that human systems need a certain amount of stability to avoid cognitive and social anxiety.

Where do solutions initially come from? Most cultural solutions in new groups and organizations originate from the founders and early leaders of those organizations.[14] Typically, the solution process is an advocacy of certain ways of doing things that are then tried out and either adopted or rejected, depending on how well they work out. Initially, the founders have the most influence, but, as the group ages and acquires its own experiences, its members will find their own solutions. Ultimately, the process of discovering new solutions will be more a result of interactive, shared experiences. But leadership will always play a key role during those times when the group faces a new problem and must develop new responses to the situation. In fact, one of the crucial functions of leadership is to provide guidance at precisely those times when habitual ways of doing things no longer work, or when a dramatic change in the environment requires new responses.

At those times, leadership must not only ensure the invention of new and better solutions, but must also provide some security to help the group tolerate the anxiety of giving up old, stable responses, while new ones are learned and tested. In the Lewinian change framework, this means that the "unfreezing stage" must involve both enough disconfirmation to motivate change and enough psychological safety to permit the individual or group to pay attention to the disconfirming data.[15]

4. Problems of External Adaptation and Internal Integration

If culture is a solution to the problems a group faces, what can we say about the nature of those problems? Most group theories agree it is useful to distinguish between two kinds of problems: (1) those that deal with the group's basic survival, which has been labeled the primary task, basic function, or ultimate mission of the group; and (2) those that deal with the group's ability to function as a group. These problems have been labeled socioemotional, group building and maintenance, or integration problems.[16]

Homans further distinguishes between the external system and the internal system and notes that the two are interdependent.[17] Even though one can distinguish between the external and internal problems, in practice both systems are highly interrelated.

Table 15.2 Problems of External Adaptation and Survival

Strategy

Developing consensus on the *primary task,* core mission, or manifest and latent functions of the group.

Goals

Developing consensus on goals, such goals being the concrete reflection of the core mission.

Means for Accomplishing Goals

Developing consensus on the *means* to be used in accomplishing the goals—for example, division of labor, organization structure, reward system, and so forth.

Measuring Performance

Developing consensus on the criteria to be used in measuring how well the group is doing against its goals and targets—for example, information and control systems.

Correction

Developing consensus on remedial or repair strategies as needed when the group is not accomplishing its goals.

Source: Reprinted, by permission of the publisher, from Edgar H. Schein, "The Role of the Founder in Creating Organizational Culture," in *Organizational Dynamics,* Summer 1983 © 1983 Periodicals Division, American Management Associations. All rights reserved.

External Adaptation Problems. Problems of external adaptation are those that ultimately determine the group's survival in the environment. While a part of the group's environment is "enacted," in the sense that prior cultural experience predisposes members to perceive the environment in a certain way and even to control that environment to a degree, there will always be elements of the environment (weather, natural circumstances, availability of economic and other resources, political upheavals) that are clearly beyond the control of the group and that will, to a degree, determine the fate of it.[18] A useful way to categorize the problems of survival is to mirror the stages of the problem-solving cycle as shown in Table 15.2.[19]

The basic underlying assumptions of the culture from which the founders of the organization come will determine to a large extent the initial formulations of core mission, goals, means, criteria, and remedial strategies, in that those ways of doing things are the only ones with which the group members will be familiar. But as an organization develops its own life experience, it may begin to modify to some extent its original assumptions. For example, a young company may begin by defining its core mission to be to "win in the marketplace over all competition," but may at a later stage find that "owning its own niche in the marketplace," "coexisting with other companies," or even "being a silent partner in an oligopolistic industry" is a more workable solution to survival. Thus for each stage of the problem-solving cycle, there will emerge solutions characteristic of that group's own history, and those solutions or ways of doing things based on learned assumptions will make up a major portion of that group's culture.

Internal Integration Problems.   A group or organization cannot survive if it cannot manage itself as a group. External survival and internal integration problems are, therefore, two sides of the same coin. Table 15.3 outlines the major issues of internal integration around which cultural solutions must be found.

While the nature of the solutions will vary from one organization to another, every organization will have to face each of these issues and develop some kind of solution. However, because the nature of that solution will reflect the biases of the founders and current leaders, the prior experiences of group members, and the actual events experienced, it is likely that

Table 15.3   Problems of Internal Integration

Language

Common language and conceptual categories. If members cannot communicate with and understand each other, a group is impossible by definition.

Boundaries

Consensus on group boundaries and criteria for inclusion and exclusion. One of the most important areas of culture is the shared consensus on who is in, who is out, and by what criteria one determines membership.

Power and Status

Consensus on criteria for the allocation of power and status. Every organization must work out its pecking order and its rules for how one gets, maintains, and loses power. This area of consensus is crucial in helping members manage their own feelings of aggression.

Intimacy

Consensus on criteria for intimacy, friendship, and love. Every organization must work out its rules of the game for peer relationships, for relationships between the sexes, and for the manner in which openness and intimacy are to be handled in the context of managing the organization's tasks.

Rewards and Punishments

Consensus on criteria for allocation of rewards and punishments. Every group must know what its heroic and sinful behaviors are; what gets rewarded with property, status, and power; and what gets punished through the withdrawal of rewards and, ultimately, excommunication.

Ideology

Consensus on ideology and "religion." Every organization, like every society, faces unexplainable events that must be given meaning, so that members can respond to them and avoid the anxiety of dealing with the unexplainable and uncontrollable.

each organizational culture will be unique, even though the underlying issues around which the culture is formed will be common.[20]

An important issue to study across many organizations is whether an organization's growth and evolution follows an inherent evolutionary *trend* (e.g., developing societies are seen as evolving from that of a community to more of a bureaucratic, impersonal type of system). One should also study whether organizational cultures reflect in a patterned way the nature of the underlying technology, the age of the organization, the size of the organization, and the nature of the parent culture within which the organization evolves.

5. Assumptions That Work Well Enough to Be Considered Valid

Culture goes beyond the norms or values of a group in that it is more of an ultimate outcome, based on repeated success and a gradual process of taking things for granted. In other words, to me what makes something "cultural" is this "taken-for-granted" quality, which makes the underlying assumptions virtually undiscussable.

Culture is perpetually being formed in the sense that there is constantly some kind of learning going on about how to relate to the environment and to manage internal affairs. But this ongoing evolutionary process does not change those things that are so thoroughly learned that they come to be a stable element of the group's life. Since the basic assumptions that make up an organization's culture serve the secondary function of stabilizing much of the internal and external environment for the group, and since that stability is sought as a defense against the anxiety which comes with uncertainty and confusion, these deeper parts of the culture either do not change or change only very slowly.

6. Taught to New Members

Because culture serves the function of stabilizing the external and internal environment for an organization, it must be taught to new members. It would not serve its function if every generation of new members could introduce new perceptions, language, thinking patterns, and rules of interaction. For culture to serve its function, it must be perceived as correct and valid, and if it is perceived that way, it automatically follows that it must be taught to newcomers.

It cannot be overlooked that new members do bring new ideas and do produce culture change, especially if they are brought in at high levels of the organization. It remains to be settled empirically whether and how this happens. For example, does a new member have to be socialized first and accepted into a central and powerful position before he or she can begin to effect change? Or does a new member bring from the onset new ways of perceiving, thinking, feeling, and acting, that produce automatic changes through role innovation?[21] Is the manner in which new members are socialized influential in determining what kind of innovation they will produce?[22] Much of the work on innovation in organizations is confusing, because it is often unclear whether the elements that are considered "new" are actually new assumptions, or simply new artifacts built on old cultural assumptions.

In sum, if culture provides the group members with a paradigm of how the world "is," it goes without saying that such a paradigm would be passed on without question to new members. It is also the case that the very process of passing on the culture provides an opportunity for testing, ratifying, and reaffirming it. For both of these reasons, the process of socialization (i.e., the passing on of the group's culture) is strategically an important process to study if one wants to decipher what the culture is and how it might change.[23]

7. Perceive, Think, and Feel

The final element in the definition reminds us that culture is pervasive and ubiquitous. The basic assumptions about nature, humanity, relationships, truth, activity, time, and space cover virtually all human functions. This is not to say that a given organization's culture will develop to the point of totally "controlling" all of its members' perceptions, thoughts, and feelings. But the process of learning to manage the external and internal environment does involve all of one's cognitive and emotional elements. As cultural learning progresses, more and more of the person's responses will become involved. Therefore, the longer we live in a given culture, and the older the culture is, the more it will influence our perceptions, thoughts, and feelings.

By focusing on perceptions, thoughts, and feelings, I am also stating the importance of those categories relative to the category of overt behavior. Can one speak of a culture in terms of just the overt behavior patterns one observes? Culture is manifested in overt behavior, but the idea of culture goes deeper than behavior. Indeed, the very reason for elaborating an abstract notion like "culture" is that it is too difficult to explain what goes on in organizations if we stay at the descriptive behavioral level.

To put it another way, behavior is, to a large extent, a joint function of what the individual brings to the situation and the operating situational forces, which to some degree are unpredictable. To understand the cultural portion of what the individual brings to the situation (as opposed to the idiosyncratic or situational portions), we must examine the individual's pattern of perceptions, thoughts, and feelings. Only after we have reached a consensus at this inner level have we uncovered what is potentially *cultural*.

The Study of Organizational Culture and Its Implications

Organizational culture as defined here is difficult to study. However, it is not so difficult as studying a different society where language and customs are so different that one needs to live in the society to get any feel for it at all. Organizations exist in a parent culture, and much of what we find in them is derivative from the assumptions of the parent culture. But different organizations will sometimes emphasize or amplify different elements of a parent culture. For example, in the two companies previously mentioned, we find in the first an extreme version of the individual-freedom ethic, and in the second one, an extreme version of the authority ethic, both of which can be derived from U.S. culture.

The problem of deciphering a particular organization's culture, then, is more a matter of surfacing assumptions, which will be recognizable once they have been uncovered. We will not find alien forms of perceiving, thinking, and feeling if the investigator is from the same parent culture as the organization that is being investigated. On the other hand, the particular pattern of assumptions, which we call an organization's cultural paradigm, will not reveal itself easily, because it is taken for granted.

How then do we gather data and decipher the paradigm? Basically, there are four approaches that should be used in combination with one another:

1. Analyzing the Process and Content of Socialization of New Members. By interviewing "socialization agents," such as the supervisors and older peers of new members, one can identify some of the important areas of the culture. But some elements of the culture will not be discovered by this method because they are not revealed to newcomers or lower members.

2. Analyzing Responses to Critical Incidents in the Organization's History. By constructing a careful "organizational biography" from documents, interviews, and perhaps even surveys of present and past key members, it is possible to identify the major periods of culture formation. For each crisis or incident identified, it is then necessary to determine what was done, why it was done, and what the outcome was. To infer the underlying assumptions of the organization, one would then look for the major themes in the reasons given for the actions taken.

3. Analyzing Beliefs, Values, and Assumptions of "Culture Creators or Carriers."
When interviewing founders, current leaders, or culture creators or carriers, one should initially make an open-ended chronology of each person's history in the organization—his or her goals, modes of action, and assessment of outcomes. The list of external and internal issues found in Tables 15.2 and 15.3 can be used as a checklist later in the interview to cover areas more systematically.

4. Jointly Exploring and Analyzing with Insiders the Anomalies or Puzzling Features Observed or Uncovered in Interviews. It is the joint inquiry that will help to disclose basic assumptions and help determine how they may interrelate to form the cultural paradigm.

The insider must be a representative of the culture and must be interested in disclosing his or her own basic assumptions to test whether they are in fact cultural prototypes. This process works best if one acts from observations that puzzle the outsider or that seem like anomalies, because the insider's assumptions are most easily surfaced if they are contrasted to the assumptions that the outsider initially holds about what is observed.

While the first three methods mentioned above should enhance and complement one another, at least one of them should systematically cover all of the external adaptation and internal integration issues. In order to discover the underlying basic assumptions and eventually to decipher the paradigm, the fourth method is necessary to help the insider surface his or her own cultural assumptions. This is done through the outsider's probing and searching.[24]

If an organization's total culture is not well developed, or if the organization consists of important stable subgroups, which have developed subcultures, one must modify the above methods to study the various subcultures.[25] Furthermore, the organizational biography might reveal that the organization is at a certain point in its life cycle, and one would hypothesize that the functions that a given kind of culture plays vary with the life-cycle stage.[26]

Implications for Culture Management and Change

If we recognize organizational culture—whether at the level of the group or the total corporation—as a deep phenomenon, what does this tell us about when and how to change or manage culture? First of all, the evolutionary perspective draws our attention to the fact that the culture of a group may serve different functions at different times. When a group is forming and growing, the culture is a "glue"—a source of identity and strength. In other words, young founder-dominated companies need their cultures as a way of holding together their organizations. The culture changes that do occur in a young organization can best be described as clarification, articulation, and elaboration. If the young company's culture is genuinely maladaptive in relation to the external environment, the company will not survive anyway. But even if one identified needed changes, there is little chance at this stage that one could change the culture.

In organizational midlife, culture can be managed and changed, but not without considering all the sources of stability identified above. The large diversified organization probably contains many functional, geographic, and other groups that have cultures of their own—some of which will conflict with each other. Whether the organization needs to enhance the diversity to remain flexible in the face of environmental turbulence, or create a more homogeneous "strong" culture (as some advocate), becomes one of the toughest strategy decisions management confronts, especially if senior management is unaware of some of its own cultural assumptions. Some form of outside intervention and "culture consciousness raising" is probably essential at this stage to facilitate better strategic decisions.

Organizations that have reached a stage of maturity or decline resulting from mature markets and products or from excessive internal stability and comfort that prevents innovation may need to change parts of their culture, provided they can obtain the necessary self-insight.[27] Such managed change will always be a painful process and will elicit strong resistance. Moreover, change may not even be possible without replacing the large numbers of people who wish to hold on to all of the original culture.

No single model of such change exists: Managers may successfully orchestrate change through the use of a wide variety of techniques, from outright coercion at one extreme to subtle seduction through the introduction of new technologies at the other extreme.[28]

Summary and Conclusions

I have attempted to construct a formal definition of organizational culture that derives from a dynamic model of learning and group dynamics. The definition highlights that culture: (1) is always in the process of formation and change; (2) tends to cover all aspects of human functioning; (3) is learned around the major issues of external adaptation and internal integration; and (4) is ultimately embodied as an interrelated, patterned set of basic assumptions that deal with ultimate issues, such as the nature of humanity, human relationships, time, space, and the nature of reality and truth itself.

If we are to decipher a given organization's culture, we must use a complex interview, observation, and joint-inquiry approach in which selected members of the group work with the outsider to uncover the unconscious assumptions that are hypothesized to be the essence of the culture. I believe we need to study a large number of organizations using these methods to determine the utility of the concept of organizational culture and to relate cultural variables to other variables, such as strategy, organizational structure, and ultimately, organizational effectiveness.

If such studies show this model of culture to be useful, one of the major implications will be that our theories of organizational change will have to give much more attention to the opportunities and constraints that organizational culture provides. Clearly, if culture is as powerful as I argue in this article, it will be easy to make changes that are congruent with present assumptions, and very difficult to make changes that are not. In sum, the understanding of organizational culture would then become integral to the process of management itself.

Notes and References

Chapter 2

Notes

Much of the research on which this article is based was done under the sponsorship of the Group Psychology branch of the Office of Naval Research. Their generous support has made continuing work in this area possible. I would also like to thank my colleagues Lotte Bailyn and John Van Maanen for many of the ideas expressed in this article.

1. See Pigors and Myers [24], and Burack [10].
2. See Hackman and Suttle [13], and Meltzer and Wickert [21].
3. See McGregor [20], Bennis [6], Pigors and Myers [24], Schein [29], Van Maanen [36], Bailyn and Schein [4], and Katz [18].
4. See Beckhard [5], Bennis [6], Schein [28], Galbraith [12], Lesieur [19], and Alfred [1].
5. Schein [31].
6. Schein [32].
7. Bailyn and Schein [4], Myers [22], Van Maanen, Bailyn, and Schein [38], and Roeber [25].
8. Van Maanen and Schein [39], Bailyn [3] and [2], and Kanter [17].
9. Sheehy [33], Troll [35], Kalish [16], and Pearse and Pelzer [23].
10. Burack [10], pp. 402–403.
11. Schein [29].
12. See Dalton and Thompson [11], Super and Bohn [34], Hall [14], and Schein [32].
13. Schein [32].
14. Schein [32].
15. Schein [26] and [32].
16. Schein [27], and Van Maanen [36].
17. Schein [26].
18. Schein [30] and [32].
19. Schein [26], Bray, Campbell, and Grant [9], Berlew and Hall [8], and Hall [14].
20. Dalton and Thompson [11], and Katz [18].
21. See Heidke [15].
22. See Bailyn [2].
23. See Katz [18].
24. See Bailyn [2].

References

[1] Alfred, T., "Checkers or Choice in Manpower Management," *Harvard Business Review,* January–February 1967, pp. 157–169.
[2] Bailyn, L., "Involvement and Accommodation in Technical Careers," in *Organiza-*

tional Careers: Some New Perspectives, J. Van Maanen, ed. (New York: John Wiley, 1977).

[3] Bailyn, L., "Career and Family Orientations of Husbands and Wives in Relation to Marital Happiness," *Human Relations,* 1970, pp. 97–113.

[4] Bailyn, L., and Schein, E. H., "Life/Career Considerations as Indicators of Quality of Employment," in *Measuring Work Quality for Social Reporting,* A. D. Biderman and T. F. Drury, eds. (New York: Sage Publications, 1976).

[5] Beckhard, R. D., *Organization Development: Strategies and Models* (Reading, MA: Addison-Wesley, 1969).

[6] Bennis, W. G., *Changing Organizations* (New York: McGraw-Hill, 1966).

[7] Bennis, W. G., *Organization Development: Its Nature, Origins, and Prospects* (Reading, MA: Addison-Wesley, 1969).

[8] Berlew, D., and Hall, D. T., "The Socialization of Managers," *Administrative Science Quarterly* 11, 1966, pp. 207–223.

[9] Bray, D. W., Campbell, R. J., and Grant, D. E., *Formative Years in Business* (New York: John Wiley, 1974).

[10] Burack, E., *Organization Analysis* (Hinsdale, IL: Dryden, 1975).

[11] Dalton, G. W., and Thompson, P. H., "Are R&D Organizations Obsolete?" *Harvard Business Review,* November–December 1976, pp. 105–116.

[12] Galbraith, J., *Designing Complex Organizations* (Reading, MA: Addison-Wesley, 1973).

[13] Hackman, J. R., and Suttle, J. L., *Improving Life at Work* (Los Angeles: Goodyear, 1977).

[14] Hall, D. T., *Careers in Organizations* (Los Angeles: Goodyear, 1976).

[15] Heidke, R., *Career Pro-Activity of Middle Managers,* Master's Thesis, Massachusetts Institute of Technology, 1977.

[16] Kalish, R. A., *Late Adulthood: Perspectives on Aging* (Monterey, CA: Brooks-Cole, 1975).

[17] Kanter, R. M., *Work and Family in the United States* (New York: Russell Sage, 1977).

[18] Katz, R., "Job Enrichment: Some Career Considerations," in *Organizational Careers: Some New Perspectives,* J. Van Maanen, ed. (New York: John Wiley, 1977).

[19] Lesieur, F. G., *The Scanlon Plan* (New York: John Wiley, 1958).

[20] McGregor, D., *The Human Side of Enterprise* (New York: McGraw-Hill, 1960).

[21] Meltzer, H., and Wickert, F. R., *Humanizing Organizational Behavior* (Springfield, IL: Charles C. Thomas, 1976).

[22] Myers, C. A., "Management and the Employee," in *Social Responsibility and the Business Predicament,* J. W. McKie, ed. (Washington, DC: Brookings, 1974).

[23] Pearse, R. F., and Pelzer, B. P., *Self-directed Change for the Mid-Career Manager* (New York: AMACOM, 1975).

[24] Pigors, P., and Myers, C. A., *Personnel Administration,* 8th ed. (New York: McGraw-Hill, 1977).

[25] Roeber, R. J. C., *The Organization in a Changing Environment* (Reading, MA: Addison-Wesley, 1973).

[26] Schein, E. H., "How to Break in the College Graduate," *Harvard Business Review,* 1964, pp. 68–76.

[27] Schein, E. H., "Organizational Socialization and the Profession of Management," *Industrial Management Review,* Winter 1968, pp. 1–16.

[28] Schein, E. H., *Process Consultation: Its Role in Organization Development* (Reading, MA: Addison-Wesley, 1969).

[29] Schein, E. H., *Organizational Psychology* (Englewood Cliffs, NJ: Prentice-Hall, 1970).

[30] Schein, E. H., "The Individual, the Organization, and the Career: A Conceptual Scheme," *Journal of Applied Behavioral Science* 7, 1971, pp. 401–426.

[31] Schein, E. H., "How 'Career Anchors' Hold Executives to Their Career Paths," *Personnel* 52, no. 3 (1975), pp. 11–24.

[32] Schein, E. H., *The Individual, the Organization and the Career: Toward Greater Human Effectiveness* (Reading, MA: Addison-Wesley, forthcoming).

[33] Sheehy, G., "Catch 30 and Other Predictable Crises of Growing Up Adult," *New York Magazine,* February 1974, pp. 30–44.

[34] Super, D. E., and Bohn, M. J., *Occupational Psychology* (Belmont, CA: Wadsworth, 1970).

[35] Troll, L. E., *Early and Middle Adulthood* (Monterey, CA: Brooks-Cole, 1975).

[36] Van Maanen, J., "Breaking In: Socialization to Work," in *Handbook of Work, Organization, and Society,* R. Dubin, ed. (Chicago: Rand McNally, 1976).

[37] Van Maanen, J., ed., *Organizational Careers: Some New Perspectives* (New York: John Wiley, 1977).

[38] Van Maanen, J., Bailyn, L., and Schein, E. H., "The Shape of Things to Come: A New Look at Organizational Careers," in *Perspectives on Behavior in Organizations,* J. R. Hackman, E. E. Lawler, and L. W. Porter, eds. (New York: McGraw-Hill, 1977).

[39] Van Maanen, J., and Schein, E. H., "Improving the Quality of Work Life: Career Development," in *Improving Life at Work,* J. R. Hackman and J. L. Suttle, eds. (Los Angeles: Goodyear, 1977).

Chapter 3

Notes

A similar version of this article appears in *General Systems* Yearbook, 1962.

1. In this article, "organization" is defined as any institution from which one receives cash for services rendered. The article deals with all such supraindividual entities, although reference is made mostly to industrial organizations.

2. For a recent historical review, see Aitken [1].

3. See also Kahn, Mann, and Seashore [35], Introduction, for other suggestions for criteria.

4. See, for example, Urwick [71].

5. Another approach, advocated by A. L. Comrey, is the deliberate (and often wise) avoidance of a definition of effectiveness or health by obtaining judgments of knowledgeable observers. "This method of defining 'effectiveness' seems to be the only feasible course of action in view of the tremendous number of meanings involved in a conceptual definition of this term and the obvious impossibility of providing a criterion which would reflect all or most of those meanings" [23, p. 362].

6. See Ridgway [59] for other criticisms of the use of performance measurements.

7. See, for example, March and Simon, [46] ch. 7; Argyris [3]; Shepard [65]; Gibb and Lippitt [29]; Lippitt, Watson, and Westley [42]; Bennis, Benne, and Chin [10]; and Walker [73].

8. Although not quoted here, a book by Selznick is also directly relevant. See [63].

9. See Bennis [9] for elaboration of this point.

10. Wilson lists six "areas of social activity, each of which contain a number of significant social institutions and social groups. These areas may be rather summarily labeled as: (i) Government, (ii) Consumers, (iii) Shareholders, (iv) Competitors, (v) Raw material and power suppliers, and (vi) Groups within the firm" [77, p. 3]. These represent some of the boundary conditions for the manager.

11. See Bennis [9].

12. See the bibliographies for chs. 6, 9, and 10 in Baritz [6].

13. Shepard notes the irony that, as research organizations expand their operations, they become more like classical, ideal-type bureaucracies. See [64] for another approach to the social conditions of science.

14. See Selznick [63] ch. 3, for similar emphasis.
15. See March and Simon [46] for a formal model of search behavior (p. 50) and an excellent discussion of organizational reality-testing (ch. 6).
16. Dr. M. B. Miles has suggested that an important omission in this approach is organization "memory" or storage of information. Organizations modeled along the lines suggested here require a "theory" based on an *accumulated* storage of information. This is implied, I believe, in the criterion of adaptability.
17. See Harbison [32] on this point.
18. It is suspected that group cohesiveness will decrease as the scientific attitude infuses organizational functioning. With the depersonalization of science, the rapid turnover, and some expected individualism, cohesiveness may not be functional or even possible.

References

[1] Aitken, H. G. J., *Taylorism at Watertown Arsenal: Scientific Management in Action 1908–1915* (Cambridge, MA: Harvard University Press, 1960).
[2] Argyris, C., "The Integration of the Individual and the Organization," paper presented at the University of Wisconsin, Madison, WI, May, 1961.
[3] Argyris, C., "Organizational Development—An Inquiry into the Esso Approach," New Haven, CT: Yale University, July 1960.
[4] Argyris, C., *Personality and Organization* (New York: Harper Brothers, 1957).
[5] Barber, B., *Science and the Social Order* (Glencoe, IL: Free Press, 1952).
[6] Baritz, L., *The Servants of Power* (Middletown, CT: Wesleyan University Press, 1960).
[7] Bateson, G., "Social Planning and the Concept of Deutero-Learning," in *Readings in Social Psychology,* T.M. Newcomb and E.L. Hartley, eds. (New York: Henry Holt, 1947), pp. 121–128.
[8] Bendix, R., *Max Weber: An Intellectual Portrait* (Garden City, NY: Doubleday, 1960).
[9] Bennis, W. G., "Leadership Theory and Administrative Behavior: The Problem of Authority," *Administrative Science Quarterly,* December 1959, pp. 259–301.
[10] Bennis, W. G., Benne, K., and Chin, R., *The Planning of Change* (New York: Henry Holt, 1961).
[11] Berkowitz, N., and Bennis, W., "Interaction in Formal Service-Oriented Organizations," *Administrative Science Quarterly,* June 1961, pp. 25–50.
[12] Bertalanffy, L.V., "The Theory of Open Systems in Physics and Biology," *Science,* Vol. 111, 1950, pp. 23–29.
[13] Blake, R. R., and Mouton, J. S., "Developing and Maintaining Corporate Health through Organic Management Training," unpublished paper, Austin, TX: University of Texas, 1961.
[14] Blake, R. R., and Mouton, J. S., "From Industrial Warfare to Collaboration: A Behavioral Science Approach," Korzybski Memorial Address, April 20, 1961.
[15] Blansfield, M. G., and Robinson, W. F., "Variations in Training Laboratory Design: A Case Study in Sensitivity Training," *Personnel Administration,* March–April, 1961, pp. 17–22, 49.
[16] Bradford, L. ed., "Theories of T-Group Training" (New York: National Training Laboratories, New York University Press, Winter 1962).
[17] Bronowski, J., *The Common Sense of Science* (New York: Modern Library, no date).
[18] Bronowski, J., *Science and Human Values* (New York: Harper Brothers, 1959).
[19] Brown, W., *Exploration in Management* (New York: John Wiley, 1960).
[20] Bruner, J., *The Process of Education* (Cambridge, MA: Harvard University Press, 1961).
[21] Bush, G. P., and Hattery, D. H., *Teamwork in Research* (Washington, DC: American University Press, 1953).
[22] Caplow, T., "The Criteria of Organizational Success," in *Readings in Human Relations,* K. Davis and W. G. Scott, eds. (New York: McGraw-Hill, 1959), p. 96.

[23] Comrey, A. L., "A Research Plan for the Study of Organizational Effectiveness," in *Some Theories of Organization*, A.H. Rubenstein and C.J. Haberstroh, eds. (Homewood, IL: Dorsey-Irwin, 1960).

[24] Emery, F.E., and Trist, E.L., "Socio-Technical Systems," paper presented at the 6th Annual International Meeting of the Institute of Management Sciences, Paris, France, September, 1959.

[25] Erikson, E., "Identity and the Life Cycle," *Psychological Issues,* I, Monograph 1, 1959.

[26] Freud, S., "Analysis Terminable and Interminable," in *Collected Papers,* V, E. Jones, ed. (New York: Basic Books, 1959).

[27] Fromm-Reichmann, F., *Principles of Intensive Psychotherapy* (Chicago, IL: University of Chicago Press, 1950).

[28] Geiger, G., "Values and Social Science," *Journal of Social Issues,* VI, 4 (1950), pp. 8–16.

[29] Gibb, J. R., and Lippitt, R., eds., "Consulting with Groups and Organizations," *Journal of Social Issues,* XV, (1959), pp. 1–74.

[30] Gouldner, A., "Locals and Cosmopolitans: Towards an Analysis of Latent Social Roles," *Administrative Science Quarterly,* II (1957), pp. 281–306.

[31] Haire, M., "What Price Value?," *Contemporary Psychology,* IV, June 1959, pp. 180–182.

[32] Harbison, F. H., "Management and Scientific Manpower," paper presented at the Centennial Symposium on Executive Development, School of Industrial Management, Massachusetts Institute of Technology, Cambridge, MA, April 27, 1961.

[33] Hartmann, H., *Ego Psychology and the Problem of Adaption* (New York: International Universities Press, 1958).

[34] Jahoda, M., *Current Concepts of Positive Mental Health* (New York: Basic Books, 1958).

[35] Kahn, R., Mann, F. C., and Seashore, S., "Human Relations Research in Large Organizations," *Journal of Social Issues,* XII, 2 (1956), p. 4.

[36] Katzell, R. A., "Industrial Psychology," in *Annual Review of Psychology,* P. R. Farnsworth, ed. (Palo Alto, CA, 1957), pp. 237–268.

[37] Kubie, L. S., "Neurotic Distortions of the Creative Process," Porter Lectures, Series 22, University of Kansas Press, Lawrence, KS, 1958.

[38] Leavitt, H. J., "Effects of Certain Communication Patterns on Group Performance," *Journal of Abnormal Social Psychology,* 46 (1951), pp. 38–50.

[39] Leavitt, H. J., "Unhuman Organizations," address presented at the Centennial Symposium on Executive Development, School of Industrial Management, Massachusetts Institute of Technology, Cambridge, MA, April 27, 1961.

[40] Leavitt, H. J., and Whisler, T.L., "Management in the 1980s," *Harvard Business Review,* November–December 1958, pp. 41–48.

[41] Likert, R., "Measuring Organizational Performance," *Harvard Business Review,* March–April 1958, pp. 41–50.

[42] Lippitt, R., Watson, J., and Westley, B., *The Dynamics of Planned Change* (New York: Harcourt, Brace, 1958).

[43] McGregor, D., *The Human Side of Enterprise* (New York: McGraw-Hill, 1960).

[44] McGregor, D., "New Concepts of Management," *Technology Review,* February 1961, pp. 25–27.

[45] Mann, F. C., and Neff, F. W., *Managing Major Change in Organizations* (Ann Arbor, MI, Foundation for Research on Human Behavior, 1961).

[46] March, J., and Simon, H., *Organizations* (New York: John Wiley, 1958).

[47] Marcson, S., *The Scientist in American Industry* (Princeton, NJ: Industrial Relations Section, Princeton University, 1960).

[48] Marvick, D., "Career Perspectives in a Bureaucratic Setting," University of Michigan Governmental Study 27 (Ann Arbor, MI: University of Michigan Press, 1954).

[49] Merton, R., "The Professions and Social Structure," in *Essays in Sociological Theory* (Glencoe, IL: Free Press, 1949).

[50] Merton, R., "The Sociology of Knowledge," ch. VIII, and "Science and Democratic

Social Structure," ch. XII, in *Social Theory and Social Structure* (Glencoe, IL, Free Press, 1949).

[51] Morison, E., "A Case Study of Innovation," *Engineering Science Monthly,* April 1950, pp. 5–11.

[52] "Muggeridge and Snow," *Encounter,* February 1962, p. 90.

[53] Oppenheimer, R., "Prospects in the Arts and Sciences," *Perspectives USA,* Spring 1955, pp. 5–14.

[54] Parsons, T., *The Social System* (Glencoe, IL: Free Press, 1951), ch. 8.

[55] Parsons, T., "Suggestions for a Sociological Approach to the Theory of Organizations," *Administrative Science Quarterly, I,* 1956, 63–85.

[56] Paul, B., "Social Science in Public Health," *American Journal of Public Health,* November 1956, pp. 1390–1393.

[57] Pfiffner, J. M., and Sherwood, F. P., *Administrative Organization* (Englewood Cliffs, NJ: Prentice-Hall, 1960).

[58] Rapaport, D., "The Theory of Ego Autonomy: A Generalization," *Bulletin of the Menninger Clinic,* January 1958, pp. 13–35. (See also "The Structure of Psychoanalytic Theory," *Psychological Issues,* vol. II, no. 2, Monograph 6, 1960.)

[59] Ridgway, V. F., "Dysfunctional Consequences of Performance Measurements," in *Some Theories of Organization,* A. H. Rubenstein and C. J. Haberstroh, eds. (Homewood, IL: Dorsey-Irwin, 1960), pp. 371–377.

[60] Rubenstein, A. H., and Shepard, H. A., "Annotated Bibliography on Human Relations in Research Laboratories," Cambridge, MA: School of Industrial Management, Massachusetts Institute of Technology, February 1956.

[61] Sanford, N., "Social Science and Social Reform," presidential address for SPSSI at the Annual Meeting of the American Psychological Association, Washington, DC, August 28, 1958.

[62] Selznick, P., "Foundations of the Theory of Organization," *American Sociological Review,* vol. 13, 1948, pp. 25–35.

[63] Selznick, P., *Leadership in Administration* (Evanston, IL: Row, Peterson, 1957).

[64] Shepard, H., "Superiors and Subordinates in Research," *Journal of Business,* October 1956, pp. 261–267.

[65] Shepard, H., "Three Management Programs and the Theories Behind Them," in *An Action Research Program for Organization Improvement* (Ann Arbor, MI: Foundation for Research on Human Behavior, 1960).

[66] Sherif, M., and Sherif, C., *Groups in Harmony and Tension* (New York: Harper Brothers, 1953).

[67] Simon, H. A., Smithburg, D. W., and Thompson, V. A., *Public Administration* (New York: Alfred A. Knopf, 1950).

[68] Smith, S., "Communication Pattern and the Adaptability of Task-Oriented Groups: An Experimental Study," unpublished paper, Massachusetts Institute of Technology, Cambridge, MA, 1950.

[69] Snow, C. P., *The Two Cultures and the Scientific Revolution* (New York: Mentor Books, 1962).

[70] Thelen, H., "Education and the Human Quest" (New York: Harper Brothers, 1960).

[71] Urwick, L. F., "The Purpose of a Business," in *Readings in Human Relations,* K. Davis and W. G. Scott, eds. (New York: McGraw-Hill, 1959), pp. 85–91.

[72] Waddington, C. H., *The Scientific Attitude* (Baltimore, MD.: Penguin, 1941).

[73] Walker, C., ed., *Modern Technology and Civilization: An Introduction to Human Problems of a Machine Age* (New York: McGraw-Hill, 1961).

[74] Wasserman, P., "Measurement and Evaluation of Organizational Performance," McKinsey Foundation Annotated Bibliography, Graduate School of Business and Public Administration, Cornell University, Ithaca, NY, 1959.

[75] White, R. W., "Motivation Reconsidered: The Concept of Competence," *Psychological Review,* September 1959, pp. 297–333.

[76] Whyte, W. H., Jr., *The Organization Man* (New York: Simon & Schuster, 1956).

[77] Wilson, A.T.M., "The Manager and His World," paper presented at the Centennial Symposium on Executive Development, School of Industrial Management, Massachusetts Institute of Technology, Cambridge, MA, April 27, 1961.

Chapter 5

Research support upon which this article is based was provided by the Office of Naval Research and the Sloan Research Fund. Much of it is based upon the published works in references 1–10.

1. Blau, P. M., and Scott, R. W., *Formal Organizations* (San Francisco: Chandler, 1962).

2. Goffman, E., *Asylums* (Garden City, NY: Doubleday Anchor, 1961).

3. Schein, E. H., Schneier, I., and Barker, C. H., *Coercive Persuasion* (New York: W. W. Norton, 1961).

4. Schein, E. H., "Management Development as a Process of Influence," *Industrial Management Review,* II, 1961, pp. 59–77.

5. Schein, E. H., "Forces Which Undermine Management Development," *California Management Review,* V, Summer 1963.

6. Schein, E. H., "How to Break in the College Graduate," *Harvard Business Review,* XLII, 1964.

7. Schein, E. H., "Training in Industry: Education or Indoctrination," *Industrial Medicine and Surgery,* XXXIII, 1964.

8. Schein, E. H., *Organizational Psychology* (Englewood Cliffs, NJ: Prentice-Hall, 1965).

9. Schein, E. H., "The Problem of Moral Education for the Business Manager," *Industrial Management Review,* VIII, 1966, pp. 3–14.

10. Schein, E. H., "Attitude Change During Management Education," *Administrative Science Quarterly,* XI, 1967, pp. 601–628.

11. Schein, E. H., "The Wall of Misunderstanding on the First Job," *Journal of College Placement,* February–March 1967.

Chapter 6

Notes

This paper was prepared for the Seventeenth Conference on Science, Philosophy and Religion, Chicago, August 1966.

1. In this discussion, I do not distinguish between concepts of "ethical" and concepts of "moral." The two terms are used interchangeably.

2. Hughes, E. C. [1]

3. One might hypothesize that legal sanctions tend to develop when vulnerability is at a maximum, there is a specific identifiable target who is potentially vulnerable, the manager's behavior is potentially observable and unambiguous, and there are immediate or short-run consequences of the managerial behavior.

4. Since the organization is an abstraction, can one view it as a client? I believe we can treat it as an "object" in the same sense in which clubs, fraternal organizations, political parties, and countries exist as objects to which we give loyalty and attention and from which we obtain material and symbolic rewards.

5. William Evan points out that in organizational life employees do not have the protection of due process of law and a system of appeals as they do in the larger society. [2]
6. Schein, E. H. [3]
7. Schein, E. H. [4]
8. Both "helping" and "hurting" are *interpersonal* concepts with limited meaning when applied merely as a trait like "helpful" or "mean". They become meaningful as we specify *who* is hurt or *who* is helped.
9. Milgram, S. [5]
10. One might speculate that the *motivation* to help or not hurt comes from the *feelings* of compassion, fear, or guilt, not from a *rational* assessment of need or vulnerability. We are more likely to give something to a beggar who confronts us than a starving country that may need our help more but that arouses no direct feeling in us. In any case this is an hypothesis worth testing.
11. Robert Kahn has suggested the further implication of organizing our enterprise as small units, possibly federated into larger ones, to ensure a maximum of close contacts among managers and their various clients. [6]
12. I am indebted to John Thomas for this point.
13. The obvious, more general case is the passive behavior of the witness to a crime, especially in cases where help is needed.
14. See Schein, 1967. [4]

References

[1] Hughes, E. C., *Men and Their Work* (Glencoe, IL: Free Press, 1958).
[2] Evan, W. M., "Due Process of Law in Military and Industrial Organizations," *Administrative Science Quarterly*, 1962, pp. 187–207.
[3] Schein, E. H., *Organizational Psychology* (Englewood Cliffs, NJ: Prentice-Hall, 1965).
[4] Schein, E. H., "Attitude Change During Management Education: A Study of Organizational Influences on Student Attitudes," *Administrative Science Quarterly*, 1967.
[5] Milgram, S., "Some Conditions of Obedience and Disobedience to Authority," in *Current Studies in Social Psychology,* I. D. Steiner and M. Fishbein, eds. (New York: Holt, Rinehart & Winston, 1965), pp. 243–262.
[6] Kahn, R. L., personal communication.

Chapter 7

1. T. Levitt, "The Managerial Merry-Go-Round," *Harvard Business Review,* July–August 1974.
2. *Business Week,* February 25, 1980.
3. It should be noted that the selection system is but one component of an overall executive human resource management system. For an overview of a total system, see E. H. Schein, *Career Dynamics: Matching Individual and Organizational Needs* (Reading, MA: Addison-Wesley, 1978), pp. 189–199.
4. A small number of corporations employ selection methods that are as comprehensive as the one presented here. However, these systems were not found to be the norm in our investigations.
5. We estimate that it takes a skilled professional approximately one day to interview an executive and to document his or her job. If the responsibilities are unclear or undergoing change, the documentation process will take longer.
6. The alternative view that performance in a position stems from the degree of "fit" between

a job's requirements and an incumbent's abilities logically suggests that jobs as well as people be evaluated in making assessment decisions. Without job analysis and comparison, results, either positive or negative, cannot be placed in proper context.

7. The perspective that the selection process focuses on the filling of a job at a given point in time is taken here. For a view of job evolution over a longer time frame, see Schein (1978), pp. 203–206.

8. See, for example, C. Hofer and D. Schendel, *Strategy Formulation: Analytical Concepts* (St. Paul, MN: West Publishing, 1978).

9. We have developed similar requirements for other key roles, such as vice-president of operations, vice-president of marketing, and vice-president of human resources.

10. Job documentation and job contracting serve as linkages between the selection-and performance-appraisal processes in the larger human resource system.

11. PDI assesses approximately 1,000 managers annually for selection purposes. See, for example, J.P. Campbell et al., *Managerial Behavior, Performance, and Effectiveness* (New York: McGraw-Hill, 1970); and J.P. Kotter, *The General Managers* (New York: Free Press, 1982). The executives interviewed were drawn from a number of industries, including financial services, manufacturing, retailing, and chemicals.

12. For a description of behavior-observation scaling methodology, see M.D. Dunnette, "Aptitudes, Abilities, and Skills," in *Handbook of Industrial and Organizational Psychology* (New York: Rand McNally, 1976), pp. 490–514.

13. The authors would like to thank Henri Tremblay and the senior executives of Steinberg, Inc., Montreal, Canada, for their support of our work on executive selection.

14. Behavioral interviewing is described in J.L. Janz, "Effective Interviewing via the Behavioral Route: The Behavior Description Interview" (Simon Fraser University, School of Business Administration and Economics Discussion Series 81-05-02, 1981).

15. For a thorough review of the assessment-center approach, see: R.B. Finkle, "Managerial Assessment Centers," in *Handbook of Industrial and Organizational Psychology* (New York: Rand McNally, 1976), pp. 861–888; and, D.W. Bray and D.E. Grant, "The Assessment Center in the Measurement of Potential Business Management," *Psychological Monographs,* 1966.

16. Shorter simulation sessions can be designed to deal with specific assessment requirements, but these shorter sessions may lack the multiexercise and multiassessor evaluations that contribute to the assessment center's high validity.

17. For example, the movement from a functional to a matrix or a product organization, or the replacement of an international division by a worldwide business structure creates tremendous changes in the jobs of most of the key positions in the top several levels of management.

18. In selecting the CEO or general manager, or in replacing a single individual on the management team, it may not be necessary to analyze the entire management team. This is a matter of judgment. In general, however, when the strategy changes markedly, we prefer to review the whole management group.

19. There are psychometric reasons for this process. Dimension-by-dimension comparisons will tend to highlight skills differences among members of the management team, while rating a single candidate for all dimensions tends to obscure them.

20. We have developed a number of tools to facilitate this process. Fundamentally, their purpose is to help senior management handle the large amount of information generated in the staffing process. Unfortunately, such tools cannot eliminate the hard judgments that must still be made.

21. The selection process must dovetail the organization's manpower–career-planning activities. The concrete point of integration, of course, is the actual selection decision.

22. Circumstances often necessitate the implementation of structural and staffing changes on a phased basis. Unfortunately, protracted changes almost always create difficulties and suboptimal organizational performance as individuals "wait for the other shoe to drop."

23. The process outlined in this article will provide a clear picture of the "development gap" between an individual's current capabilities and those required in particular positions. This can provide vital input to a short-term development planning activity, thus linking the selection and development processes within the human resource system.

    Compensation for a manager's weaknesses may take a variety of forms including hiring assistants or subordinates, contracting for outside consultants, or "filling in" by the boss. Most important for success, however, is recognition by the incumbent that something important is lacking and must be provided by some means.

24. One tendency, often couched as "consideration," is to delay staffing changes until an incumbent's inability to handle the new circumstances has resulted in a substantial deterioration in performance. While the other extreme (making snap judgments) is an equally serious mistake, a third option is preferable. One can negotiate fairly explicit expectations, often called a "psychological contract," with incumbents so that they know in concrete terms what is expected. In addition, one can provide them with some additional resources during the early days of the transition to the new strategy, so that they need not "go it alone."

Chapter 9

Notes

This article is adapted from a chapter by the author in *Laboratory Method of Changing and Learning,* Benne, Bradford, Gibb, and Lippitt, eds., (Palo Alto, CA: Science and Behavior Books, 1975).

1. For a more detailed explanation of the author's views concerning organization development and intervention, see Beckhard [1].
2. See Lawrence and Lorsch [4].
3. See Krone [3].
4. For one view of this, see Beckhard [2].

References

[1] Beckhard, R., *Organization Development: Strategies and Models* (Reading, MA: Addison-Wesley, 1969).
[2] Beckhard, R., "The Confrontation Meeting," *Harvard Business Review,* March–April 1967.
[3] Krone, C., "Open Systems Redesign," in *Theory and Method in Organization Development: An Evolutionary Process,* J. Adams, ed. (Rosslyn, VA: NTL Institute, 1974).
[4] Lawrence, P. R., and Lorsch, J. W., *Organization and Environment: Managing Differentiation and Integration* (Boston: Harvard Business School, Division of Research, 1967).

Chapter 10

1. See M. Mace, "The Board and the New CEO," *Harvard Business Review,* March–April 1977, p. 16.
2. A.D. Chandler, Jr., *Strategy and Structure* (Cambridge, MA: MIT Press, 1978).
3. Mace (March–April 1977).

Chapter 11

1. A. D. Chandler, *Strategy and Structure* (Cambridge, MA:MIT Press, 1962).
2. J. Thompson, *Organizations in Action* (New York: McGraw-Hill, 1967).
3. W.J. Abernathy, K.B. Clark, and A.M. Kantrow, *Industrial Renaissance: Producing a Competitive Future for America* (New York: Basic Books, 1983).
4. "A New Strategy for No. 2 in Computers: Will Digital Equipment Corp's Massive Overhaul Pay Off?" *Business Week,* May 2, 1983.
5. "Black and Decker's Gamble on Globalization," *Fortune,* May 14, 1984.
6. "Slimming Down: Beatrice Foods Moves to Centralize Business to Reverse Its Decline," *Wall Street Journal,* September 27, 1983.
7. G.L. Reuber, "Bits, Bytes, and Banking," *Business Quarterly,* Spring 1983.
8. W.B. Tunstall, "Cultural Transition at AT&T," *Sloan Management Review,* Fall 1983, pp. 15–26; "Culture Shock is Shaking the Bell System," *Business Week,* September 26, 1983; "AT&T Manager Finds His Effort to Galvanize Sales Meets Resistance," *Wall Street Journal,* December 16, 1983; A. van Auw, *Heritage and Destiny: Reflections on the Bell System Transition* (New York: Praeger, 1983); and P. Drucker, "Beyond the Bell Breakup," *The Public Interest* 77, Fall 1984.
9. J. Galbraith, "Strategy and Organization Planning," *Human Resource Management* 22, Spring–Summer 1983.
10. "Monsanto Slowly but Deliberately Shifts Emphasis to Research, Patented Products," *Wall Street Journal,* January 13, 1983.
11. "The $5-Billion Man: Pushing the New Strategy at GE," *Fortune,* April 18, 1983.
12. "Financial Forays: Sears Expansion Brings Increased Competition to Bankers and Brokers," *Wall Street Journal,* October 12, 1981.
13. "Eaton: Spinning Its Wheels on the Road to High-Tech Profits," *Business Week,* March 28, 1983.
14. J.B. Quinn, *Strategies for Change* (Homewood, IL: Irwin, 1980).
15. "LaMauvaise Année des Autres, une Autre Année Record Chez Imasco," *Commerce,* July 1983.
16. "Philip's High-Tech Crusade," *Business Week,* July 18, 1983.
17. "High-Tech Track: Cincinnati Milacron, Mainly a Metal-Bender, Now Is a Robot Maker," *Wall Street Journal,* April 7, 1983.
18. "Rousing a Giant: David Roderick Tries to Recast U.S. Steel by Redeploying Assets," *Wall Street Journal,* February 7, 1983.
19. "Singer: Sewing Machines Finally Take a Backseat as It Expands into Aerospace," *Business Week,* June 13, 1983.
20. "Changing a Corporate Culture: Can Johnson & Johnson Go from Band-Aids to High Tech?" *Business Week,* May 14, 1984.
21. "New Bache Chief Pushes a Host of Changes, Including New Name, to Lift Firm's Image," *Wall Street Journal,* October 29, 1982; and "After a Year, Prudential's Takeover of Bache Mostly Causing Problems," *Wall Street Journal,* July 16, 1982.
22. "Continental Corp. Still Drifts despite Moves to Reorganize, Lift Its Insurance Earnings," *Wall Street Journal,* April 19, 1983.
23. "With New Chairman, Corning Tries to Get Tough and Revive Earnings," *Wall Street Journal,* April 22, 1983.
24. "Burroughs Tightens Up and Aims for IBM, but Many New Obstacles Stand in the Way," *Wall Street Journal,* July 20, 1982.
25. "Driving Ahead: Chief's Style and Ideas Help to Keep Goodyear No. 1 in the Radial Age," *Wall Street Journal,* January 18, 1983.
26. "Sears' Overdue Retailing Revival," *Fortune,* April 4, 1983.

27. "J.C. Penney Goes After Affluent Shoppers, but Store's New Image May Be Hard to Sell," *Wall Street Journal,* February 15, 1983.
28. "Operation Turnaround: How Westinghouse's New CEO Plans to Fire Up an Old-Line Company," *Business Week,* December 5, 1983.
29. "Sherwin-Williams Makes Big Turnaround under Chairman's Aggressive Leadership," *Wall Street Journal,* December 14, 1983.
30. Quinn has provided a review of the tactics and processes used by leaders in their efforts to carry out far-reaching changes in organizations. See Quinn (1980).
31. *Business Week,* May 14, 1984.
32. *Business Week,* June 18, 1984.
33. "Counter Strategy, Woolworth, Defeated in Discounting Aims at Specialty Markets," *Wall Street Journal,* November 3, 1983.
34. Tunstall (Fall 1983).
35. M. Firsirotu, "Strategic Turnaround as Cultural Revolutions," unpublished Ph.D. thesis, McGill University, Montreal, Canada, 1984.
36. "Weak Chain: Mobil Grows Impatient for Profit Turnaround at Montgomery Ward," *Wall Street Journal,* February 16, 1983.
37. P.M. Warren, "Canada Post Corporation's President: Address to the Canadian Club," Montreal, Canada, March 28, 1984.
38. T.J. Peters, "Symbols, Patterns, and Settings: An Optimistic Case for Getting Things Done," *Organizational Dynamics,* 1978.
39. *Wall Street Journal,* February 16, 1983.
40. "GM's Unlikely Revolutionist," *Fortune,* March 19, 1984.
41. "Borden: Putting the Shareholder First Starts to Pay Off," *Business Week,* April 2, 1984.
42. *Business Week,* September 26, 1983.

Chapter 12

The author would like to acknowledge the Centre d'Etudes Industrielle, Geneva, Switzerland, for its support in developing the ideas on culture. This paper was developed from a project supported by the Chief of Naval Research, Psychological Sciences Division (Code 452). Organizational Effectiveness Research, Office of Naval Research, Arlington, VA 22217 (under contract N00014–80–C0905; NR 170–911). Special thanks go to Gibb Dyer, who helped to develop the ideas on how to analyze cultures.

1. See P. Slater, *The Pursuit of Loneliness* (Boston, MA: Beacon, 1970).
1a. W. Ouchi, *Theory Z: How American Business Can Meet the Japanese Challenge* (Reading, MA: Addison-Wesley, 1981); and R.T. Pascale and A.G. Athos, *The Art of Japanese Management: Applications for American Executives* (New York: Simon & Schuster, 1981).
2. E.H. Schein, "Management Development as a Process of Influence," *Industrial Management Review* (now *Sloan Management Review*), May 1961, pp. 59–77; and E.H. Schein, *Coercive Persuasion* (New York: Norton, 1961).
3. W.H. Whyte, Jr., *The Organization Man* (New York: Simon & Schuster, 1956).
4. C. Argyris, *Integrating the Individual and the Organization* (New York: John Wiley, 1964); A.H. Maslow, *Motivation and Personality* (New York: Harper & Row, 1954); and D.M. McGregor, *The Human Side of Enterprise* (New York: McGraw-Hill, 1960).
5. S. Silverzweig and R.F. Allen, "Changing the Corporate Culture," *Sloan Management Review,* Spring 1976, pp. 33–49; A.M. Pettigrew, "On Studying Organizational Cultures," *Administrative Science Quarterly,* 1979, pp. 570–581; and H. Schwartz and S.M. Davis, "Matching Corporate Culture and Business Strategy," *Organizational Dynamics,* Summer 1981, pp. 30–48.
6. E.H. Schein, "The Individual, the Organization, and the Career: A Conceptual Scheme,"

Journal of Applied Behavioral Science, 1971, pp. 401–426; and E.H. Schein, *Career Dynamics: Matching Individual and Organizational Needs* (Reading, MA: Addison-Wesley, 1978).

7. J. Van Maanen and E.H. Schein, "Toward a Theory of Organizational Socialization," in *Research in Organizational Behavior* (Vol. 1) B. Staw, ed. (Greenwich, CT: JAI Press, 1979).

8. See, for example, F. Harbison and C.A. Myers, *Management in the Industrial World* (New York: McGraw-Hill, 1959).

9. W.J. Dickson and F.J. Roethlisberger, *Counseling in an Organization: A Sequel to the Hawthorne Researches* (Boston: Division of Research, Harvard Business School, 1966); and H.W. Johnson, "The Hawthorne Studies: The Legend and the Legacy," in *Man and Work in Society,* E.L. Cass and F.G. Zimmer, eds. (New York: Van Nostrand Reinhold, 1975).

10. E.H. Schein and W.G. Bennis, *Personal and Organizational Change through Group Methods* (New York: John Wiley, 1965).

11. McGregor (1960); and Argyris (1964).

12. R. Likert, *The Human Organization* (New York: McGraw-Hill, 1967); and A.H. Maslow, *The Farthest Reaches of Human Nature* (New York: Viking, 1971).

13. A. Etzioni, *Complex Organizations* (New York: Holt, Rinehart, & Winston, 1961).

14. Pascale and Athos, (1981), p. 102.

15. *Ibid.,* p. 106.

16. *Ibid.,* p. 105.

17. E.H. Schein, *Process Consultation* (Reading, MA: Addison-Wesley, 1969).

18. Schein and Bennis (1965).

19. A.S. Waterman, "Individualism and Interdependence," *American Psychologist,* 1981, pp. 762–773.

20. J. McLendon, *Rethinking Japanese Groupism: Individual Strategies in a Corporate Context,* unpublished paper, Harvard University, 1980.

21. E.H. Schein, *Organizational Psychology,* 3d ed. (Englewood Cliffs, NJ: Prentice-Hall, 1980).

22. J. Galbraith, *Designing Complex Organizations* (Reading, MA: Addison-Wesley, 1973).

23. W.M. Fruin, "The Japanese Company Controversy," *Journal of Japanese Studies,* 1978, pp. 267–300; and B.S. Lawrence, *Historical Perspective: Seeing through Halos in Social Research,* unpublished paper, MIT, 1981.

24. G. Hofstede, *Culture's Consequences: Internatonal Differences in Work-Related Values* (Beverly Hills, CA: Sage Publications, 1980); and G.W. England, *The Manager and His Values* (Cambridge, MA: Ballinger, 1975).

25. Some excellent efforts in this direction can be found in W.H. Newman, "Cultural Assumptions Underlying U.S. Management Concepts," in *Management in an International Context,* J.L. Massie and Luytjes, eds. (New York: Harper & Row, 1972); and in J.J. O'Toole, "Corporate Managerial Cultures," in *Behavioral Problems in Organizations,* C.L. Cooper, ed. (Englewood Cliffs, NJ: Prentice-Hall, 1979).

26. F.R. Kluckhohn and F.L. Stodtbeck, *Variations in Value Orientations* (Evanston, IL: Row, Peterson, 1961).

27. J.M. Evans, *America: The View from Europe* (Stanford, CA: The Portable Stanford, 1976).

Chapter 13

1. P. Drucker, "Behind Japan's Success," *Harvard Business Review,* January–February 1981, pp. 83–90; G. Hofstede, *Culture's Consequences: International Differences in Work Related Values* (Beverly Hills, CA: Sage Publications, 1980); E.H. Schein, "Does Japanese Management Style Have a Message for American Managers?" *Sloan Management Review,* Fall 1981, pp. 55–68; R.T. Pascale and A.G. Athos, *The Art of Japanese Management* (New

York: Simon & Schuster, 1981); and W.G. Ouchi, *Theory Z: How American Business Can Meet the Japanese Challenge* (Reading, MA: Addison-Wesley, 1981).

2. See Schein (1981).
3. I was one of twelve people recruited to conduct a demonstration project at the Shanghai Institute of Mechanical Engineering in China. Our mission was to transfer the technology involved in a two-year graduate management degree program as it might be conducted at a major U.S. university. My function was to teach a course in organization psychology and to serve as the senior faculty person for the first semester's program.
4. H. Yaobang, "Speech in Honor of the 60th Anniversary of the Founding of the Communist Party of China," *Beijing Review,* July 13, 1981, pp. 9–24.
5. W.H. Newman, "Cultural Assumptions Underlying U.S. Management Concepts," in *Management in an International Context,* J.L. Massie and J. Luytjes (New York: Harper & Row, 1972); and G.C. Lodge, *The New American Ideology* (New York: Alfred A. Knopf, 1979).
6. J. Veroff, E. Douvan, and R.A. Kulka, *The Inner American* (New York: Basic Books, 1981).
7. A.H. Maslow, *Motivation and Personality* (New York: Harper & Brothers, 1954).
8. D. Yankelovich, *New Rules: Searching for Self-Fulfillment in a World Turned Upside Down* (New York: Random House, 1981); Lodge (1979); J.W. Driscoll, "Individual Myths and Collective Realities: The Emergence of Theory 'C' Management," Sloan School of Management Working Paper 11530–30, October 1981.
9. It is interesting to note that industrial managers and other leaders were much taken with group dynamics in their T-Group experiences in the 1940s and 1950s. By 1960, however, the self-actualizing, freeing-up aspects of these experiences predominated, supported by changes in the objectives and outlook of the professionals conducting these programs.
10. See Yankelovich (1981).
11. Schein (1981).
12. J. Rawls, *A Theory of Justice* (Cambridge, MA: Belknap Press, 1971).
13. R. Beckhard, "Presentation at M.I.T. Industrial Liaison Symposium," Cambridge, MA: December 15, 1981.
14. B. Bedell, "Give the Money to the Real Innovators," *New York Times,* November 29, 1981.
15. D. Birch, "Why Things Aren't As Bad As They Seem," *Inc.,* September 1981, pp. 41–43.
16. Veroff, Douvan, and Kulka (1981).
17. R. Katz, "The Effects of Group Longevity on Project Communication and Performance," *Administrative Science Quarterly,* March 1982, pp. 81–104.
18. A.H. Raskin, "The Cooperative Economy," *New York Times,* February 14, 1982.
19. R. Pear, "Coalition Seeks to Curb Rising Health Care Cost," *New York Times,* January 15, 1982.

Chapter 14

1. The development of such a model might most profitably proceed along four dimensions: (1) corporate identity, including purpose and mission, corporate symbols, community and government relations, and attitudes toward investors; (2) psychological contract, including employee perceptions of trust and fair treatment, reward systems, management expectations of employees, and employee communications; (3) concepts of responsibility and authority, including both management style and organizational structure; and (4) orientation to the customer, especially including attitudes of employees toward product quality and service. Generally, these four dimensions form the backdrop against which AT&T's experience is examined throughout this article.

2. See A.M. Pettigrew, "On Studying Organizational Cultures," *Administrative Science Quarterly,* December 1979.

3. E.L. Baker, "Managing Organizational Culture," *Management Review,* July 1980.

4. R.H. Kilmann, "Getting Control of the Corporate Culture," *Managing,* 1982.

5. "Bell System Workers Ponder Their Future. . . ," *Wall Street Journal,* January 11, 1982.

6. S. Salmans, "New Vogue: Corporate Culture," *New York Times,* January 7, 1983.

7. T.E. Deal and A.A. Kennedy, *Corporate Cultures: The Rites and Rituals of Corporate Life* (Reading, MA: Addison-Wesley, 1982).

8. Every corporation has subcultures within its total culture, each with its own priority-oriented subset of values. In extolling technical competence as its first priority, Bell Laboratories originated values that were different from Western Electric (which espoused manufacturing efficiency and distribution know-how as primary) and from the operating companies (which cherished the service ethic first and foremost). However, this article addresses that set of overarching values that are common to all: values that transcend the subordinate organizational units.

9. A. Page, *The Bell Telephone System* (New York: Harper & Bros., 1941).

10. B. Utall, "Breaking Up the Phone Company," *Fortune,* June 27, 1983.

11. "Some Thoughts on Regulation," Speech presented by former AT&T Chairman John deButts before the Communications Law Section, Federal Bar Association, Washington, DC, on January 31, 1977.

12. W.B. Tunstall, "A Heritage of Idealism," *Bell Telephone Magazine,* ed. 6, 1980.

13. R.G. Schaeffer, "Top Management Staffing Challenges: CEOs Describe Their Needs," *The Conference Board,* 1982.

14. W. Kiechel III, "Corporate Strategies under Fire," *Fortune,* December 27, 1982.

15. "Meeting Change with Change," Speech presented by then president of AT&T Charles L. Brown before the Commercial Club, Chicago, on November 21, 1978.

16. "The Premium Now Is on Leadership," *Bell Telephone Magazine,* no. 1, 1983.

17. W. Skinner, "Big Hat, No Cattle," *Harvard Business Review,* September–October 1981.

18. M. Maccoby, *The Gamesman* (New York: Simon & Schuster, 1976).

19. A.L. Wilkins, "Exchange," Brigham Young University School of Management, Fall 1981.

20. "The Premium Now . . ." (1983).

Chapter 15

The research on which this article is based was supported by the Chief of Naval Research, Psychological Sciences Division (Code 452), Organizational Effectiveness Research Programs, Office of Naval Research, Arlington, VA 22217, under Contract Number N00014–80–C–0905, NR 170–911.

Special thanks go to my colleagues Lotte Bailyn, John Van Maanen, and Meryl Louis for helping me to think through this murky area, and to Gibb Dyer, Barbara Lawrence, Steve Barley, Jan Samzelius, and Mary Nur whose research on organizational culture has begun to establish the utility of these ideas.

1. See J. Martin and C. Siehl, "Organizational Culture and Counterculture: An Uneasy Symbiosis," *Organizational Dynamics,* Autumn 1983, pp. 52–64.

2. C. Argyris, "The Executive Mind and Double-Loop Learning," *Organizational Dynamics,* Autumn 1982, pp. 5–22.

3. E.H. Schein, "Does Japanese Management Style Have a Message for American Managers?" *Sloan Management Review,* Fall 1981, pp. 55–68; and E.H. Schein, "The Role of the Founder in Creating Organizational Culture," *Organizational Dynamics,* Summer 1983, pp. 13–28.

4. R. Evered and M.R. Louis, "Alternative Perspectives in the Organizational Sciences: 'Inquiry from the Inside' and 'Inquiry from the Outside,' " *Academy of Management Review,* 1981, pp. 385–395.

5. F.R. Kluckhohn and F.L. Strodtbeck, *Variations in Value Orientations* (Evanston, IL: Row Peterson, 1961). An application of these ideas to the study of organizations across cultures, as contrasted with the culture of organizations, can be found in W.M. Evan, *Organization Theory* (New York: John Wiley, 1976), ch. 15. Other studies of cross-cultural comparisons are not reviewed in detail here. See, for example, G. Hofstede, *Culture's Consequences* (Beverly Hills, CA: Sage Publications, 1980); and G.W. England, *The Manager and His Values* (Cambridge, MA: Ballinger, 1975).

6. E.T. Hall, *The Silent Language* (New York: Doubleday, 1959).

7. W.G. Dyer, Jr., *Culture in Organizations: A Case Study and Analysis,* Cambridge, MA: Sloan School of Management, MIT, Working Paper #1279–82, 1982.

8. T.E. Deal and A.A. Kennedy, *Corporate Culture* (Reading, MA: Addison-Wesley, 1982); and T.J. Peters and R.H. Waterman, Jr., *In Search of Excellence* (New York: Harper & Row, 1982).

9. See: J. Van Maanen and S.R. Barley, "Occupational Communities: Culture and Control in Organizations," Cambridge, MA: Sloan School of Management, November 1982; and L. Bailyn, "Resolving Contradictions in Technical Careers," *Technology Review,* November–December 1982, pp. 40–47.

10. R.L. Solomon and L.C. Wynne, "Traumatic Avoidance Learning: The Principles of Anxiety Conservation and Partial Irreversibility," *Psychological Review* 61, 1954, p. 353.

11. D.O. Hebb, "The Social Significance of Animal Studies," in *Handbook of Social Psychology,* G. Lindzey, ed. (Reading, MA: Addison-Wesley, 1954).

12. E.H. Schein, *Coercive Persuasion* (New York: Norton, 1961).

13. E.L. Trist and K.W. Bamforth, "Some Social and Psychological Consequences of the Long-Wall Method of Coal Getting," *Human Relations,* 1951, pp. 1–38; and I.E.P. Menzies, "A Case Study in the Functioning of Social Systems as a Defense against Anxiety," *Human Relations,* 1960, pp. 95–121.

14. A.M. Pettigrew, "On Studying Organizational Cultures," *Administrative Science Quarterly,* 1979, pp. 570–581; and Schein (Summer 1983), pp. 13–28.

15. Schein (1961); and E.H. Schein and W.G. Bennis, *Personal and Organizational Change through Group Methods* (New York: John Wiley, 1965).

16. A.K. Rice, *The Enterprise and Its Environment* (London: Tavistock, 1963); R.F. Bales, *Interaction Process Analysis* (Chicago, IL: University of Chicago Press, 1950); and T. Parsons, *The Social System* (Glencoe, IL: The Free Press, 1951).

17. See G. Homans, *The Human Group* (New York: Harcourt Brace, 1950).

18. K.E. Weick, "Cognitive Processes in Organizations," in *Research in Organizational Behavior,* ed. B. Staw (Greenwich, CT: JAI Press, 1979), pp. 41–74; J. Van Maanen, "The Self, the Situation, and the Rules of Interpersonal Relations," in *Essays in Interpersonal Dynamics,* W.G. Bennis, J. Van Maanen, E.H. Schein, and F.I. Steele (Homewood, IL: Dorsey Press, 1979).

19. See E.H. Schein, *Process Consultation* (Reading, MA: Addison-Wesley, 1969).

20. When studying different organizations, it is important to determine whether the deeper paradigms that eventually arise in each organizational culture are also unique, or whether they will fit into certain categories such as those that the typological schemes suggest. For example, Handy describes a typology based on Harrison's work that suggests that organizational paradigms will revolve around one of four basic issues: (1) personal connections, power, and politics; (2) role structuring; (3) tasks and efficiency; or (4) existential here and now issues.

    See: C. Handy, *The Gods of Management* (London: Penguin, 1978); and R. Harrison, "How to Describe Your Organization," *Harvard Business Review,* September–October 1972.

21. E.H. Schein, "The Role Innovator and His Education," *Technology Review,* October–November 1970, pp. 32–38.
22. J. Van Maanen and E.H. Schein, "Toward a Theory of Organizational Socialization," in *Research in Organizational Behavior,* Vol. 1, ed. B. Staw (Greenwich, CT: JAI Press, 1979).
23. *Ibid.*
24. Evered and Louis (1981).
25. M. R. Louis, "A Cultural Perspective on Organizations," *Human Systems Management,* 1981, pp. 246–258.
26. H. Schwartz and S.M. Davis, "Matching Corporate Culture and Business Strategy," *Organizational Dynamics,* Summer 1981, pp. 30–48; and J.R. Kimberly and R.H. Miles, *The Organizational Life Cycle* (San Francisco: Jossey Bass, 1981).
27. R. Katz, "The Effects of Group Longevity of Project Communication and Performance," *Administrative Science Quarterly,* 1982, pp. 27, 81–194.
28. A fuller explication of these dynamics can be found in my forthcoming book on organizational culture.

Index

A&P, 193

Abernathy, W. J., 190

Accountability, in China, 235t

Acquisitions: effects on corporate culture, 195; and executive selection, 125t; situation characteristics, 123t

Adaptability, and organizational health, 60

Adaptation: and culture, 270–271; problems of, 270t

Adjustment, preemptive, 189–190

Administration, as dimension of management effectiveness, 135

Affirmative-action programs, 238t

Allaire, Yvan, 4

Allis-Chalmers, 193

Alternative work patterns, 42

Ambition, as value, 225

American Express, 192

American Federation of Labor and Congress of Industrial Organizations, 244

American Hospital Association, 244

American Medical Association, 244

American Motors, 193

AM International, 193

Amstutz, 75

Anxiety avoidance, in culture formation, 268, 272

Application aspects, of management science, 73, 74

Appraisal, difficulty of, 46. See also Assessment; Evaluation

Argyris, C., 48, 212

Assessment: difficulty of, 121; in strategic selection system, 131; techniques for, 127–128, 139–140. See also Appraisal; Evaluation

Assessment-center testing, 128

Assignment. See Job assignment

Assumptions, basic: and organizational culture, 262–266, 272

AT&T (Bell System), 190, 205–206; balanced responsibilities at, 250, 251; breakup of, 192, 245–260; corporate culture, 199, 200, 266–267; universal service ideal, 250, 251, 253

AT&T Information Systems, 192, 247, 248

AT&T International, 248, 257

Athos, A. G., 209, 216–218, 220, 221, 225, 226, 228

Authority, and individualism, 218–220

Autocracy, in management, 215, 217

Automation, 242

Baker, E. L., 246

Bank of Montreal, 192

Barber, B., 57

Bateson, G., 60

Bavelas, Alex, 13, 90

Beatrice Foods, 191

Beckhard, Richard, 3, 4, 241

Behavior: management's levers on, 14–15; and socialization, 85, 86

Behavioral interviewing, 127–128, 139–140

Behavioral sciences: in-house programs, 22; and management, 9–24, 70–71, 79, 109

Bell, Alexander Graham, 250

Bell Advanced Management Program, 258–259

Bell Laboratories, 192, 248, 250, 257

Bell System. See AT&T

Benefits, 38, 42

Bennis, Warren G., 3, 49, 70

Bertalanffy, L. V., 54

Bethel, 9

Black and Decker, 191

Blake, R. R., 64–65

Blansfield, M. G., 64

Blue Cross and Blue Shield Associations, 244

Boise Cascade, 193

Borden, 205

Boss: manager's responsibility to, 108–110; as mentor, in Japanese companies, 218

Boundaries, of group, and culture, 271

297